INTRODUCTION

"The Great Tattoo Book" Vol. 3 "Your Ultimate Tattoo Design Resource"

Looking for fresh tattoo design inspiration? You've found it!
"The Great Tattoos Book" series, is the definitive source for tattoo enthusiasts and artists alike.

In this book Vol. 3, you'll explore an exquisite collection of 1438 unique and original grayscale tattoo designs spanning from 3 - 23+ cm in size in a total of 185 design pages.
A big range of minimalist , calligraphy , flash tattoo designs as well as realism and tattoos that are good for photorealism even in minimal are covered in this book
In the next page you can see the table of contents including category, pages on each category and total of designs in each category in total.

Each design is a masterpiece in itself, providing a multitude of creative opportunities.
This book contains theme selections of the other 2 Volumes BUT All the designs are unique and cannot be found in the other 2 volumes.

So you can buy all 3 volumes and get over 6500 unique and original designs, or any combination and still have all different designs.

Moreover since we have included more in total categories and the volume is with less pages this volume is a more budget volume with less themes than the other 2 combined, and less pages for every theme. Make no mistake though that this volume also contains amazing tattoo designs in the fashion of the other 2 books of the series (Vol.1 & 2).

These designs cater to every skill level, from those starting with small, minimalist tattoos, to those craving intricate, hyper-realistic creations.

Your clients will be captivated, and have the ability to boost your earnings with ease having a great recourse of popular tattoo designs

What makes these designs truly special is their uniqueness and originality.
You won't find them on the internet or in other tattoo books, and are made by artist for artists

All tattoo designs in this book are grayscale and as a bonus, we've included free downloadable PDF(see instructions inside the book) that showcase all color designs where apploicable

Grab this opportunity to elevate your tattoo artistry with "The Great Tattoo Book." Series,

This volume covers a wide range of 51 category themes, ensuring that you have a vast selection to choose from demonstrated in the next page table.

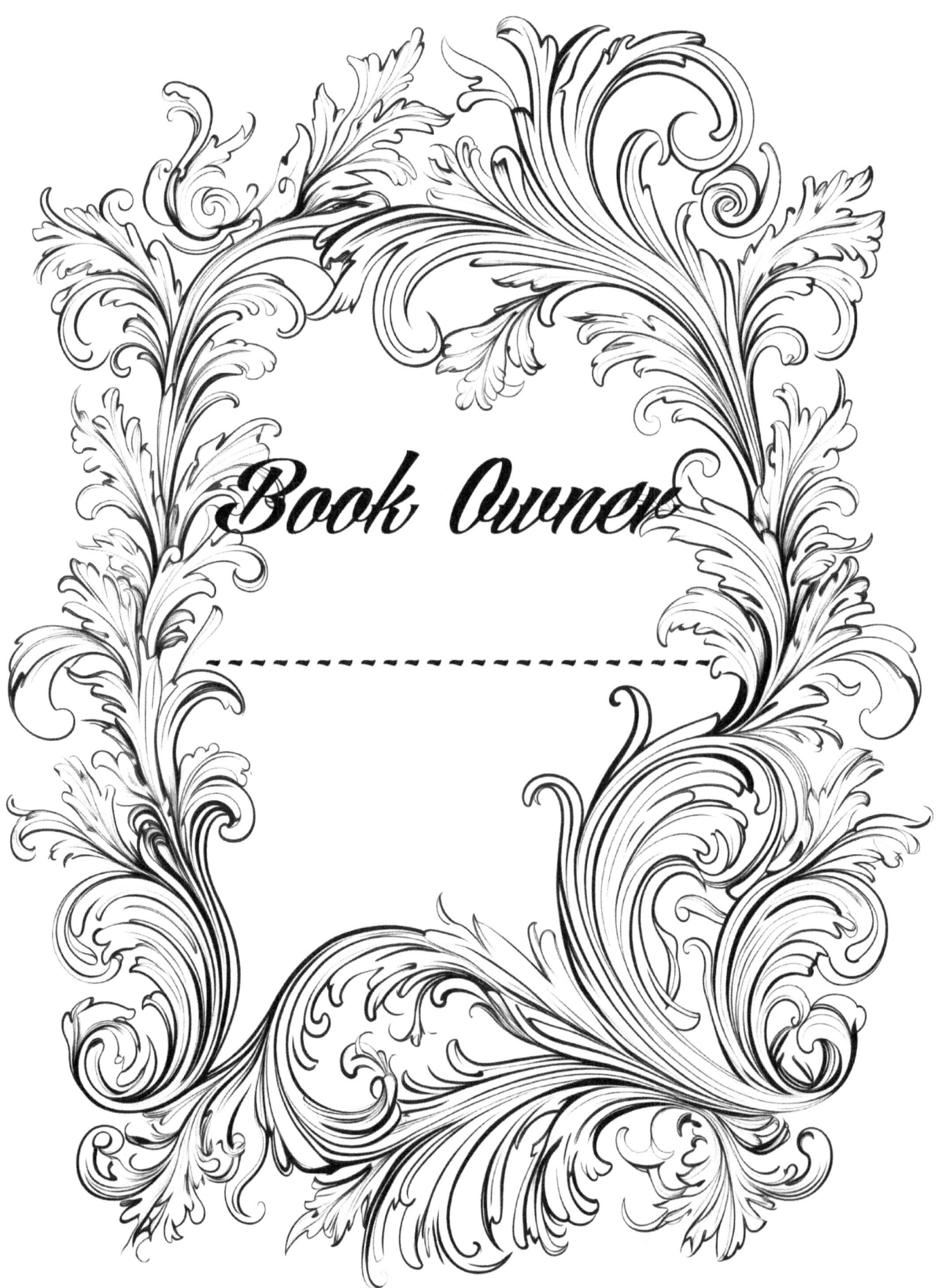

Book Owner

COPYRIGHT

ISBN 9798870424903
Find more of my books here :   amazon.com/author/alexartbooks

ABOUT THE AUTHOR

Immerse yourself in the captivating world of art, where imagination knows no bounds. With over three decades of experience as a painter, tattoo artist, and author, I have dedicated my life to the pursuit of artistic excellence.
Through countless hours of dedication, I have honed my skills in charcoal, pencils, and acrylic colors, specializing in the realms of realism, photorealism, and impressionism. My unique style blends elements of fantasy and impressionism, resulting in mesmerizing works of art that evoke deep emotions and leave a lasting impact.

In the realm of tattoo artistry, I have emerged as a trailblazer, revolutionizing the industry with my fresh and distinctive designs. Recognizing the need for innovation, I have created a new age of tattoo art that seamlessly combines my preferred style with eye-catching aesthetics. My designs not only captivate the eye but also empower individuals to express their individuality and uniqueness.

Expanding my creative horizons, I have delved into the world of coloring books. Gone are the days of simplistic designs with thick lines. I am on a mission to introduce the realms of realism and impressionism to the coloring book landscape. Each page of my coloring books offers intricate details and a chance for individuals to unleash their inner artist, resulting in remarkable and vibrant creations.

But my artistic endeavors don't stop there. I am currently engrossed in the creation of photo reference books that showcase wildlife and nature in unprecedented ways. These books will transport you to a world of vivid colors, breathtaking imagery, and seemingly impossible poses.

 Prepare to be captivated by the untamed beauty of the natural world, brought to life through my keen eye for detail and my passion for pushing artistic boundaries.

Join me on an awe-inspiring journey where creativity knows no limits. Together, let's explore new dimensions of artistry, where fresh perspectives, remarkable designs, and boundless inspiration await.

Welcome to my world of art, where dreams become reality, and the extraordinary is transformed into tangible beauty

Albatros - Seagull

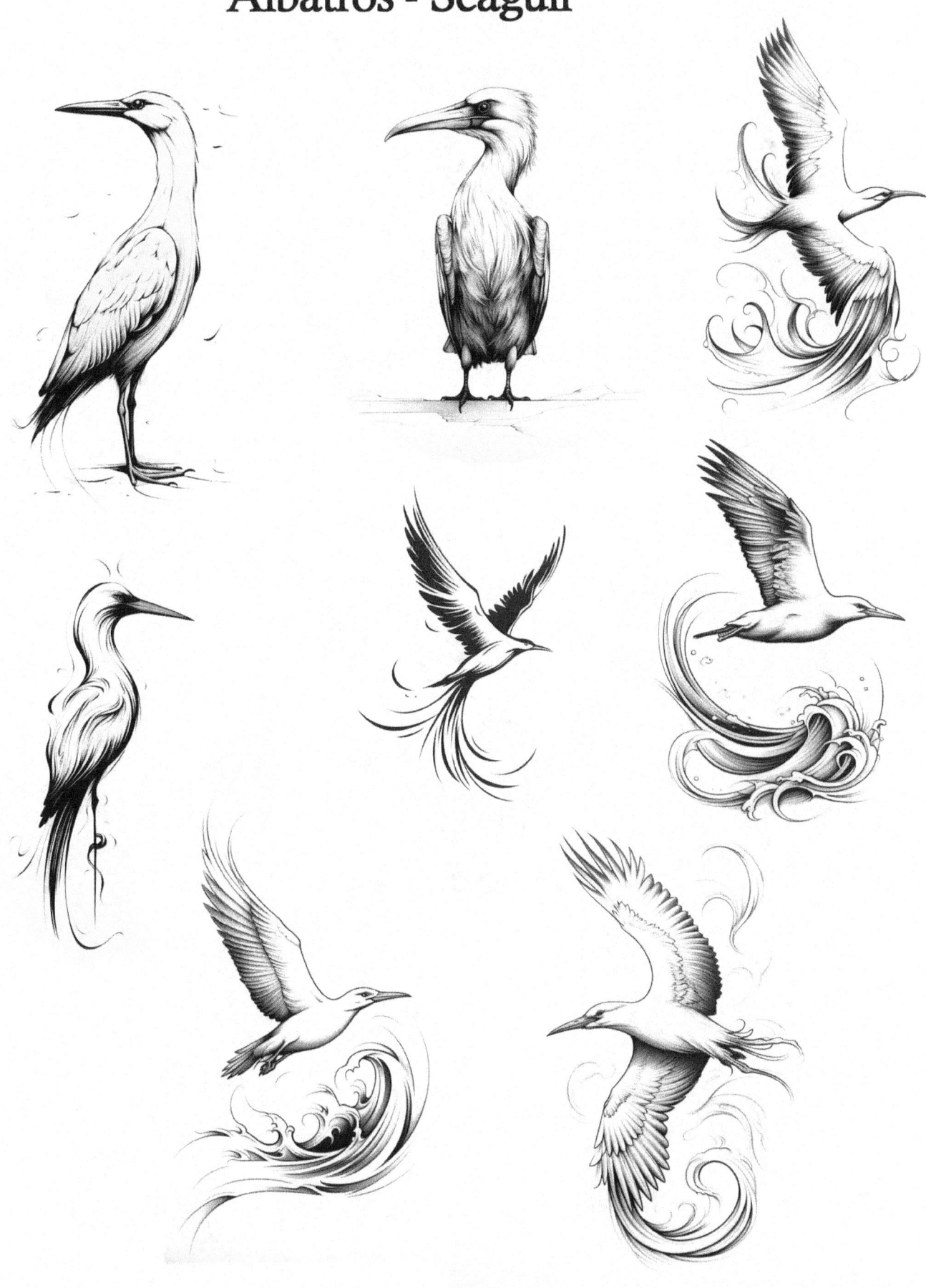

Seagull

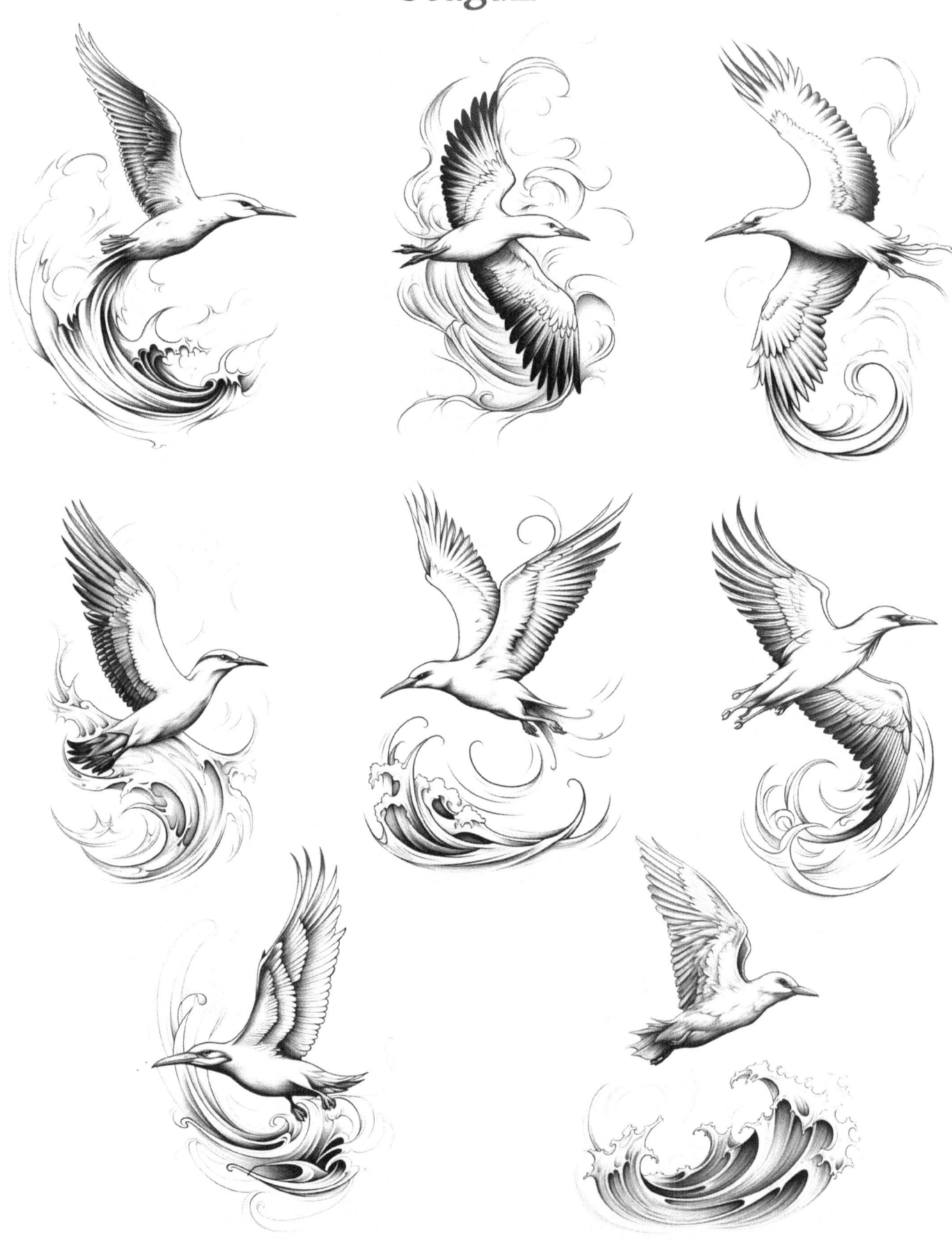

ANCHOR

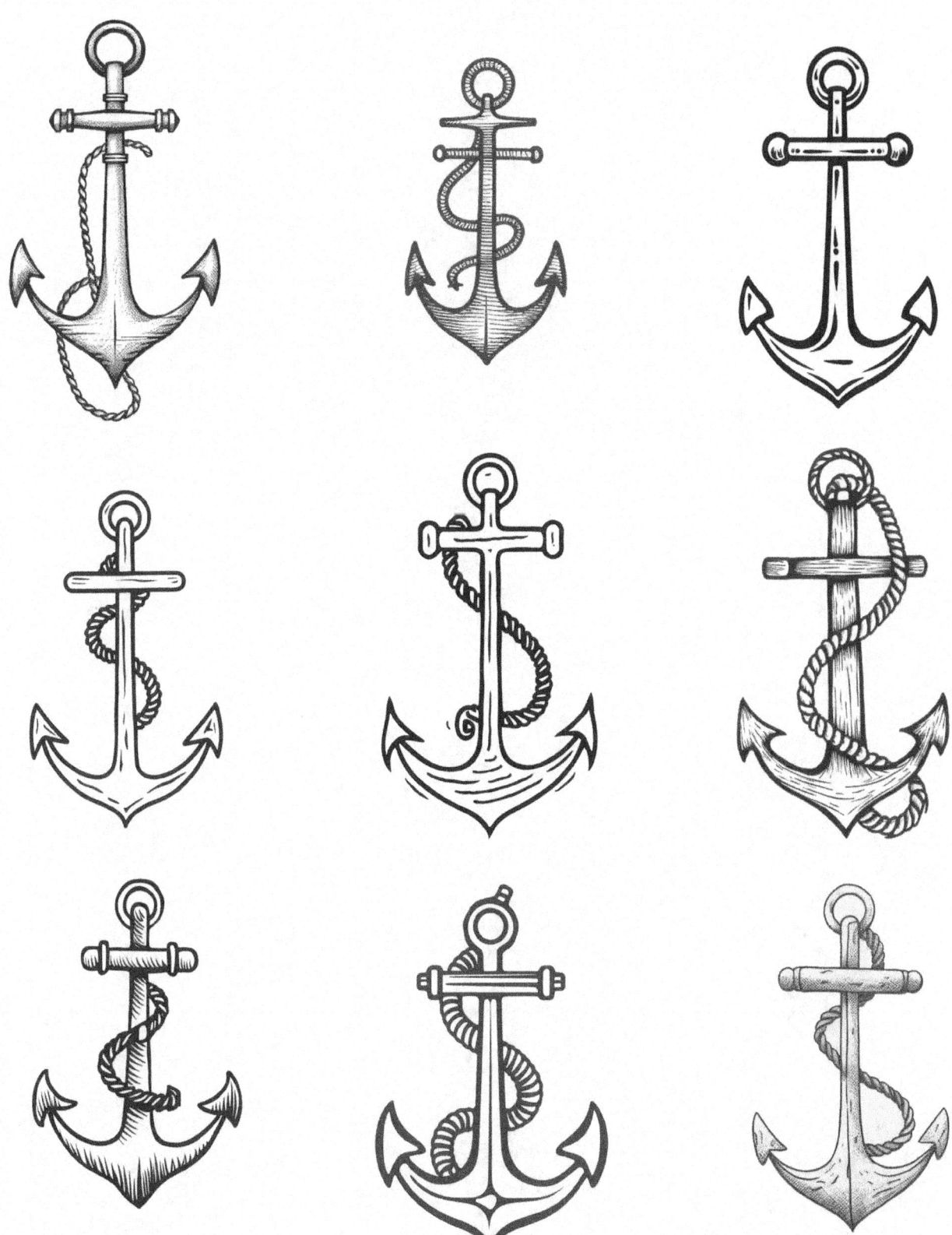

ANCHOR

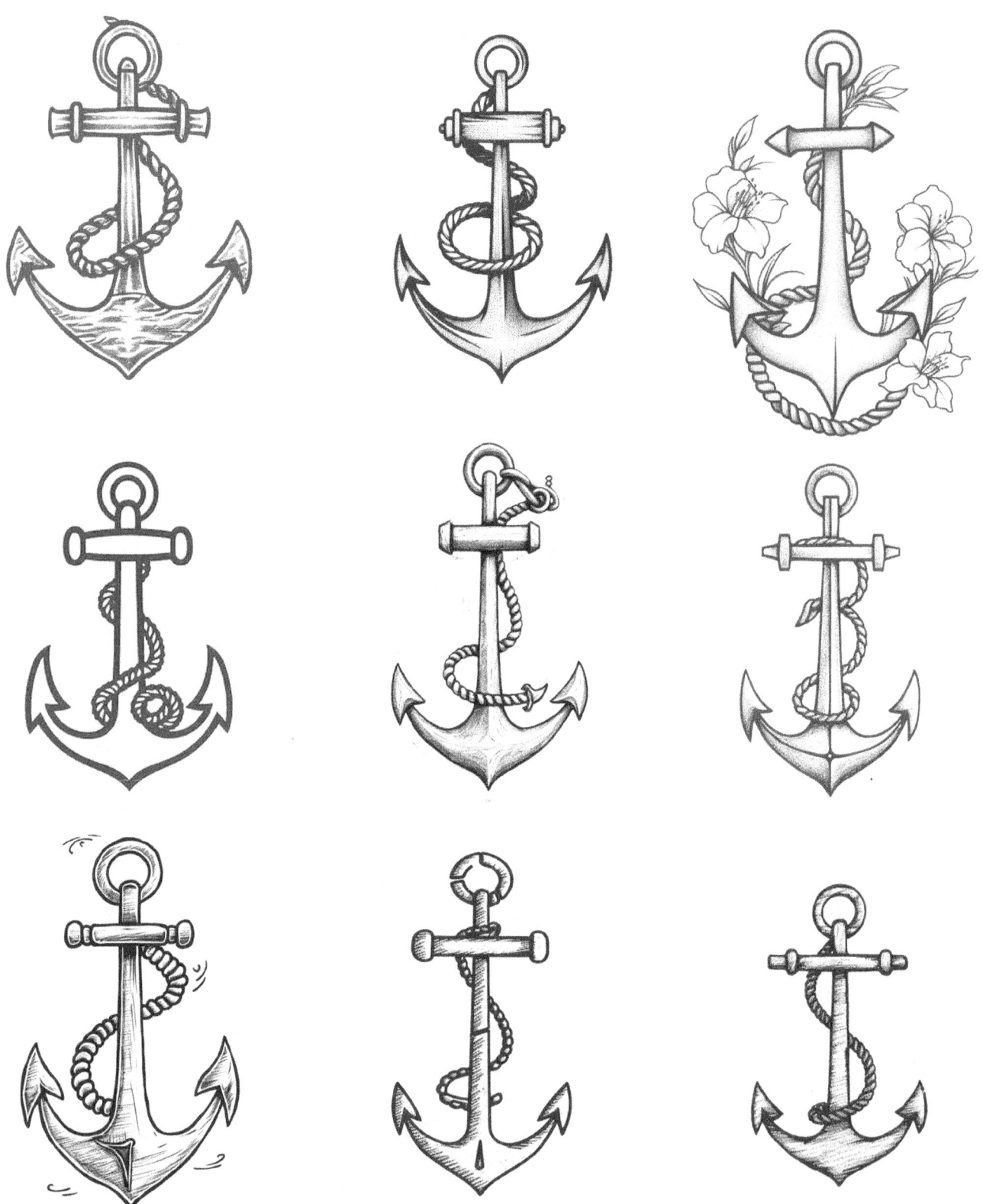

ANCHOR

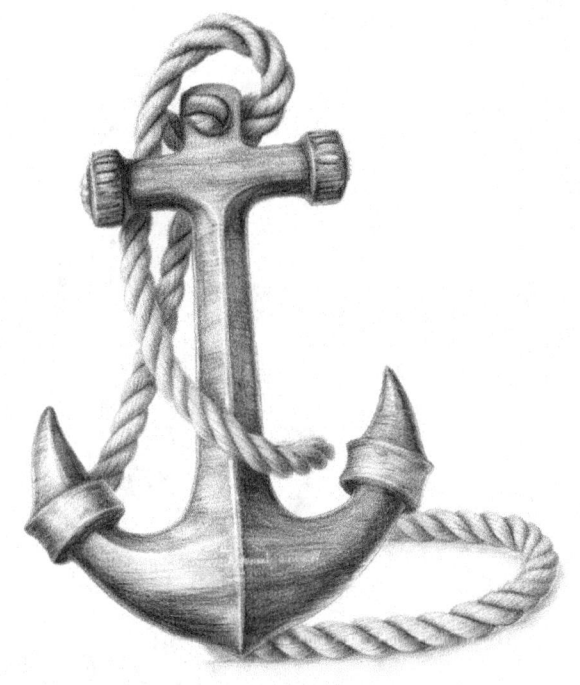

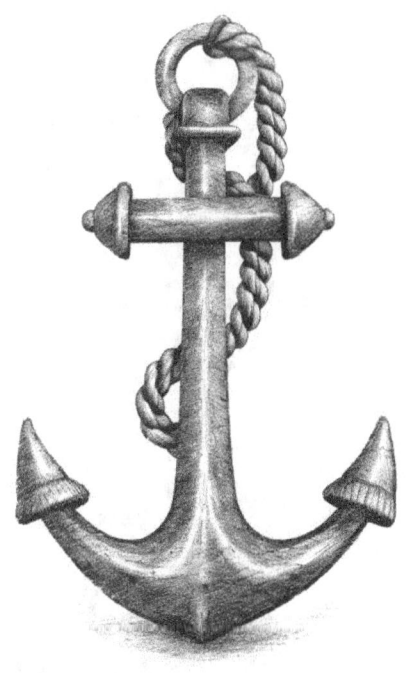

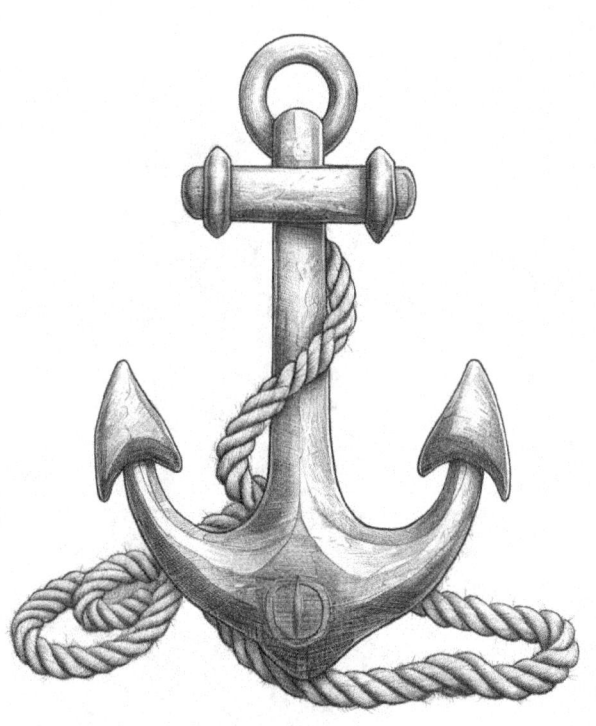

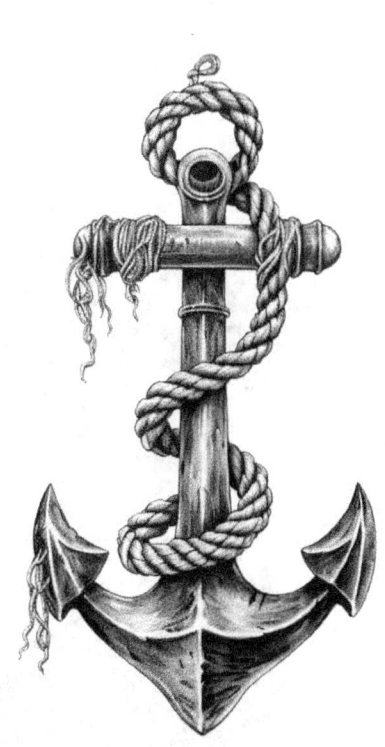

ANCHOR

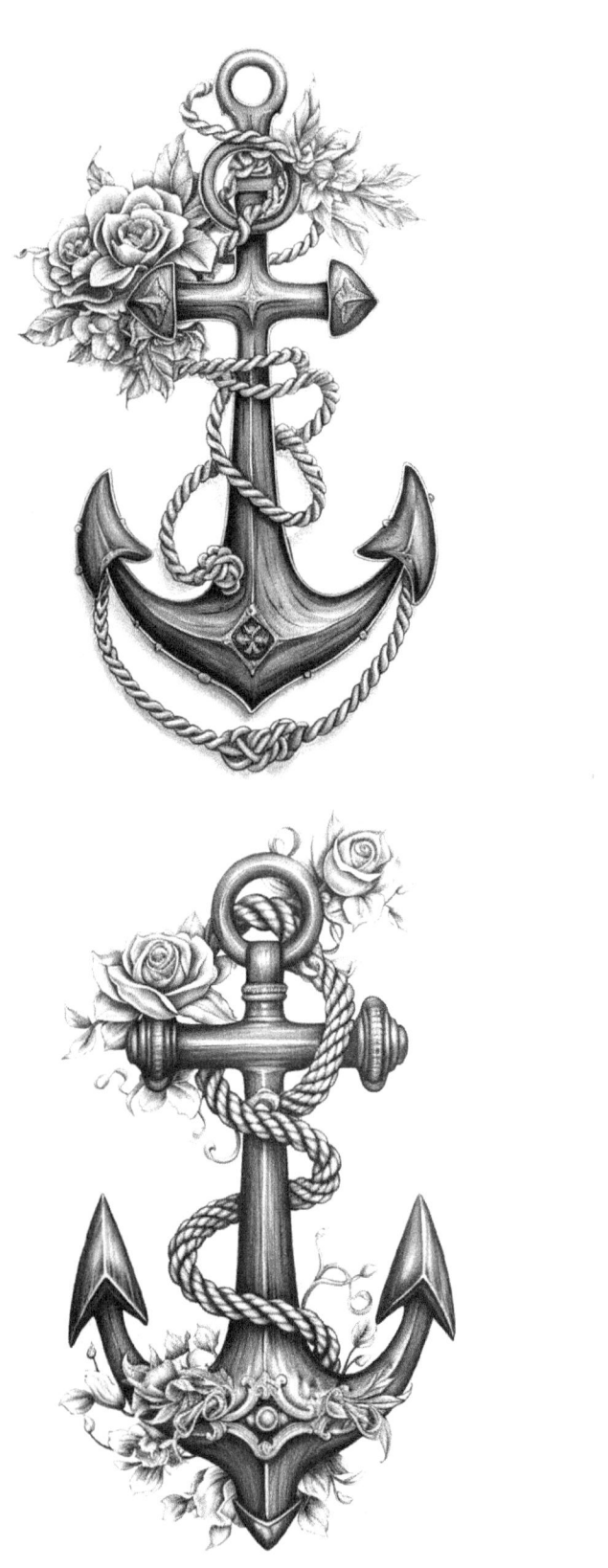

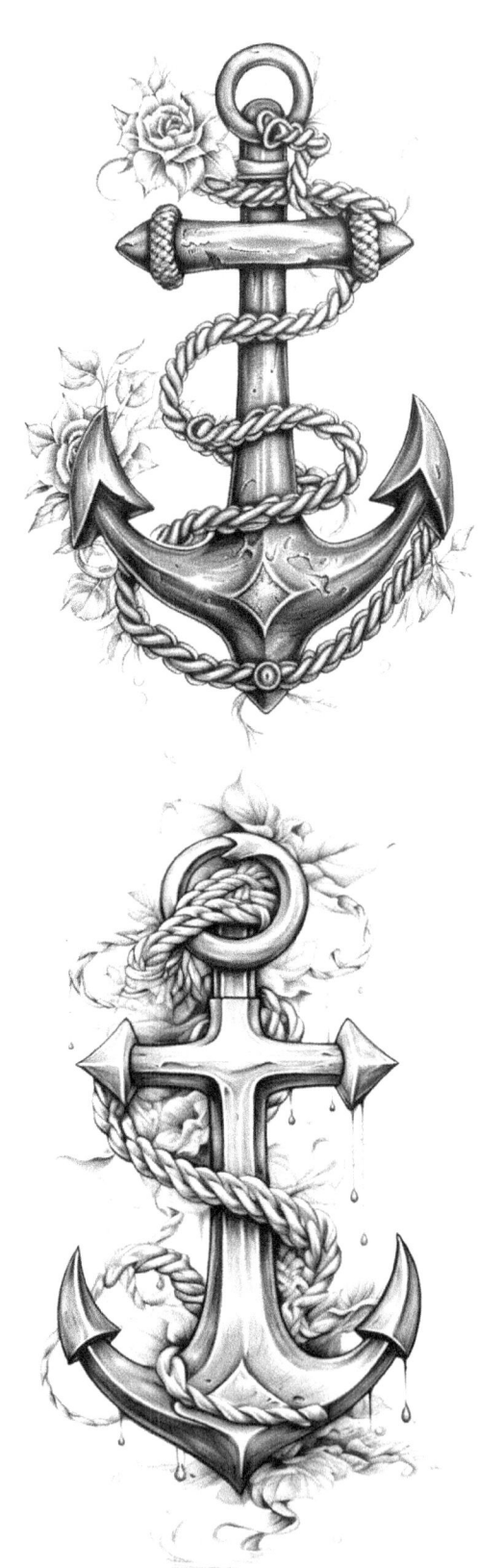

ANCHOR

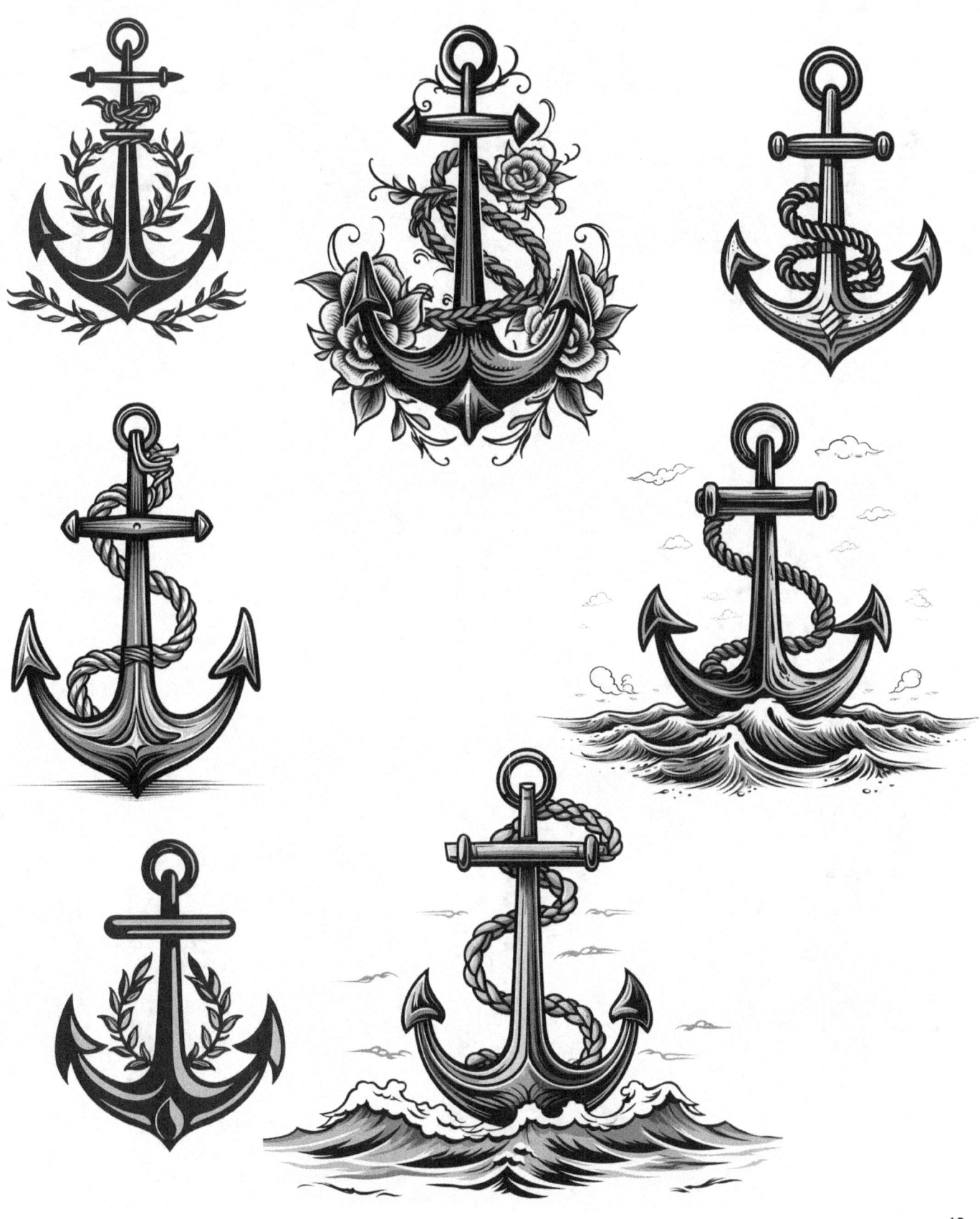

ANGEL - WINGS

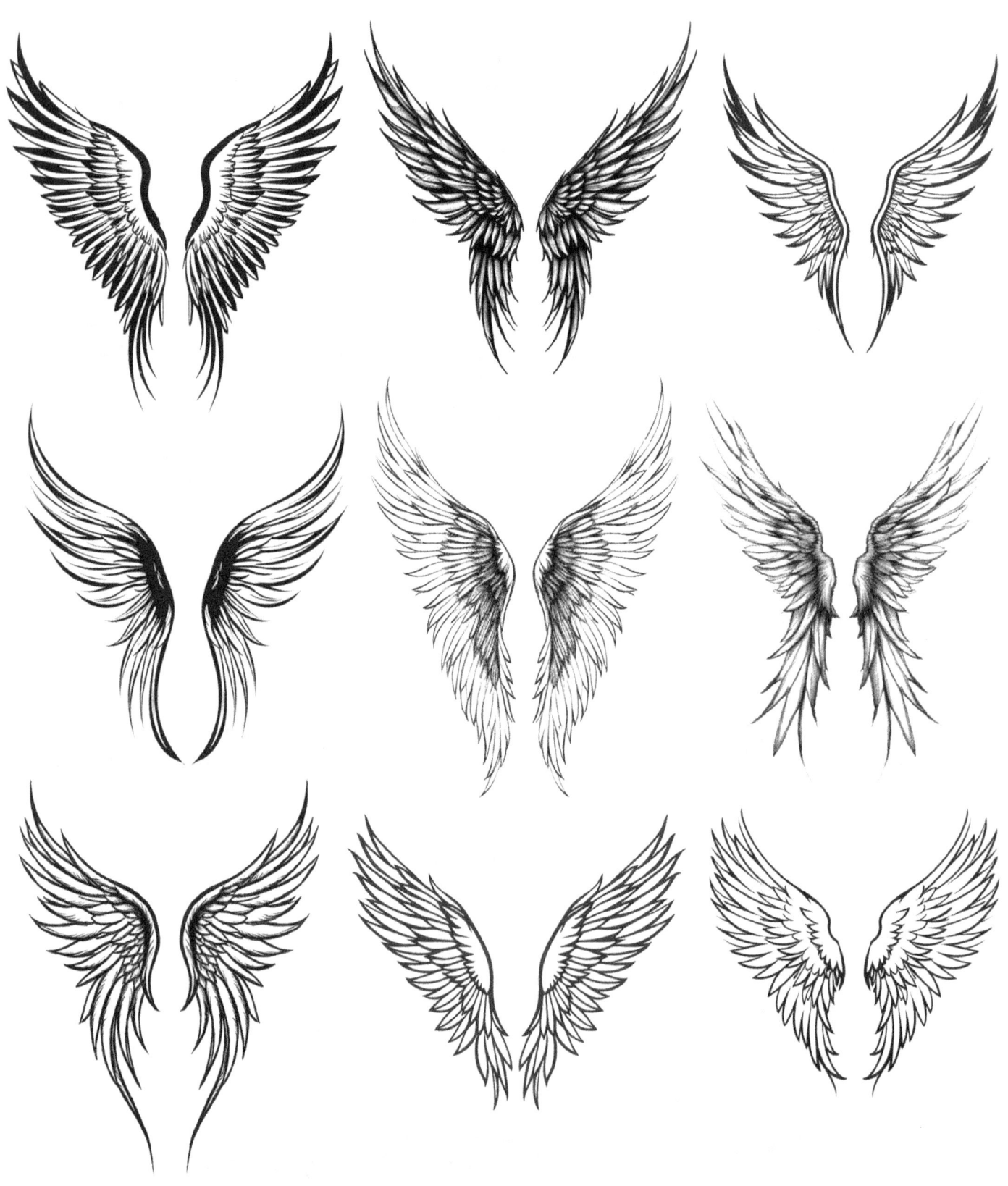

ANGEL - WINGS

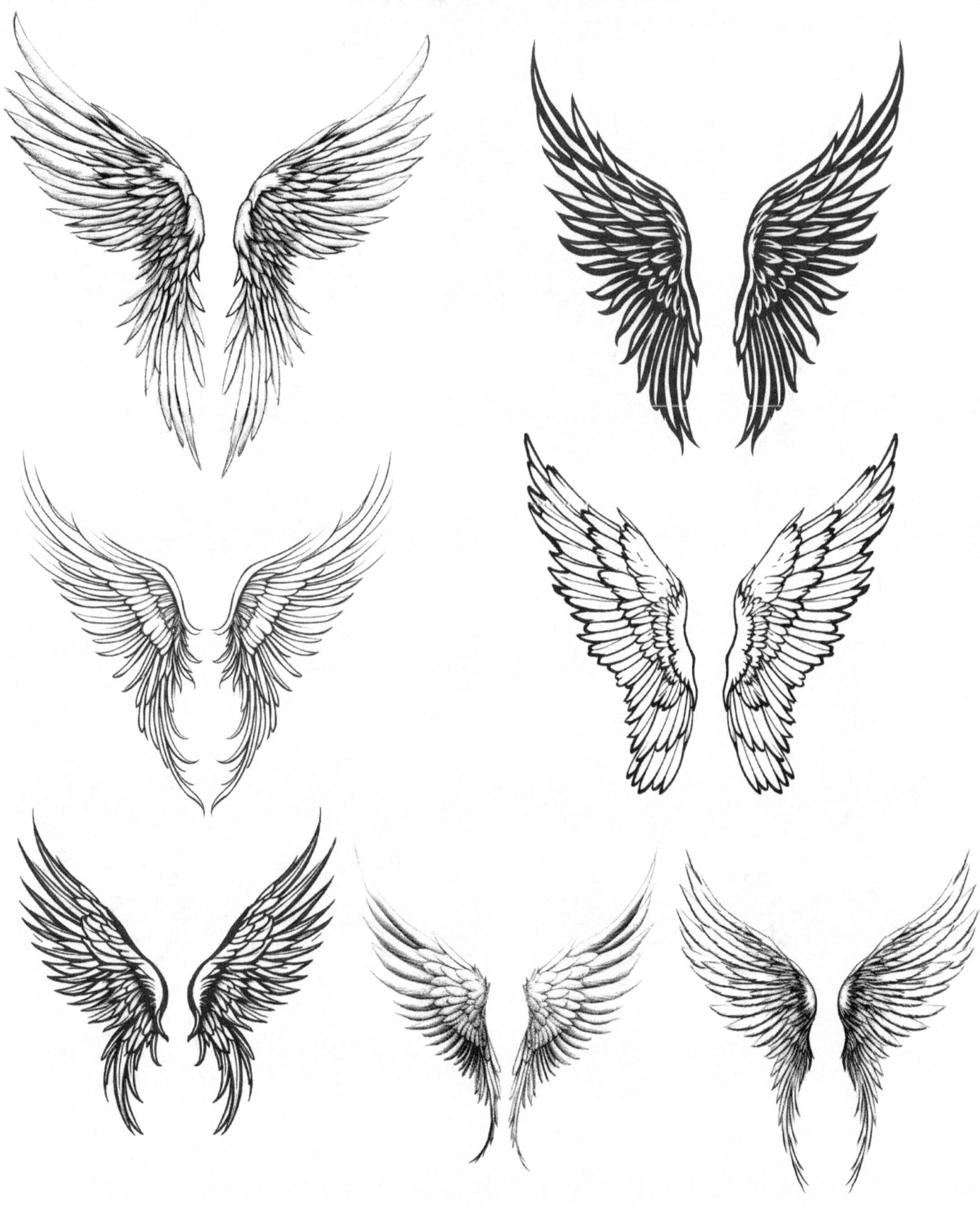

ANGEL - WINGS

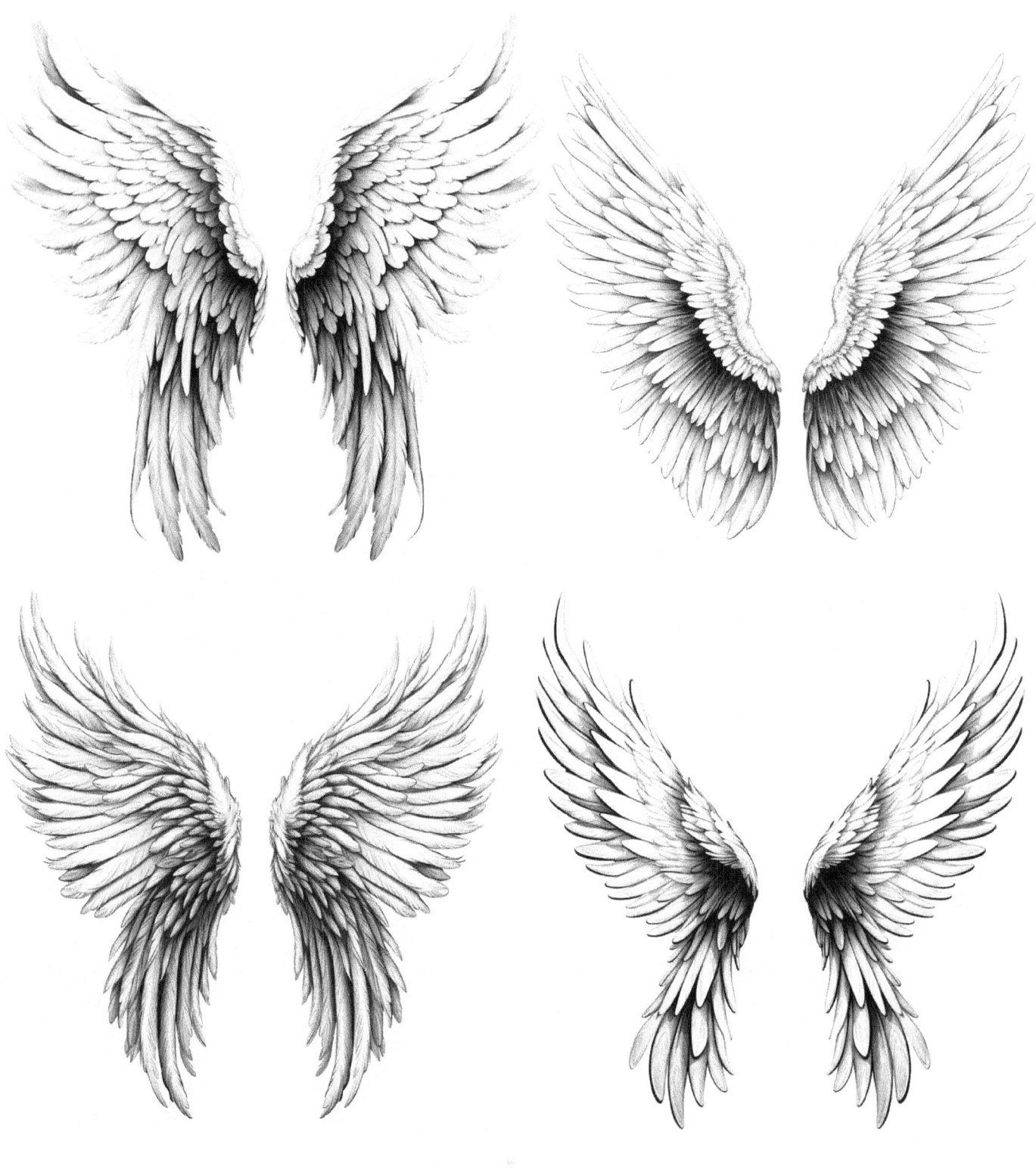

WATCH

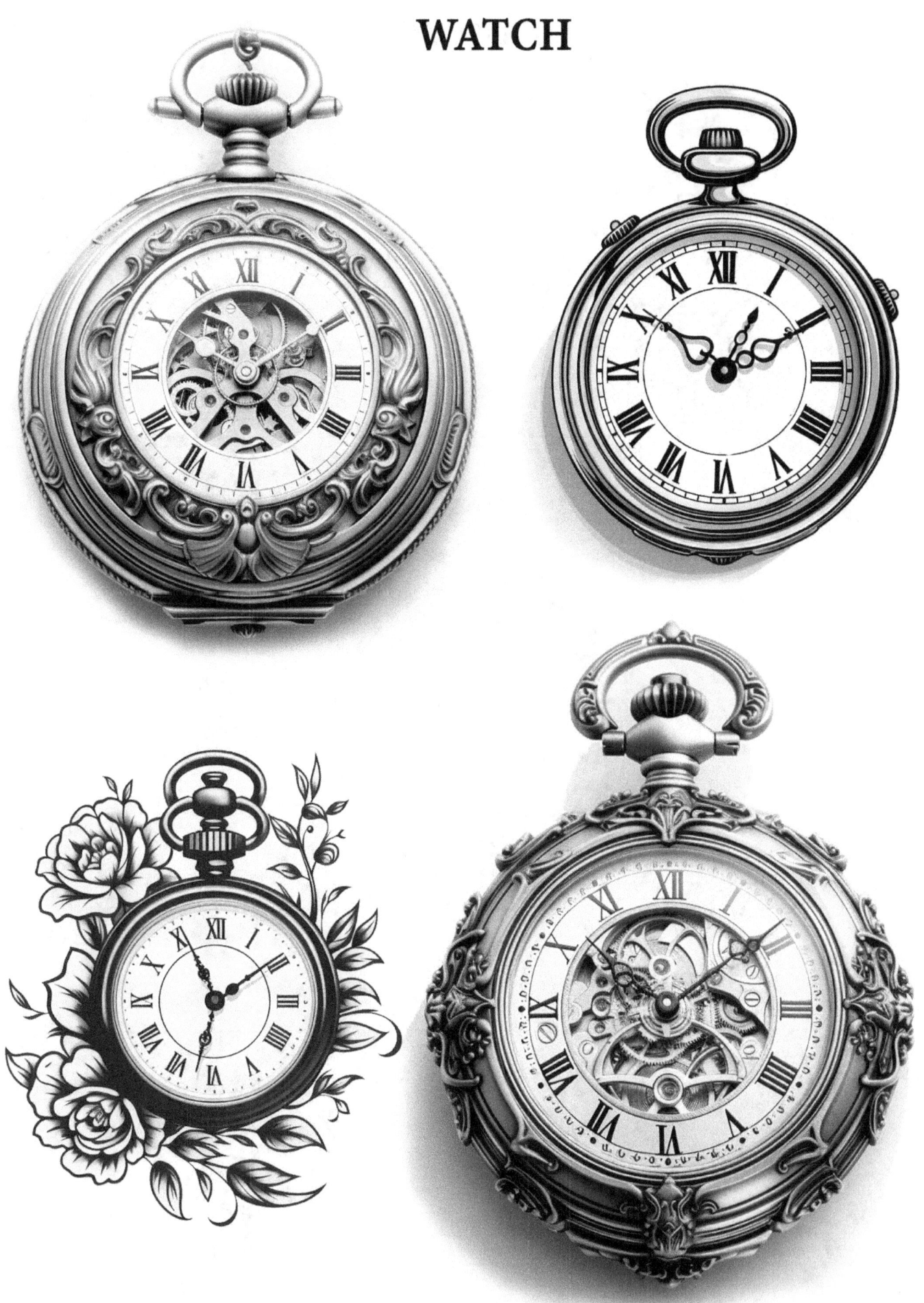

WATCH

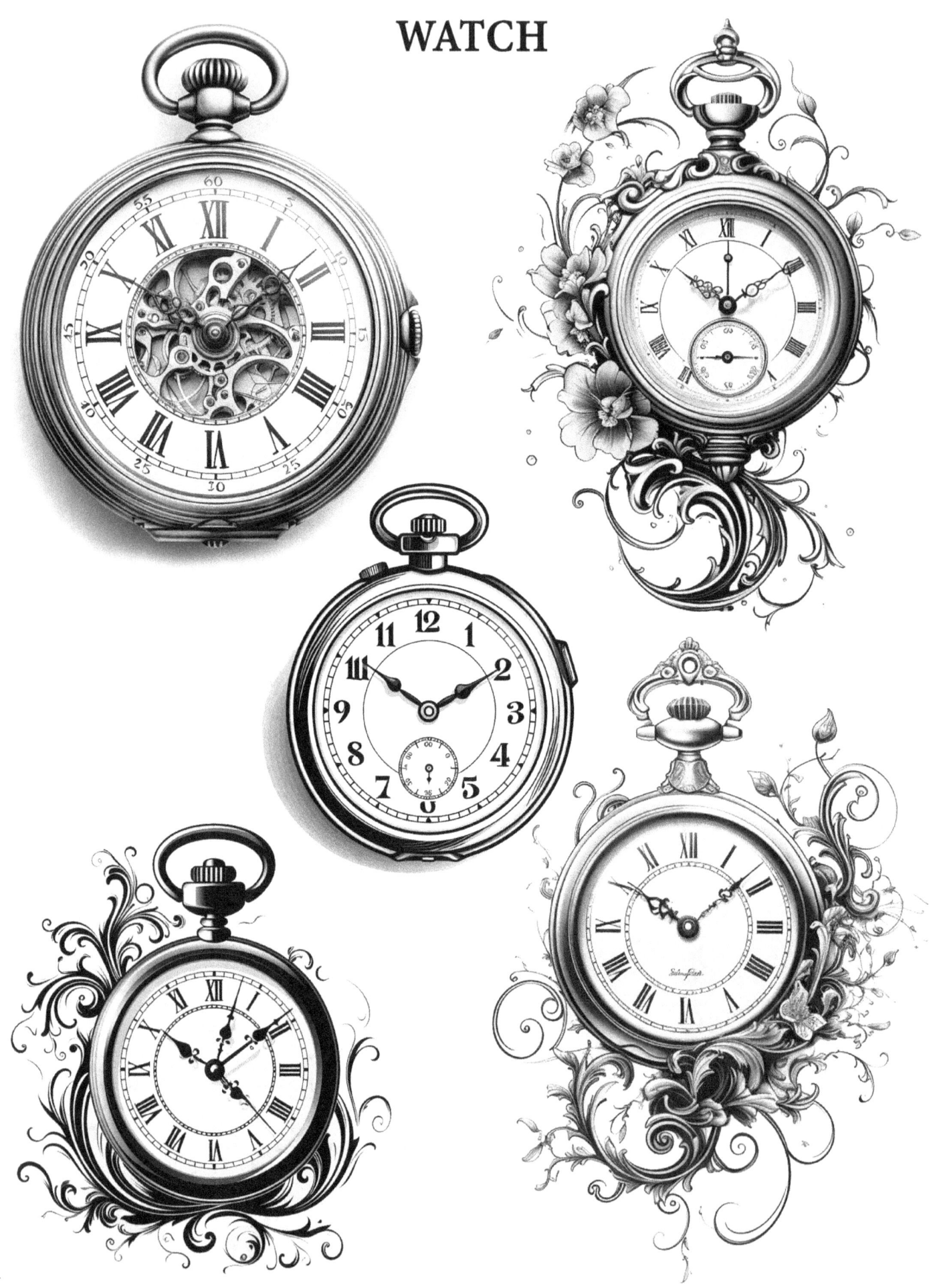

ANTIQUE WATCH

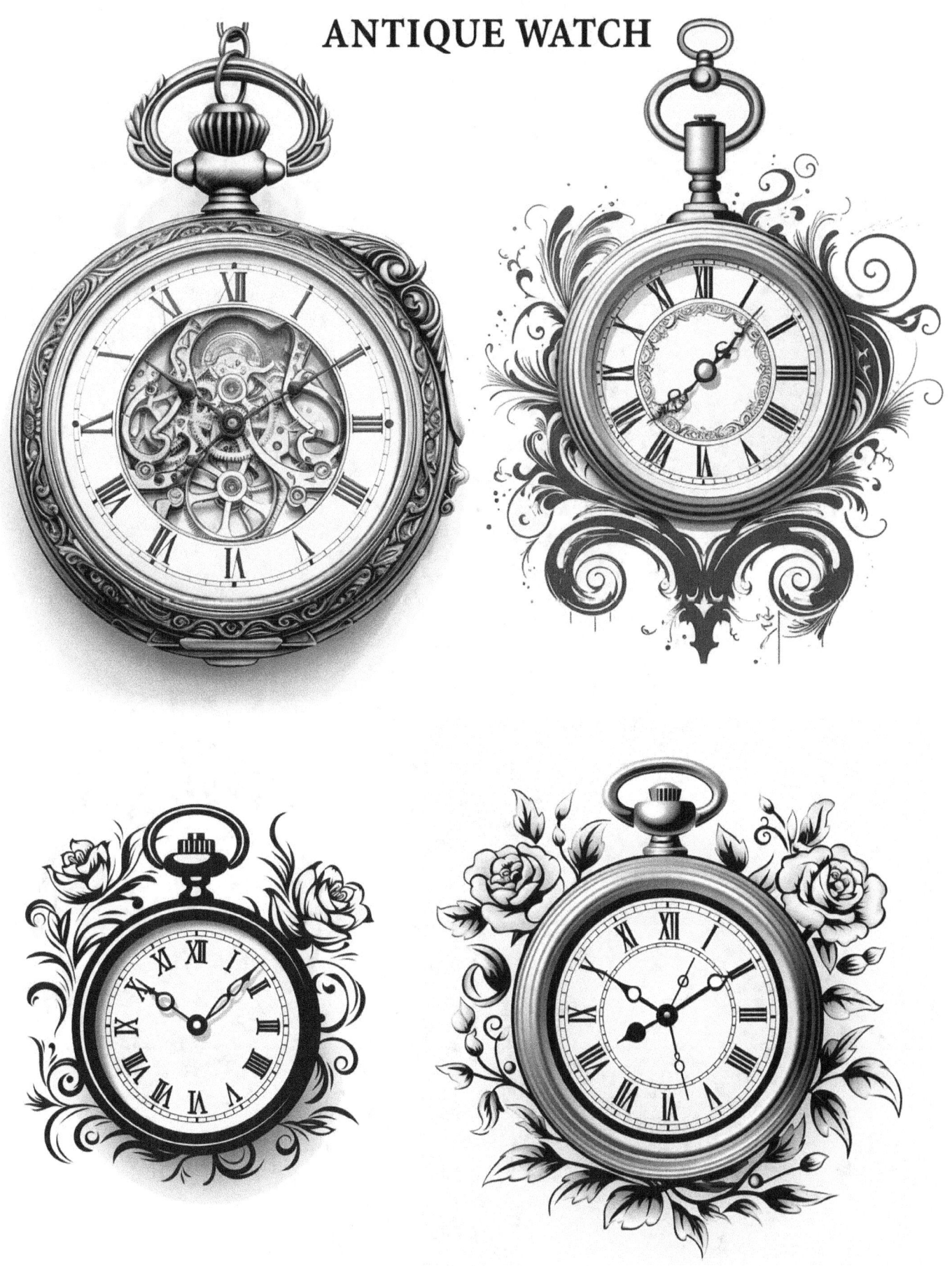

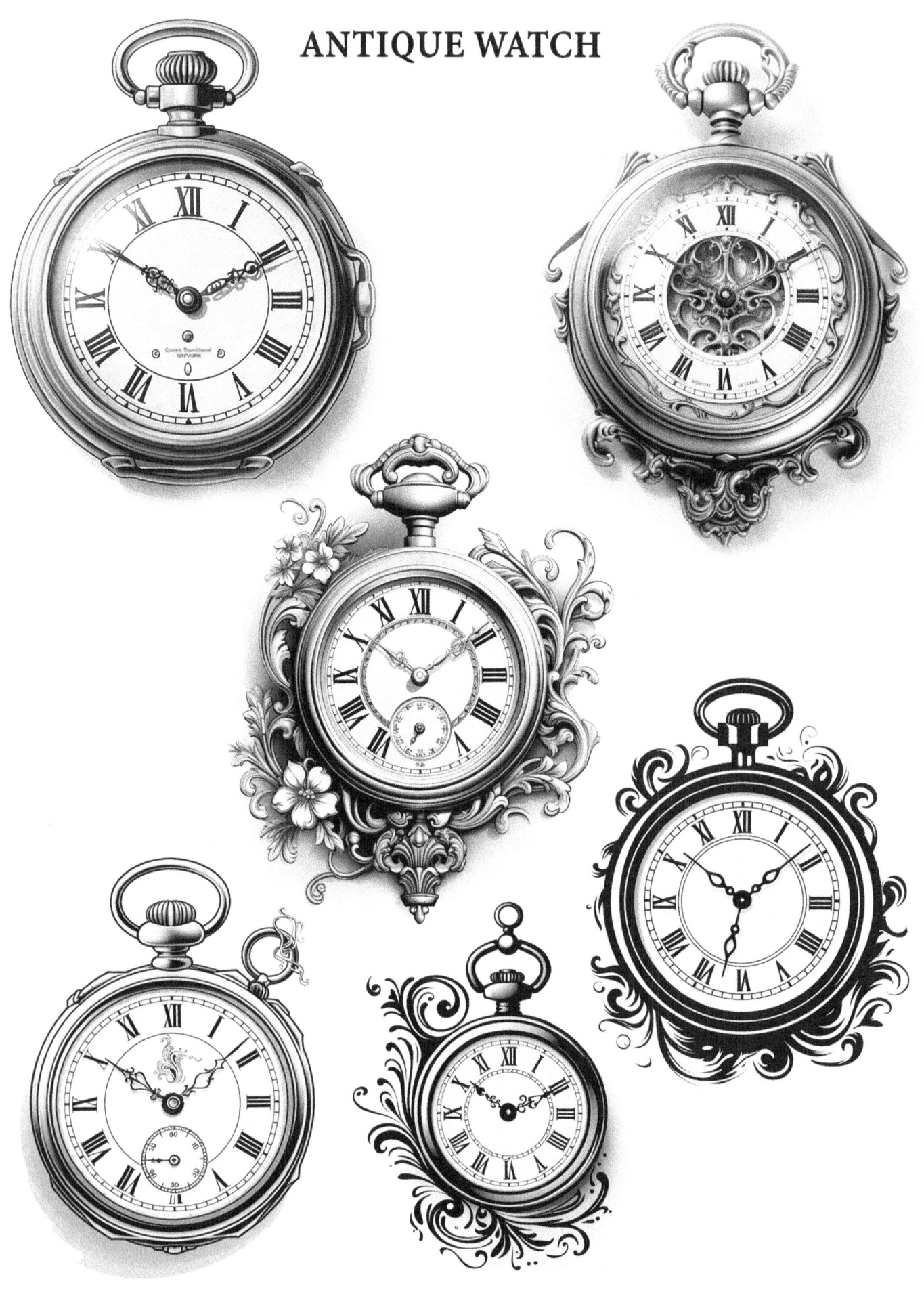

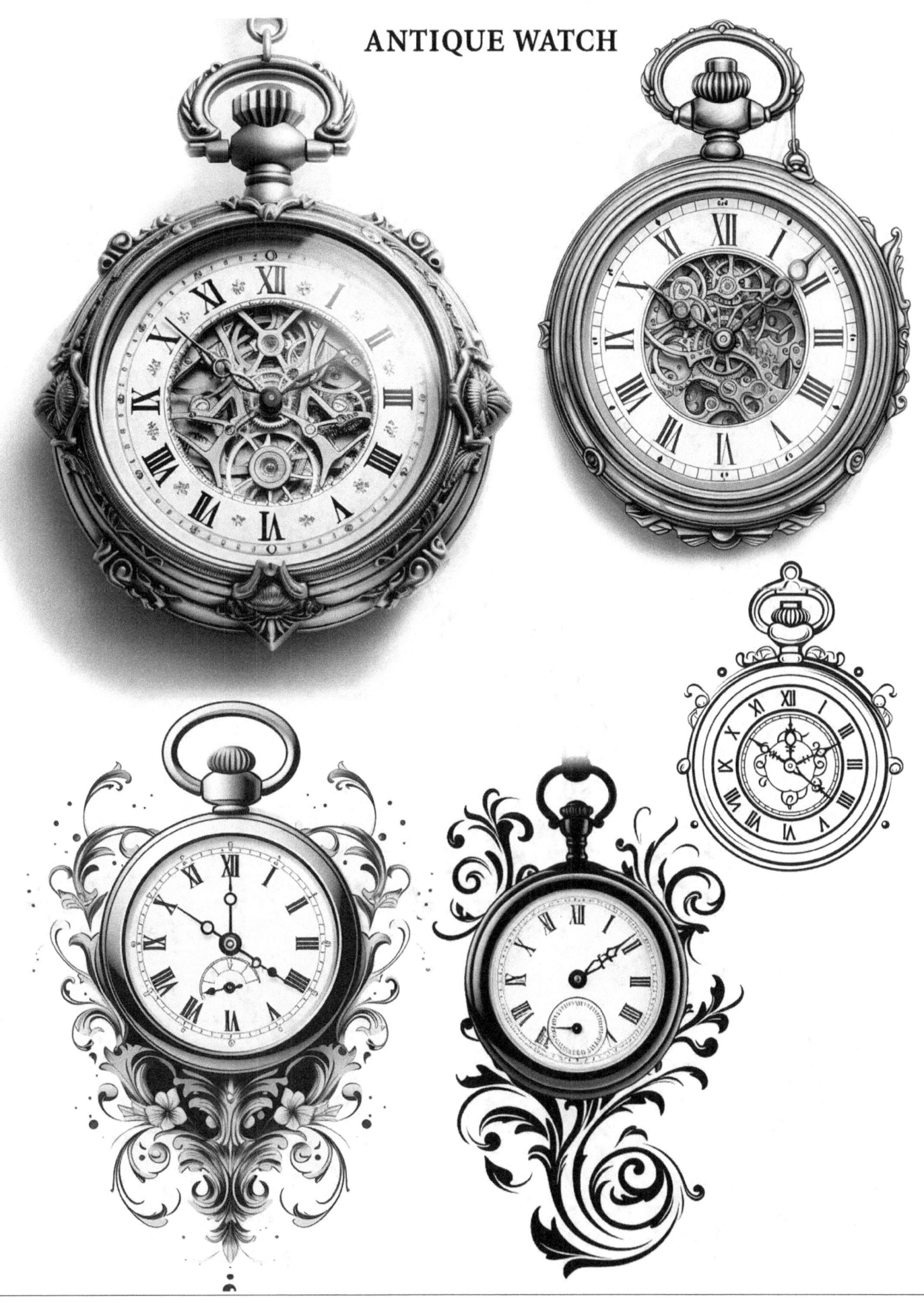

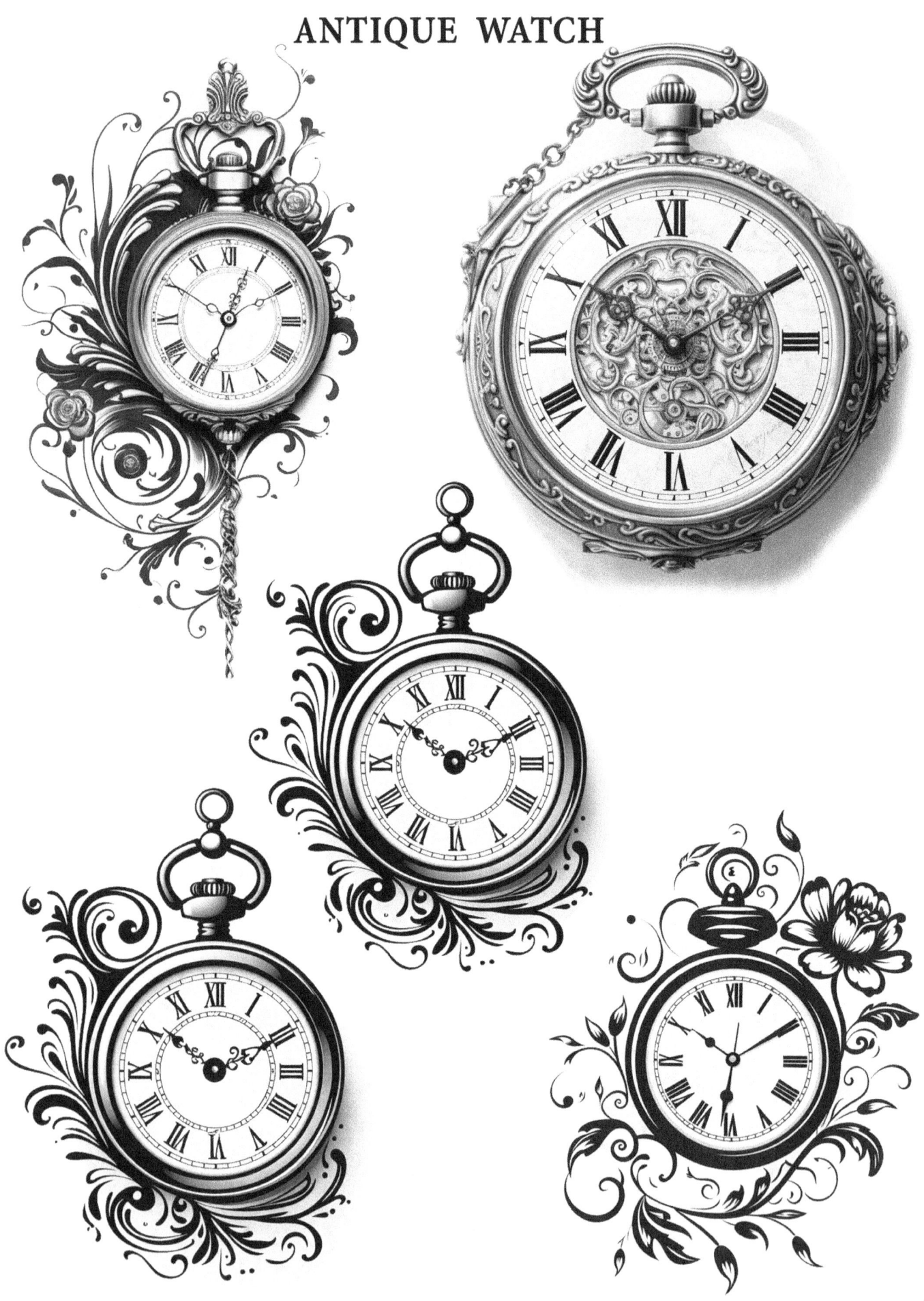

APPLE

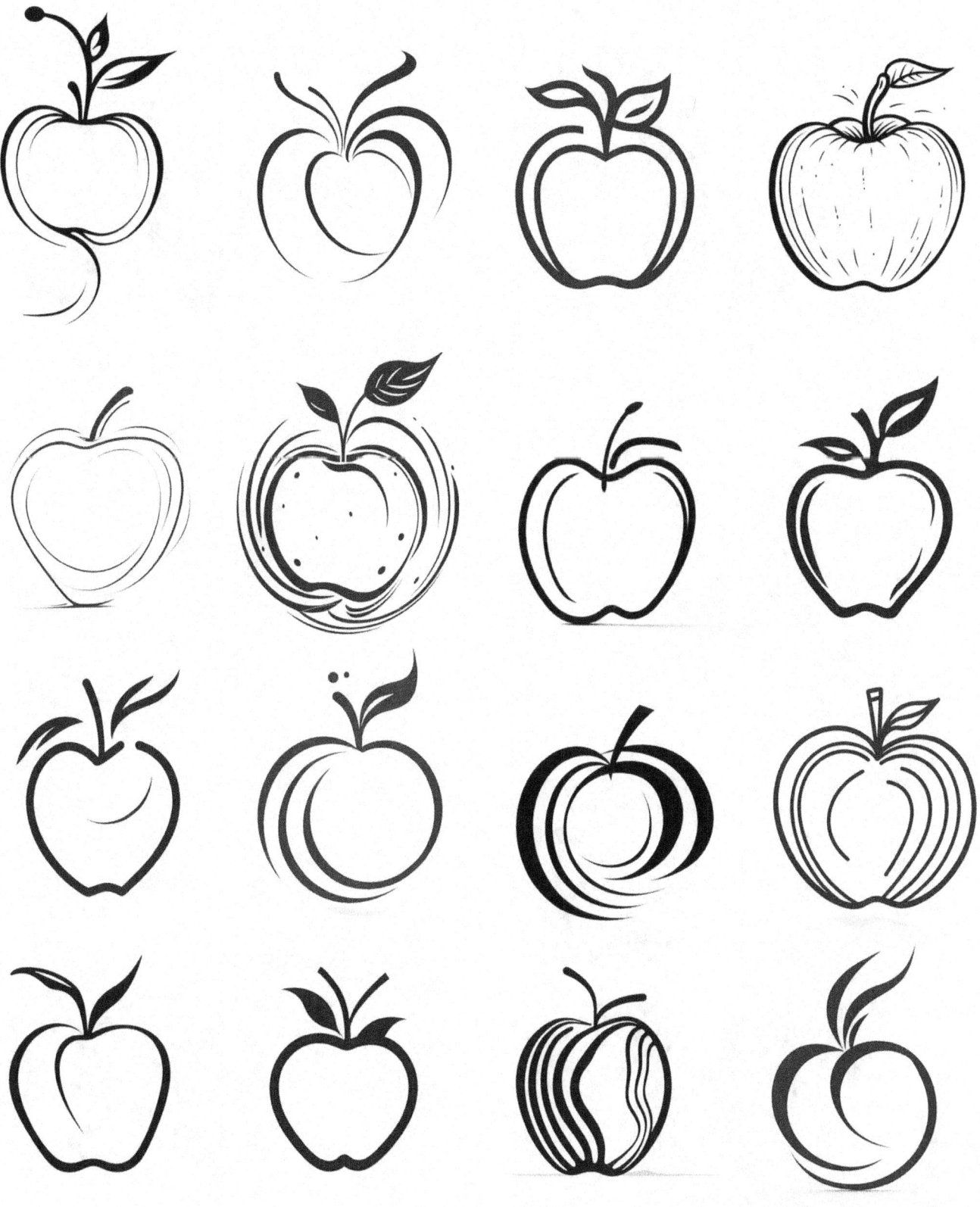

BEAR

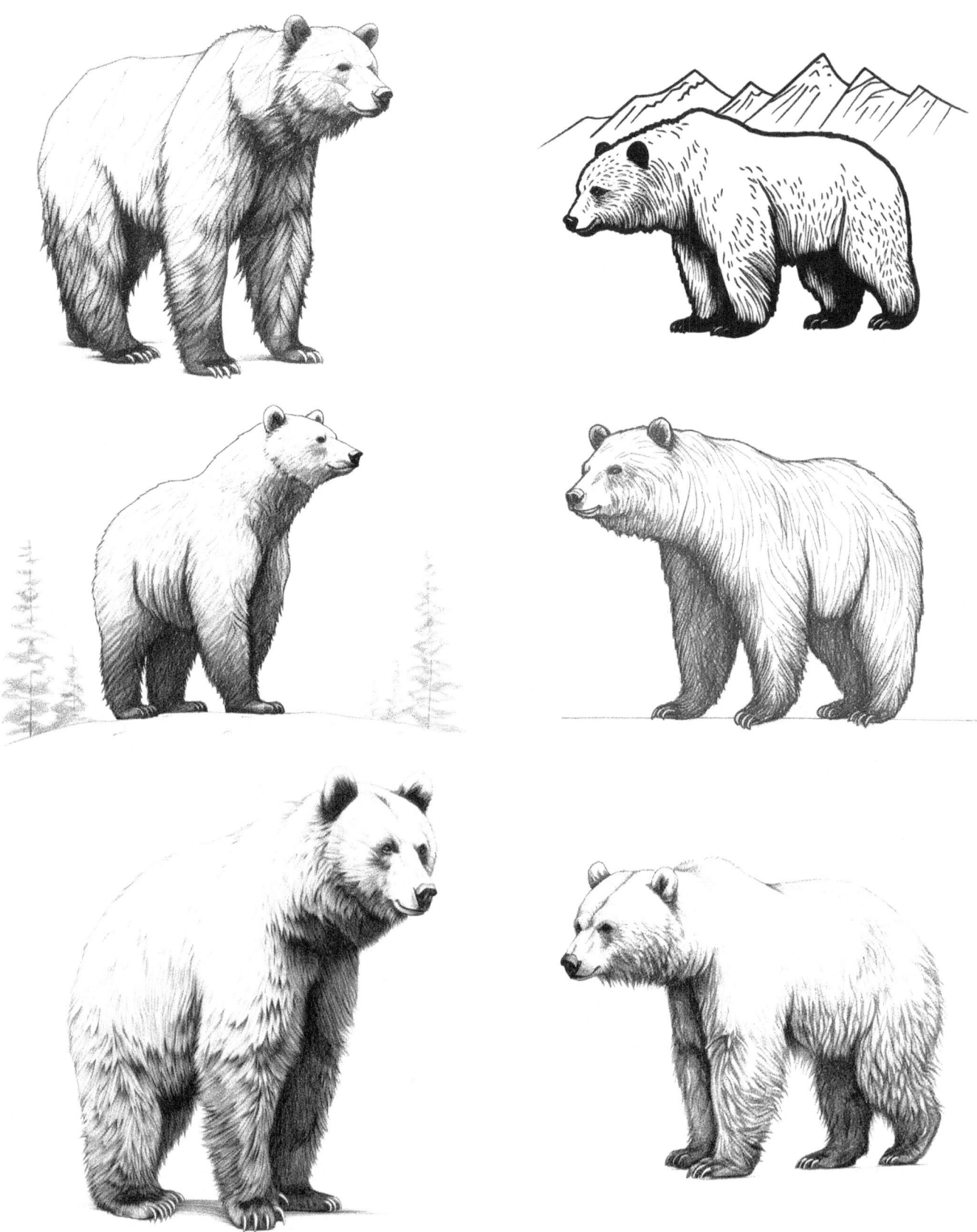

BEAR

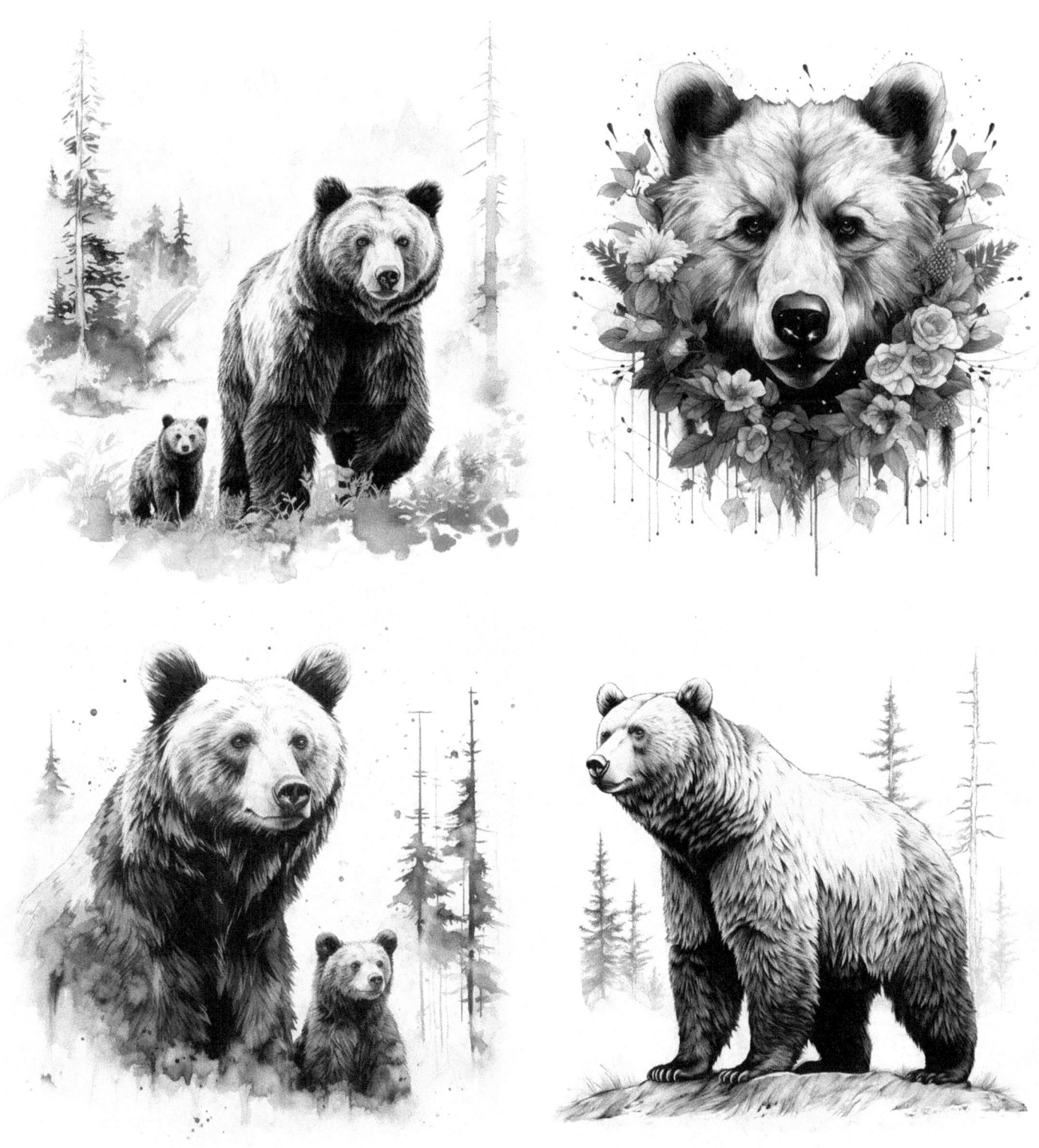

BEAR

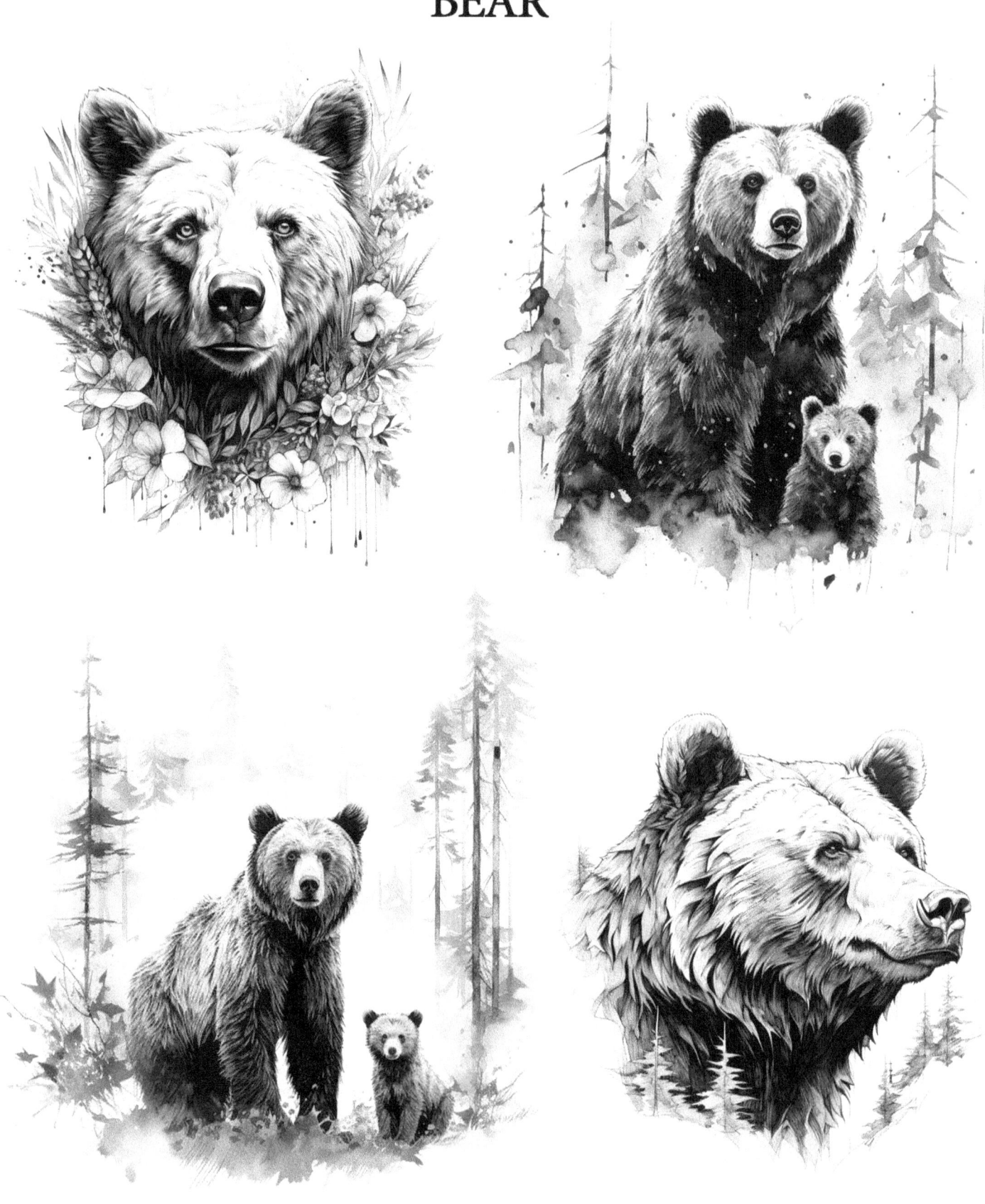

BEAVER

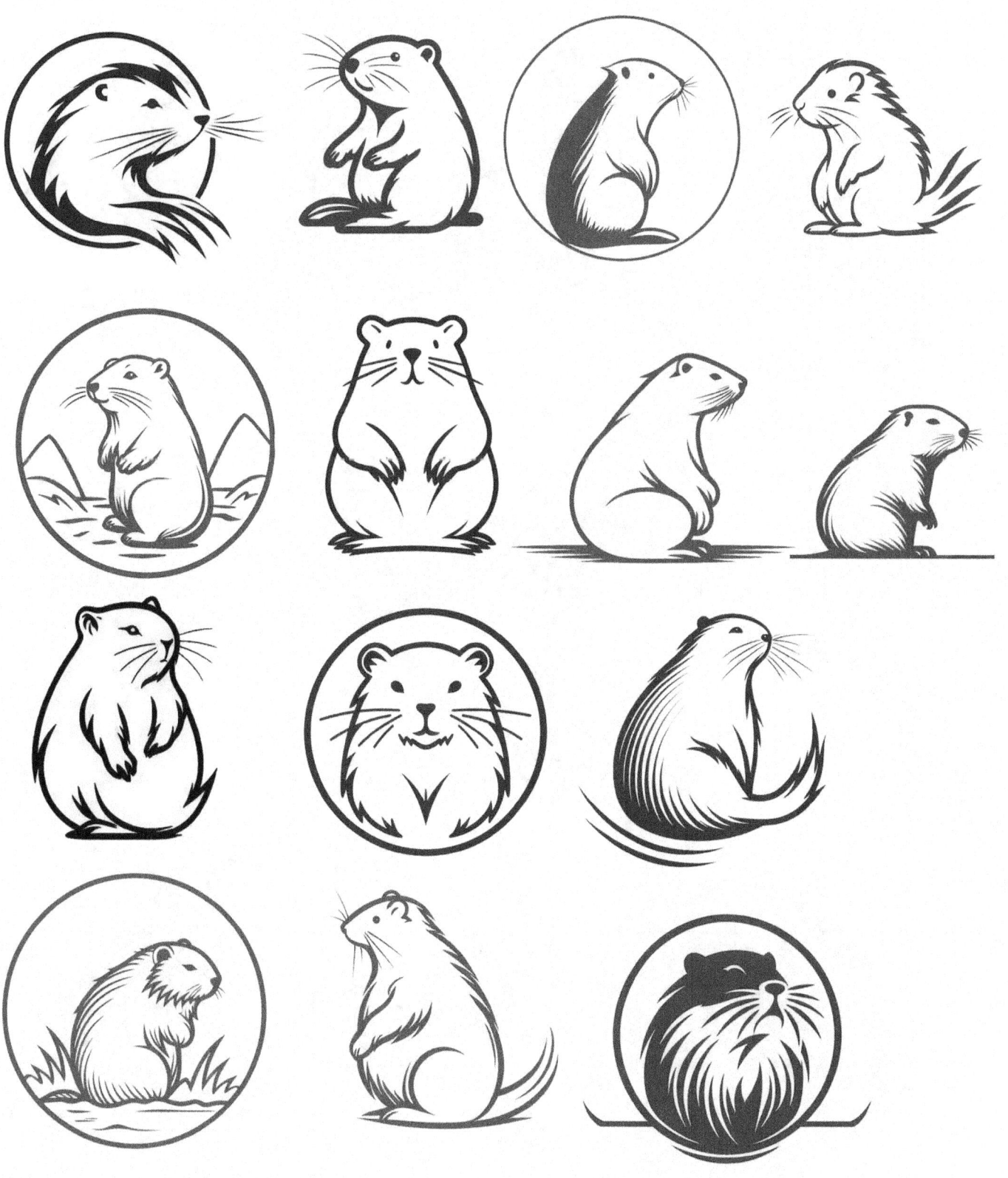

BLUE JAY

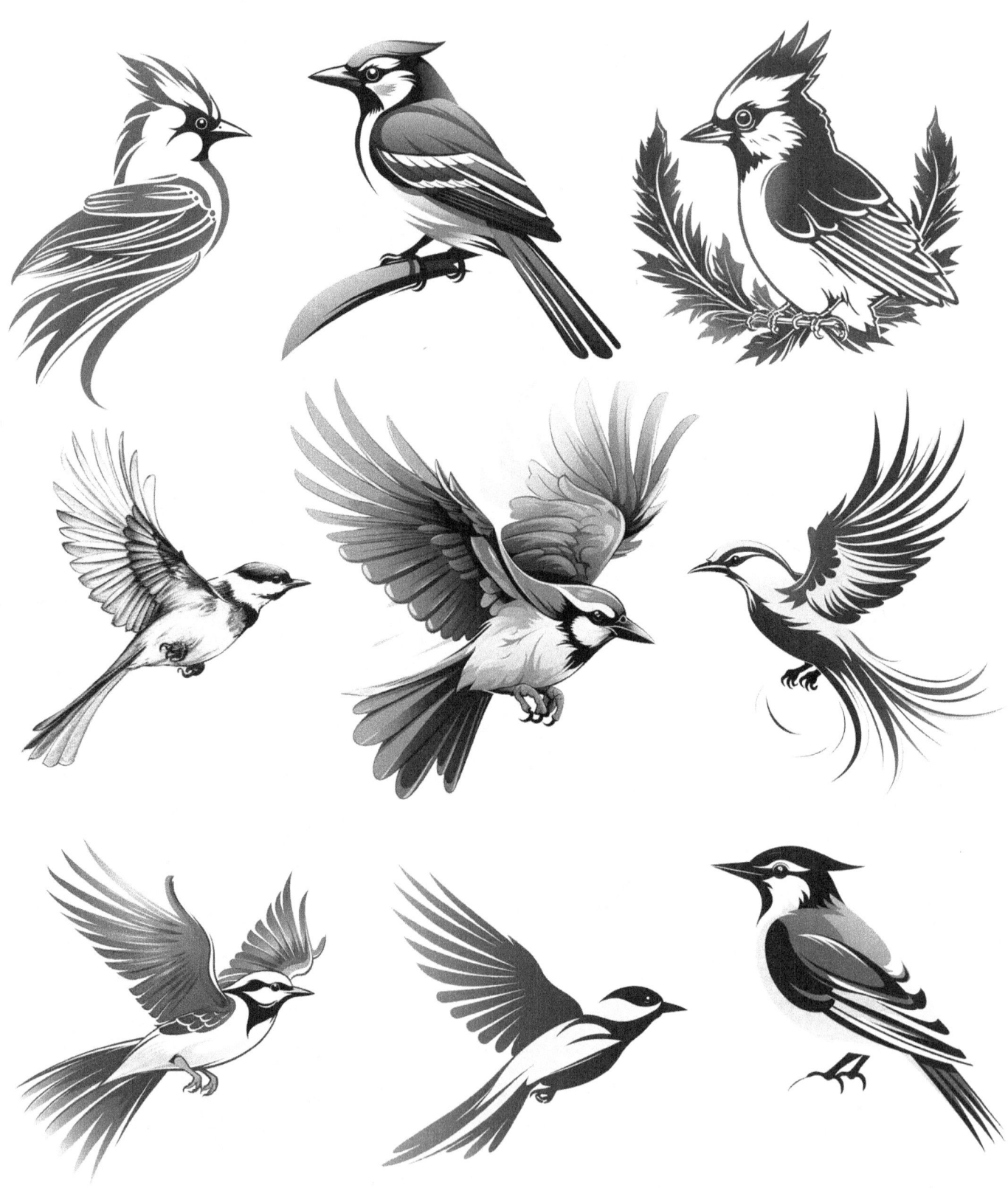

BLUE JAY

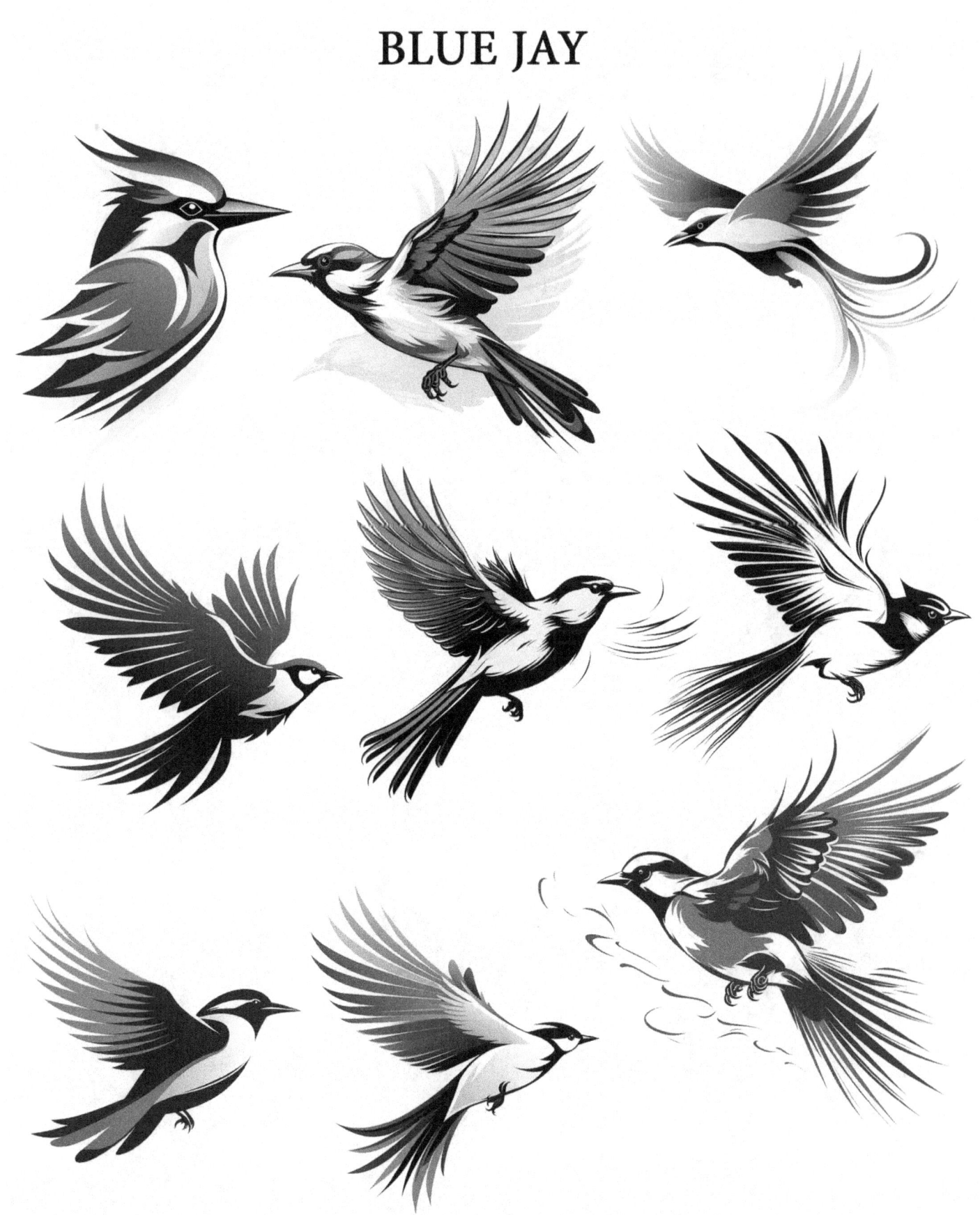

BUTTERFLY

BUTTERFLY

BUTTERFLY

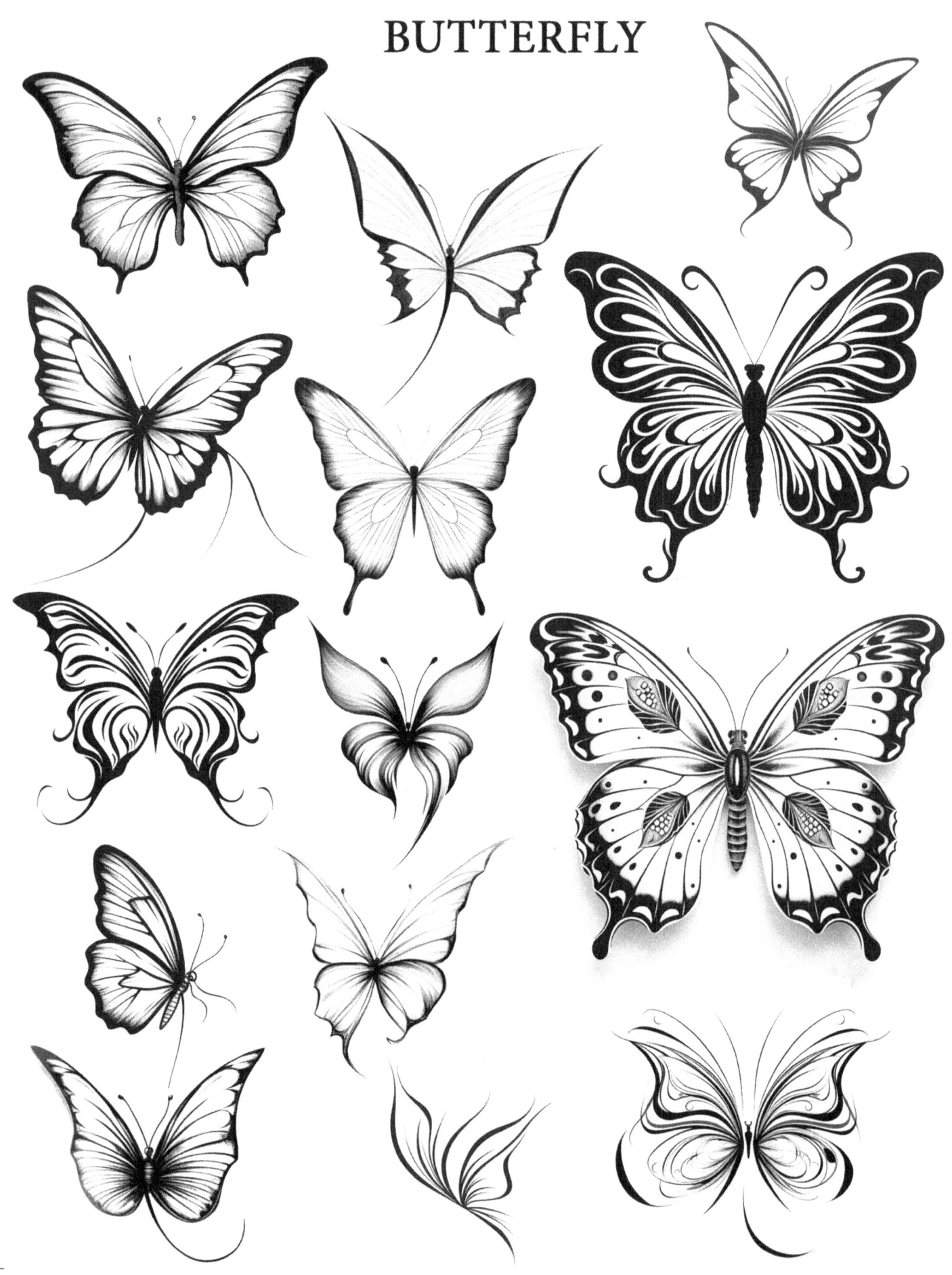

BUTTERFLY

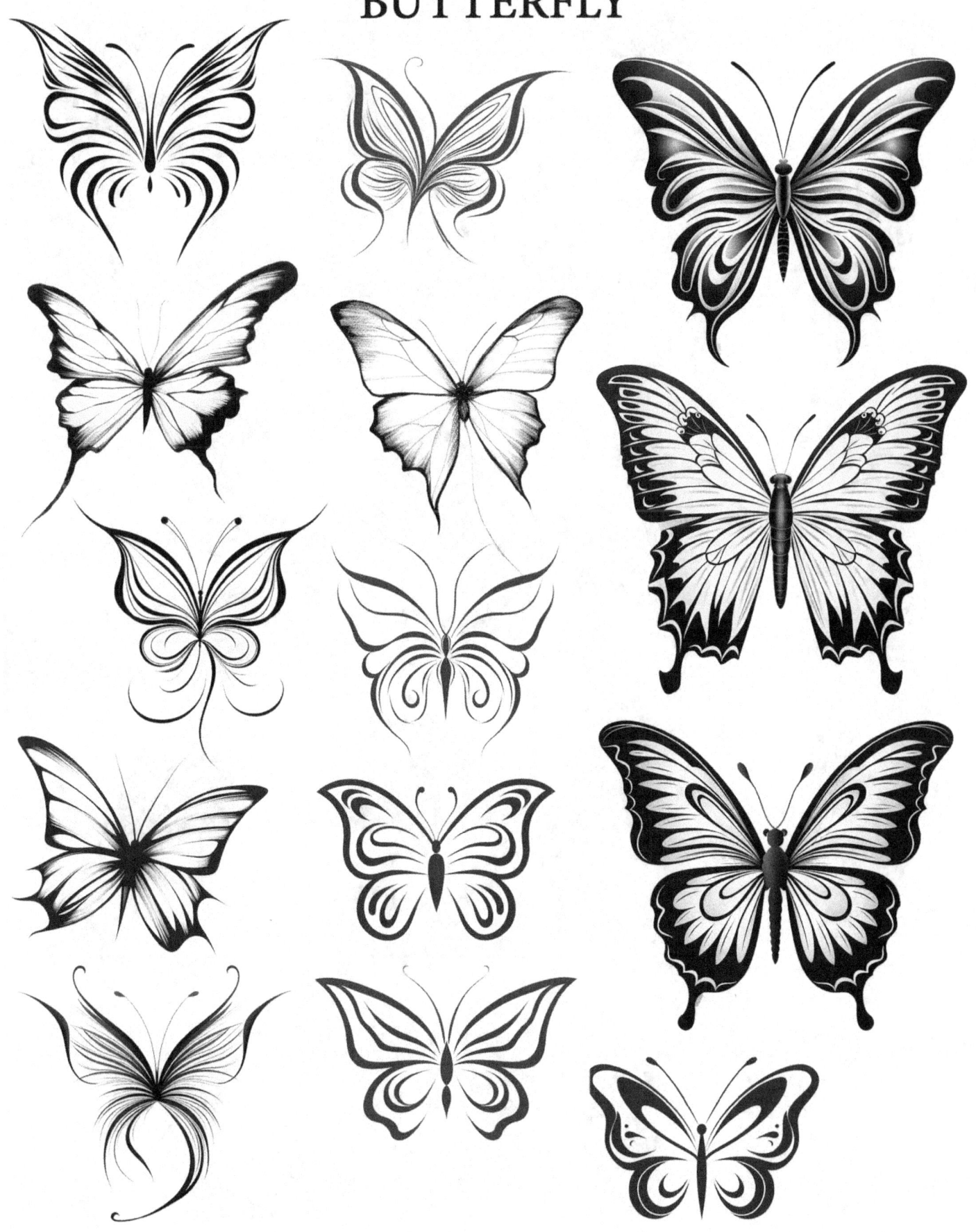

CATS

CATS

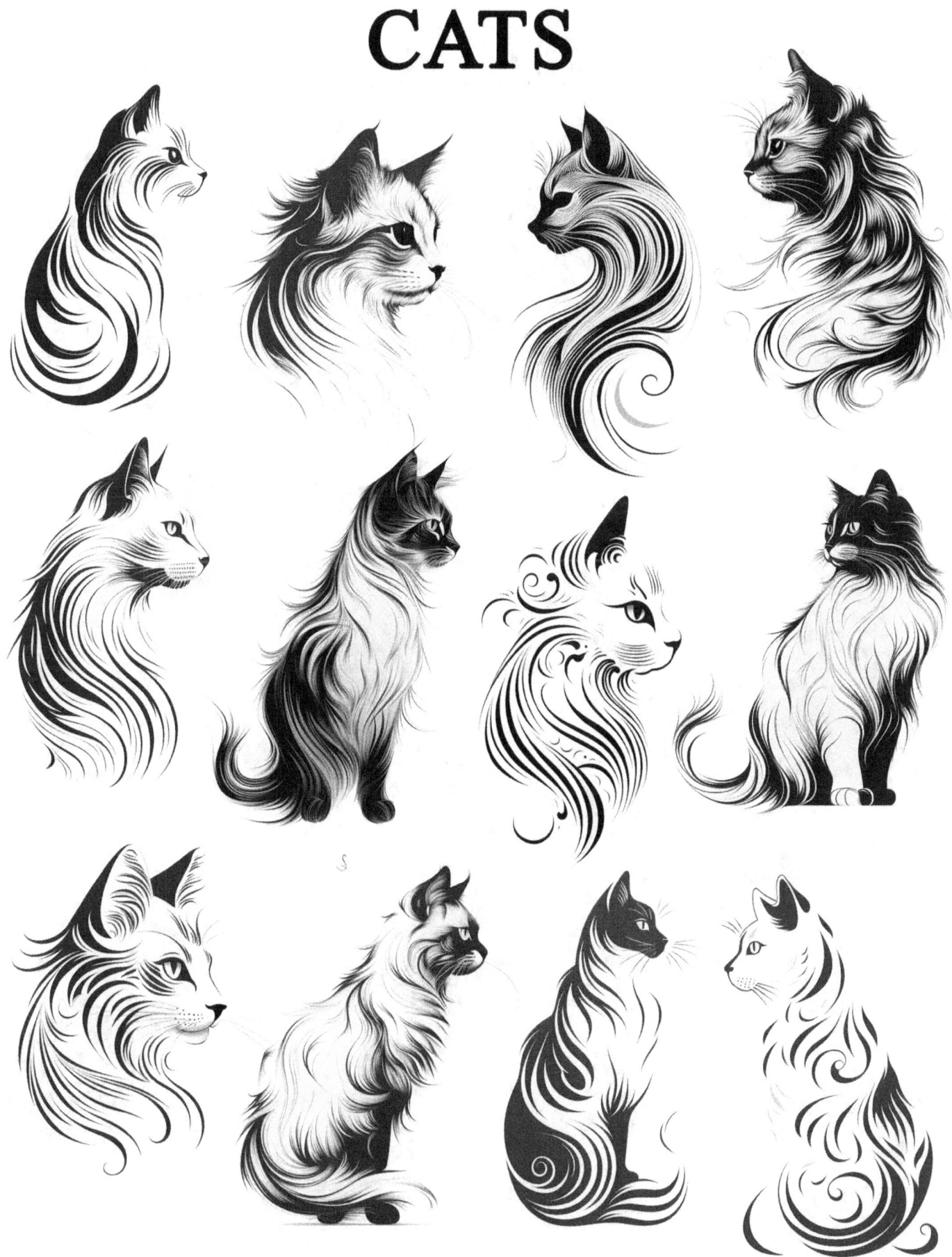

CATS

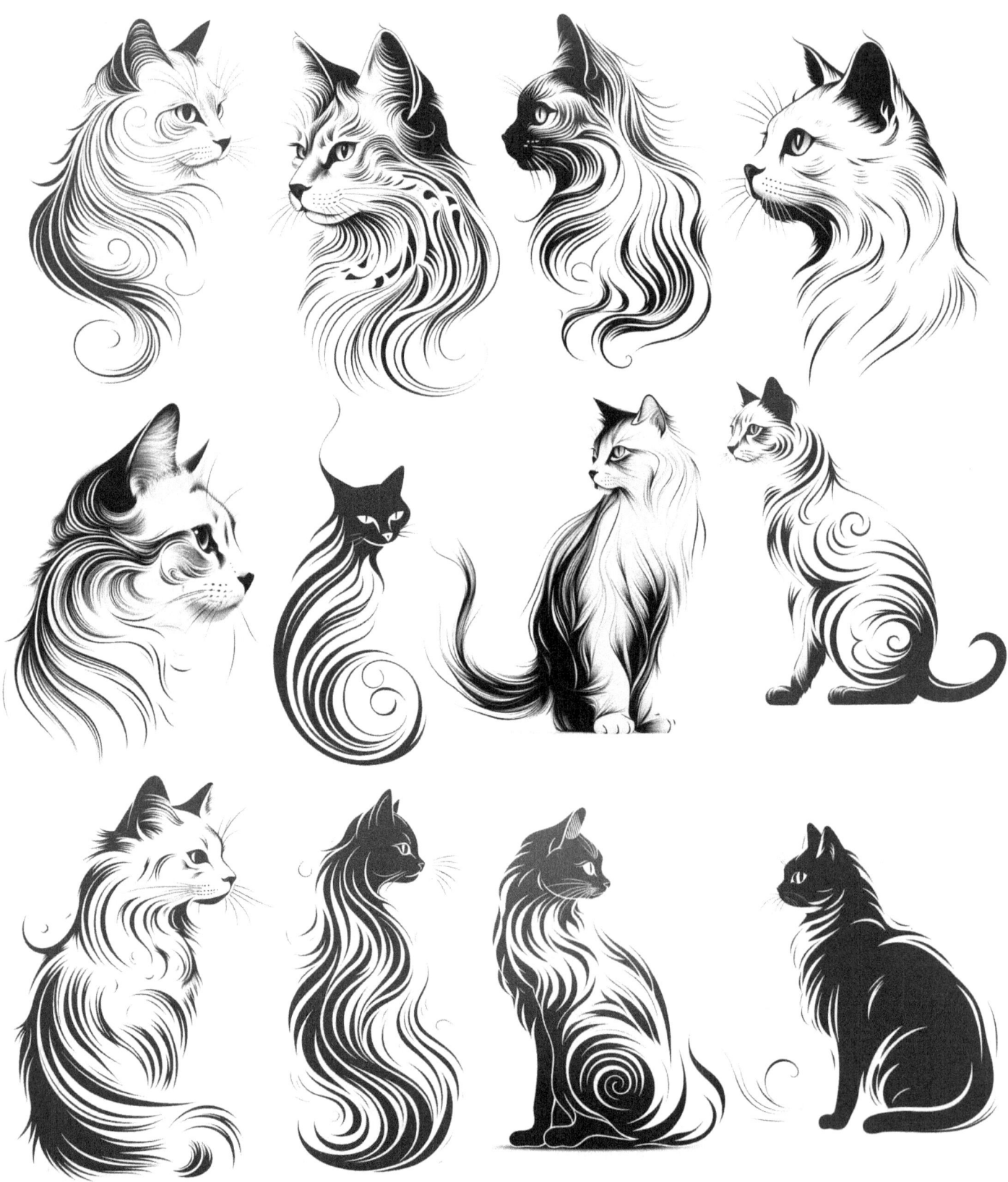

CATS

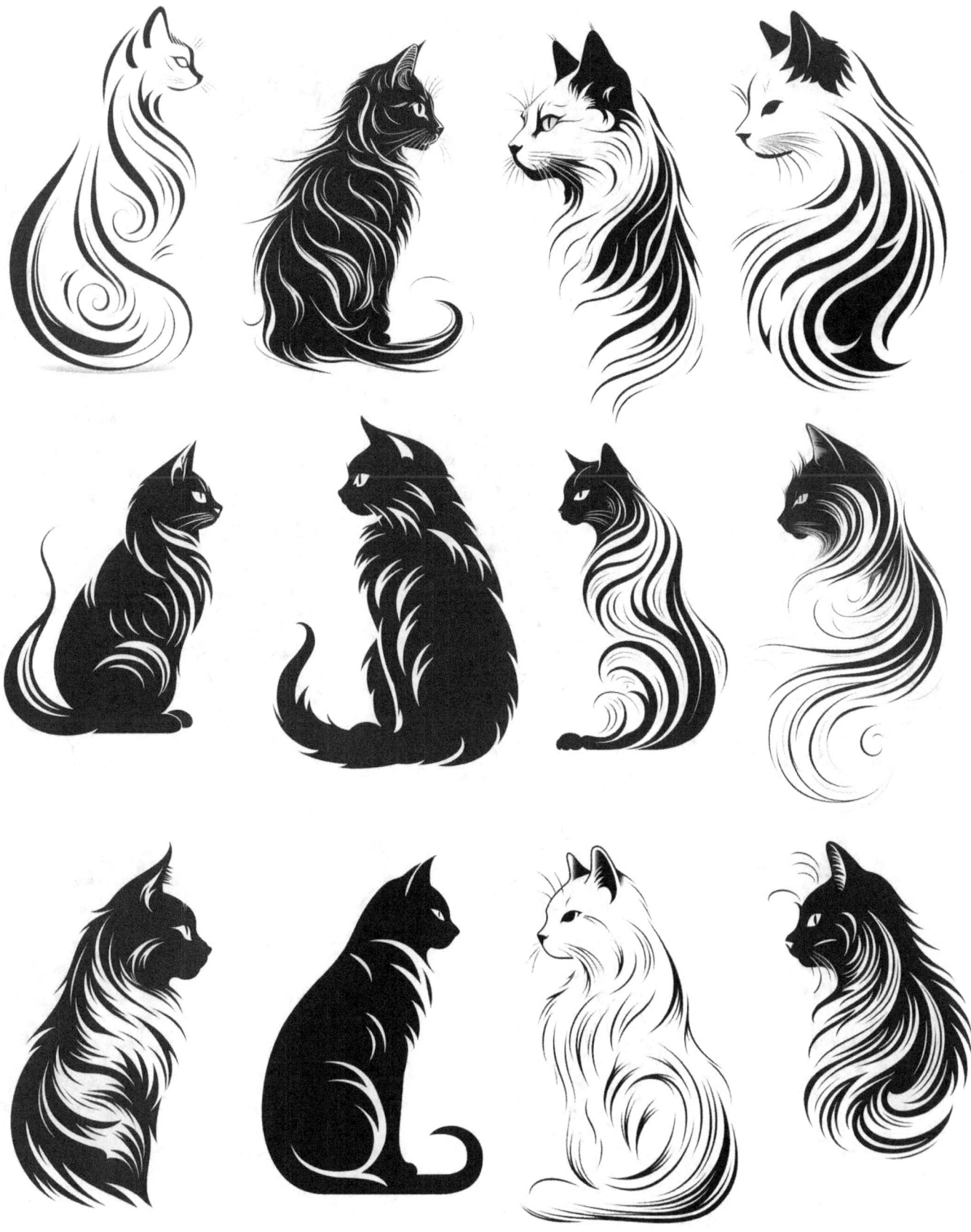

CATS

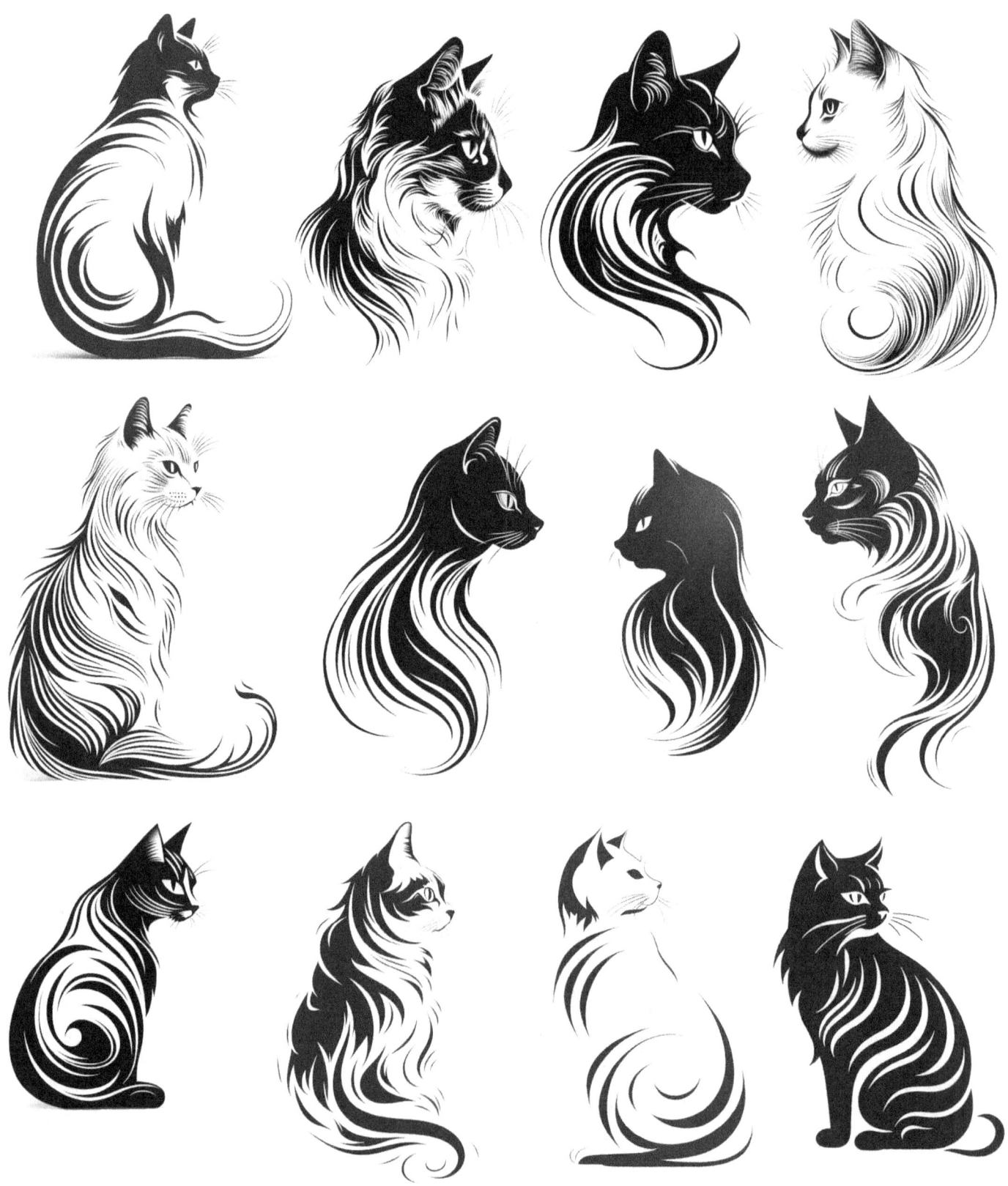

CHEETAH

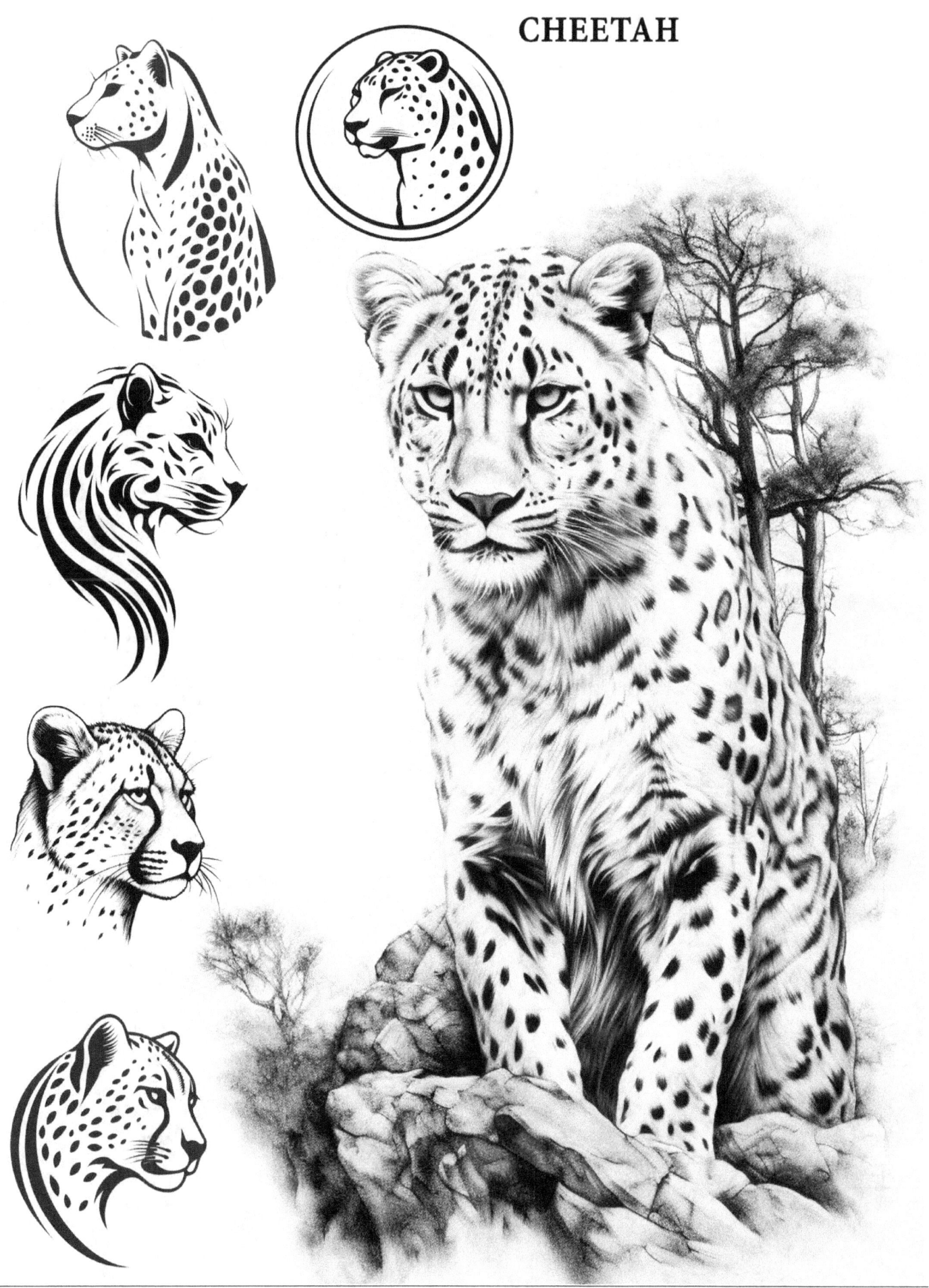

CHEETAH

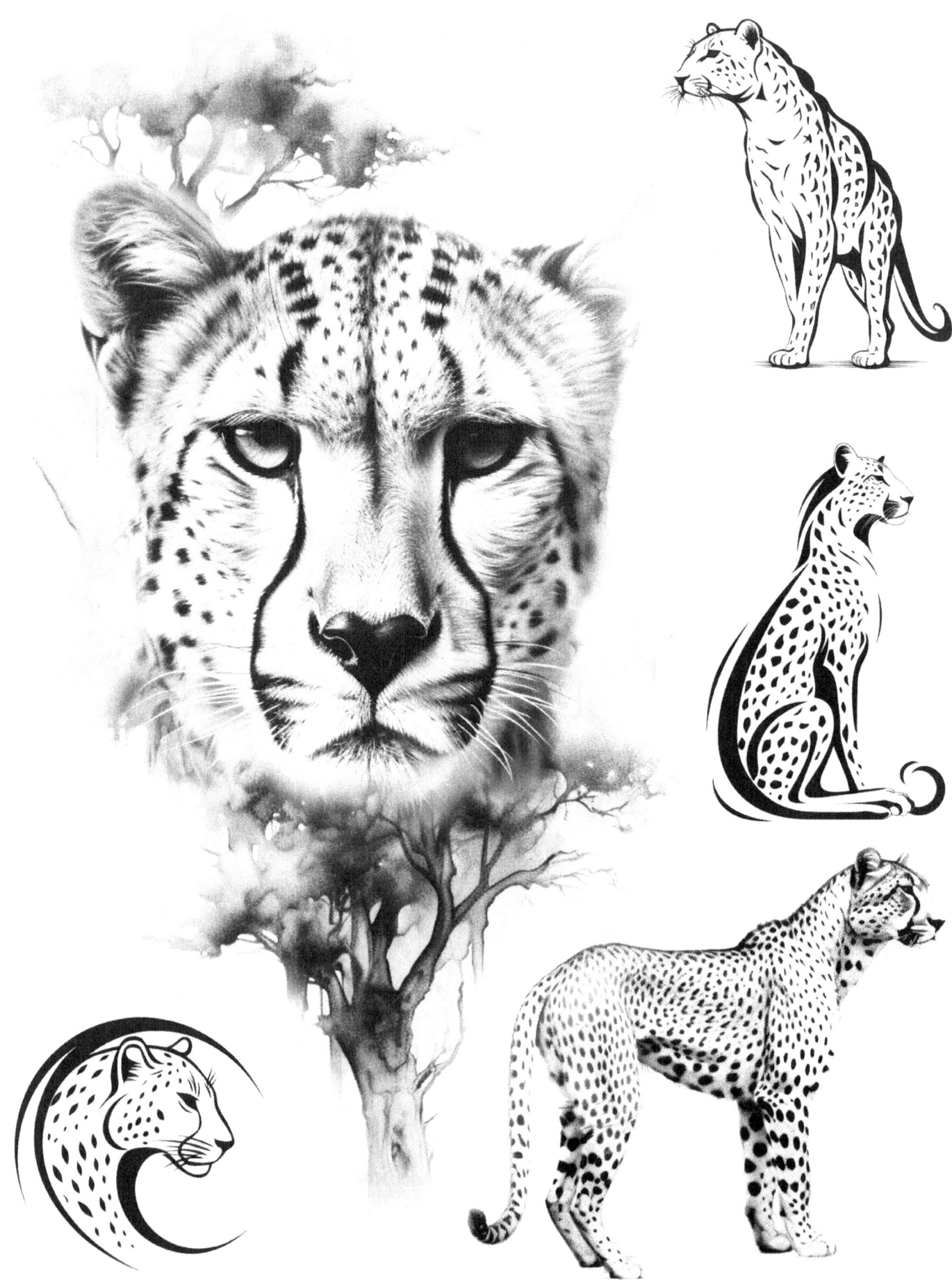

CHEETAH

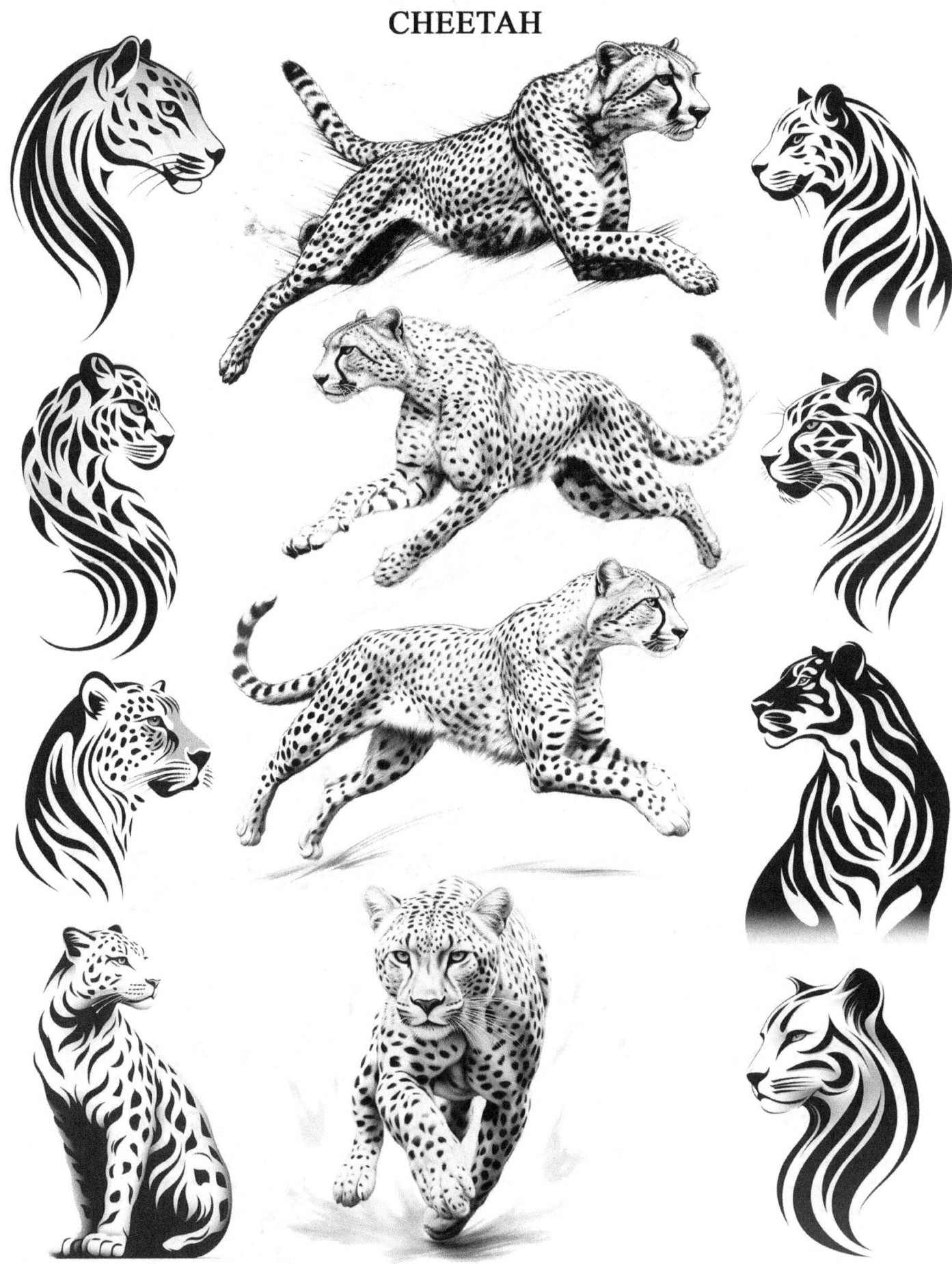

CHERUB

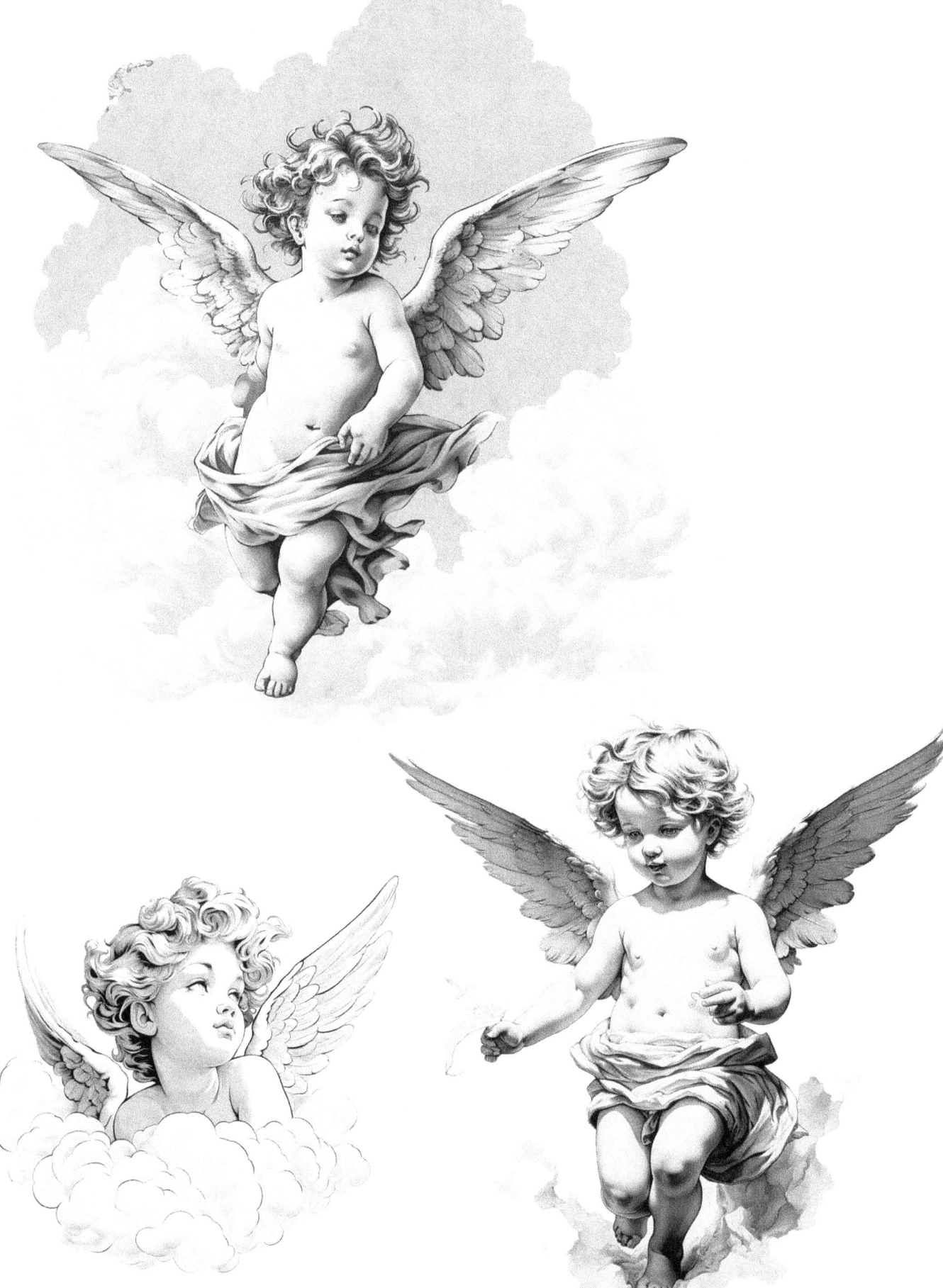

CHERUB

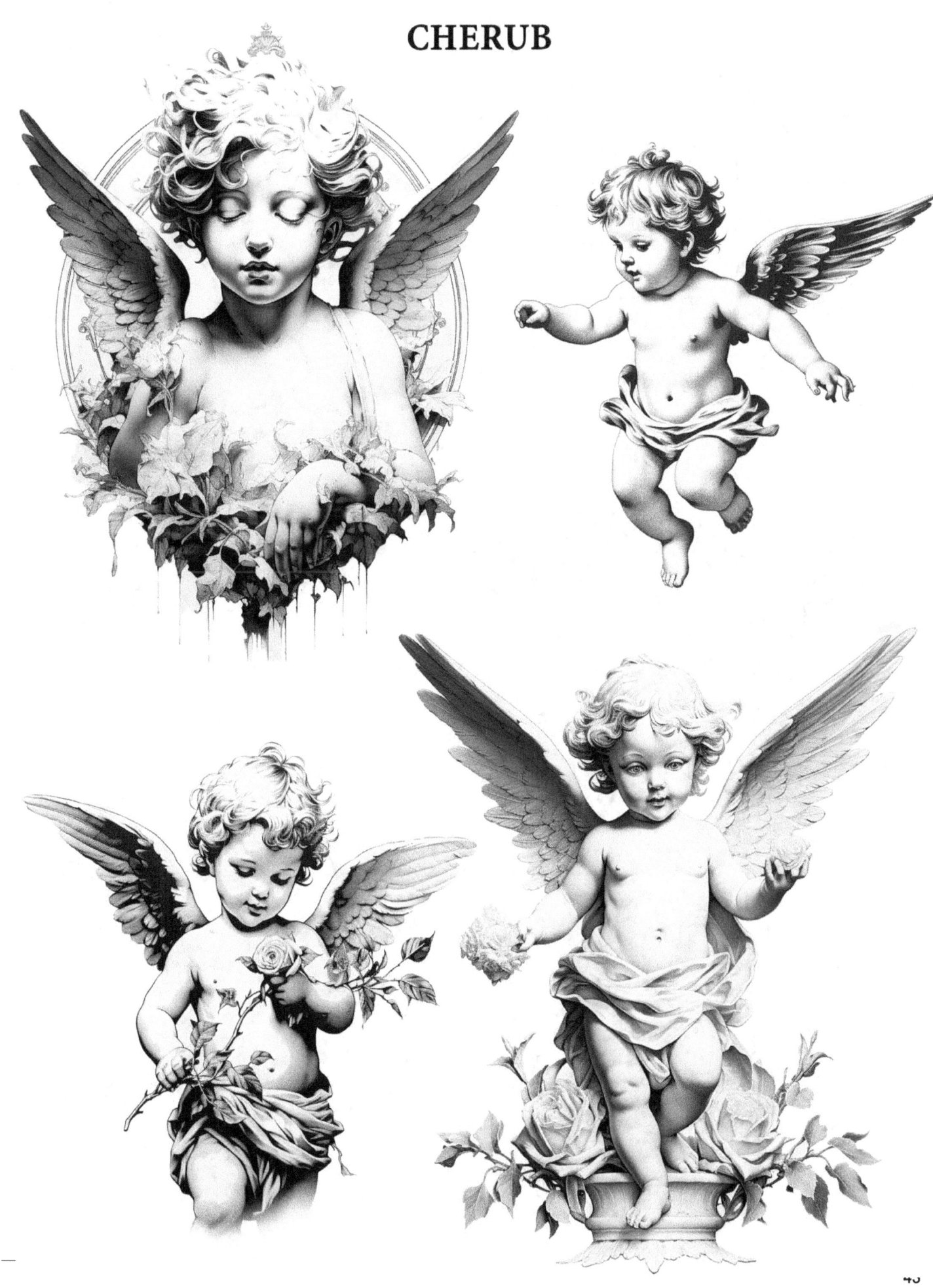

CHERUB

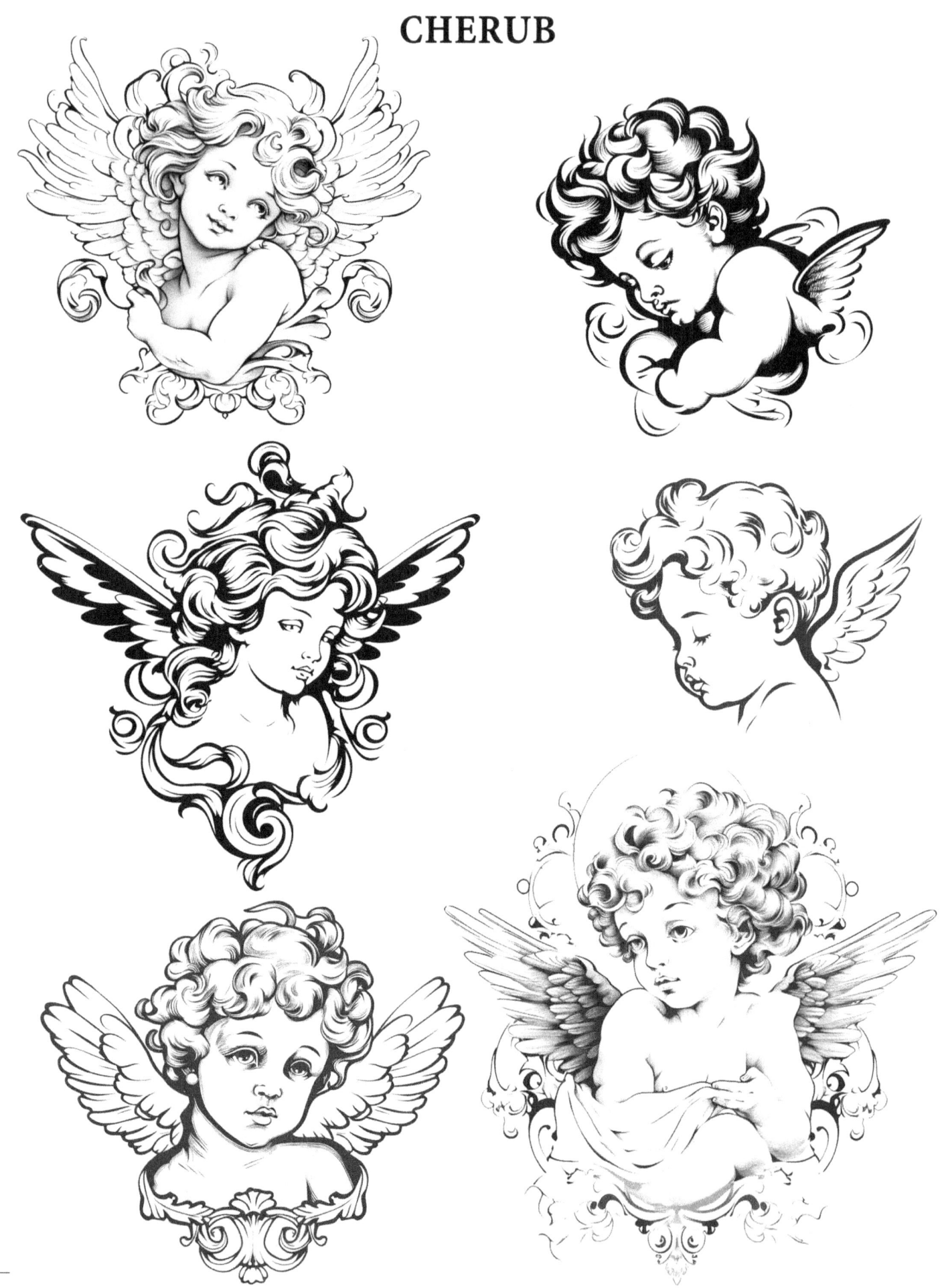

KING's CROWN

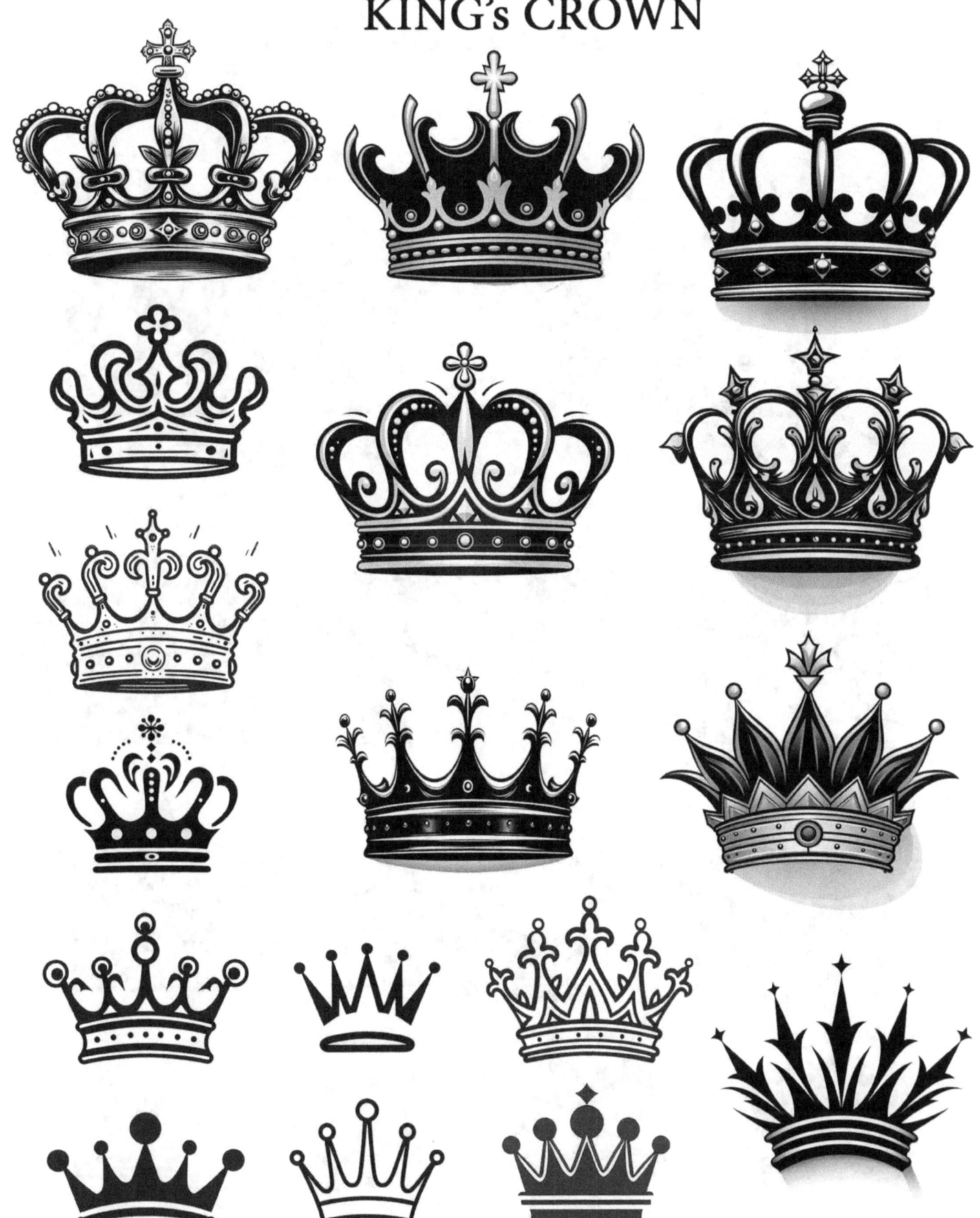

KING's CROWN

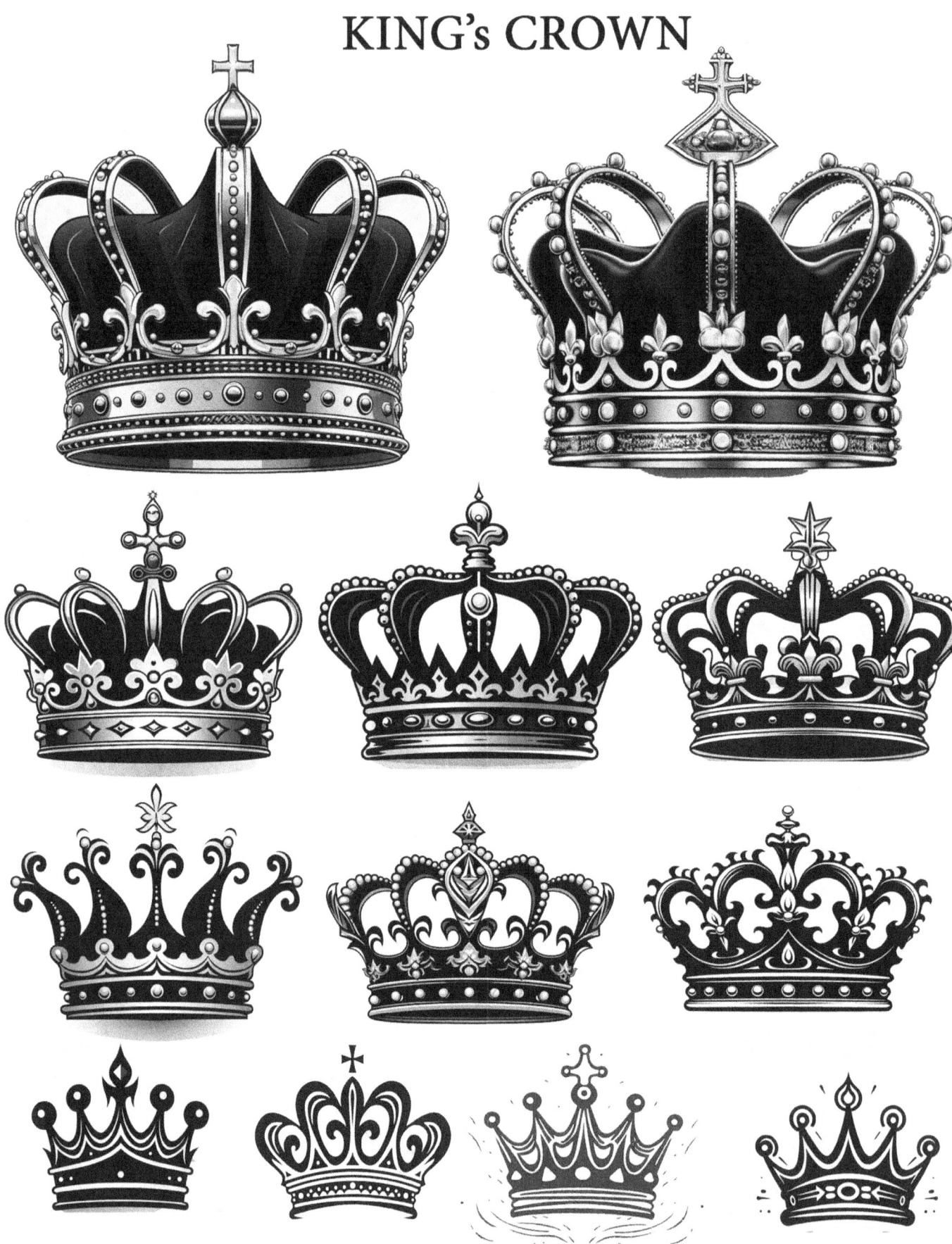

QUEEN's CROWN

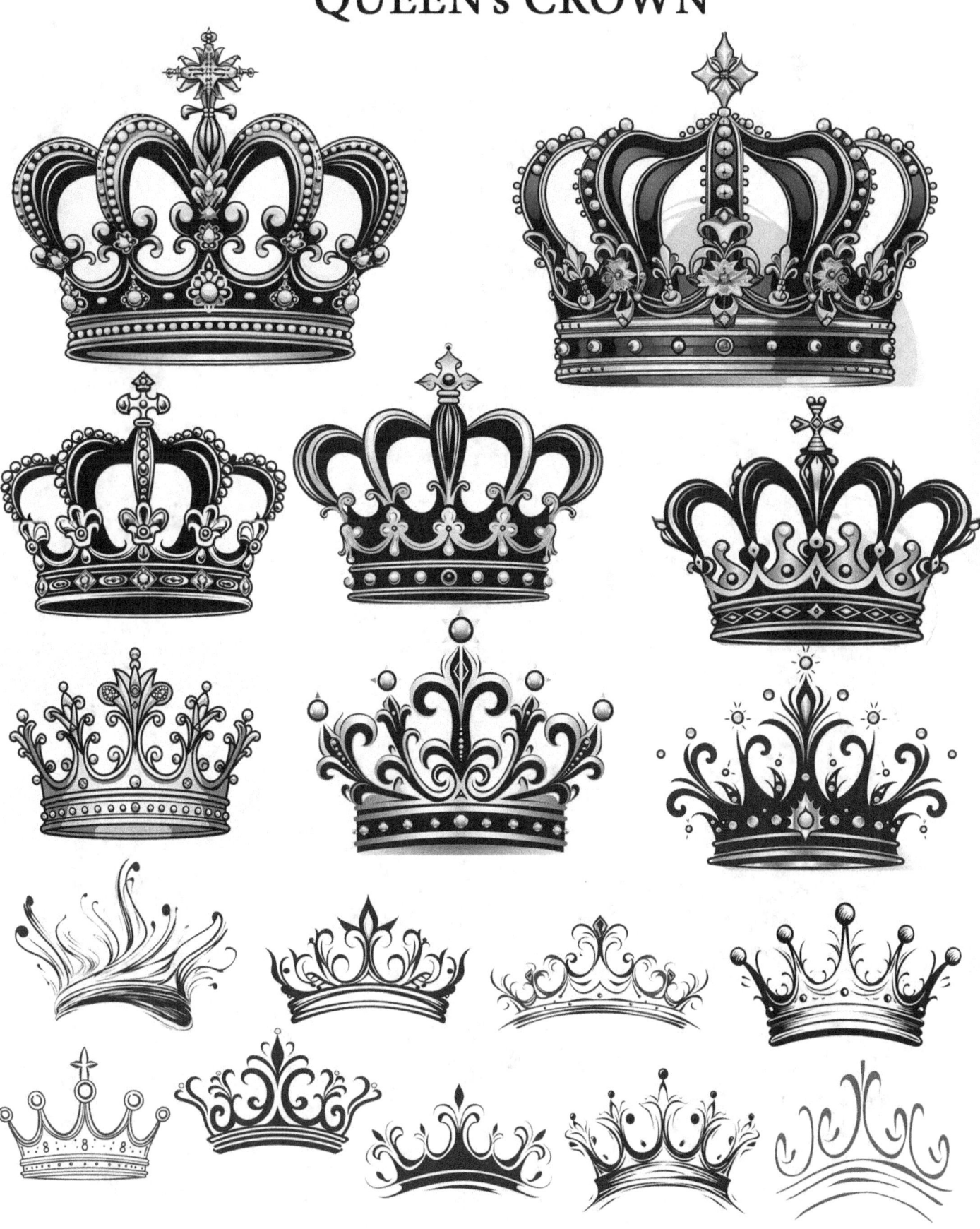

DOLPHIN

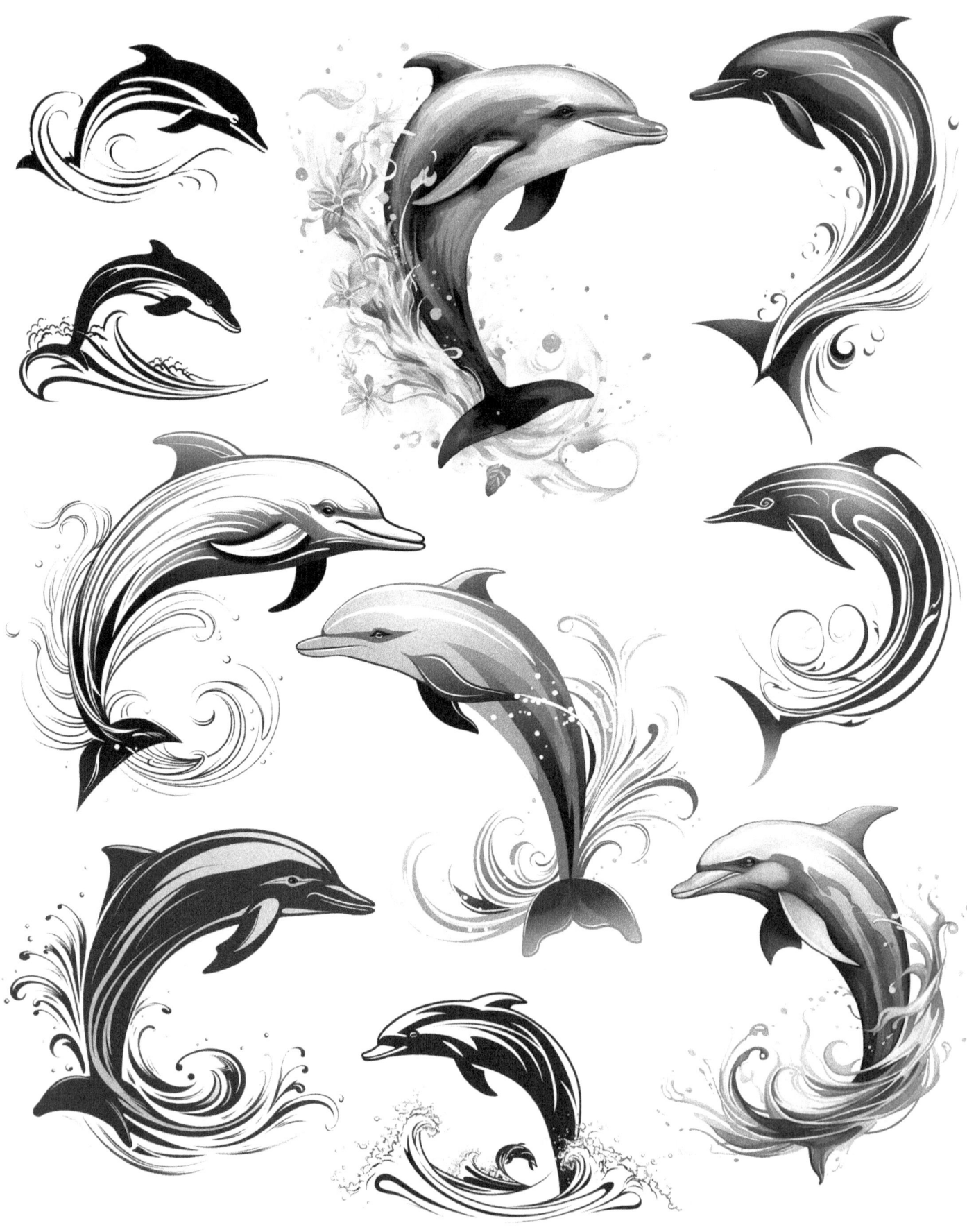

DOLPHIN

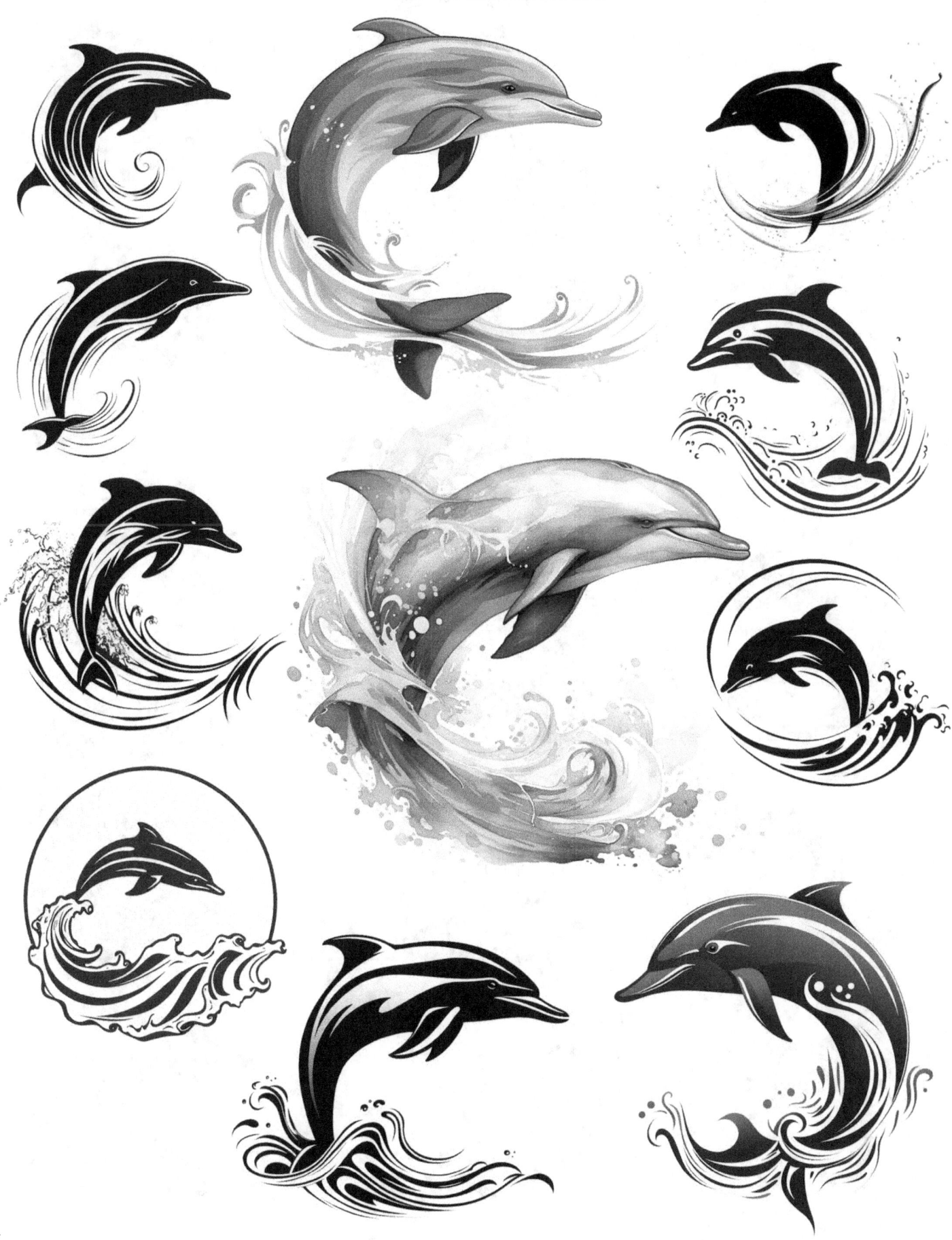

DOLPHIN

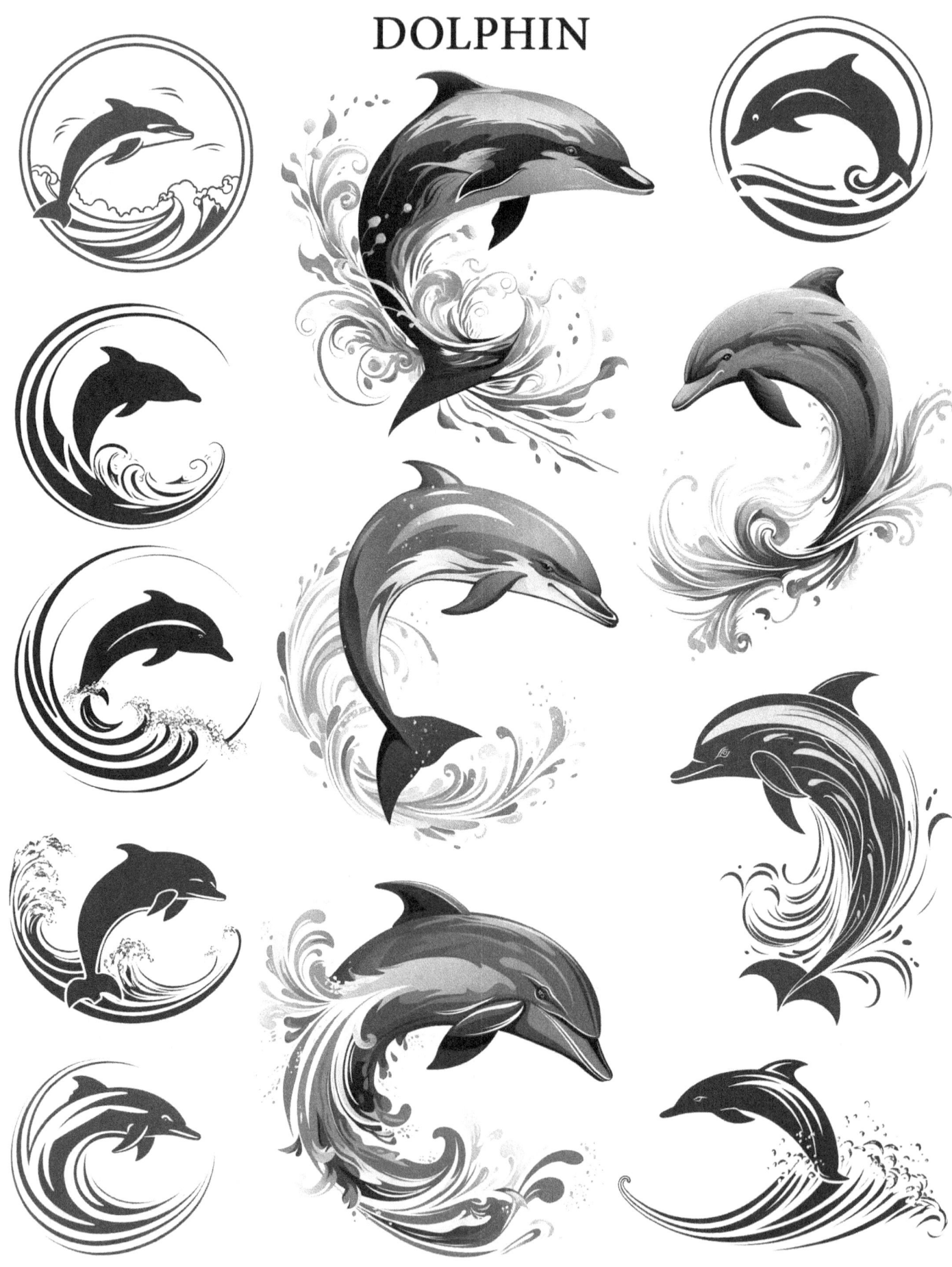

DOLPHIN

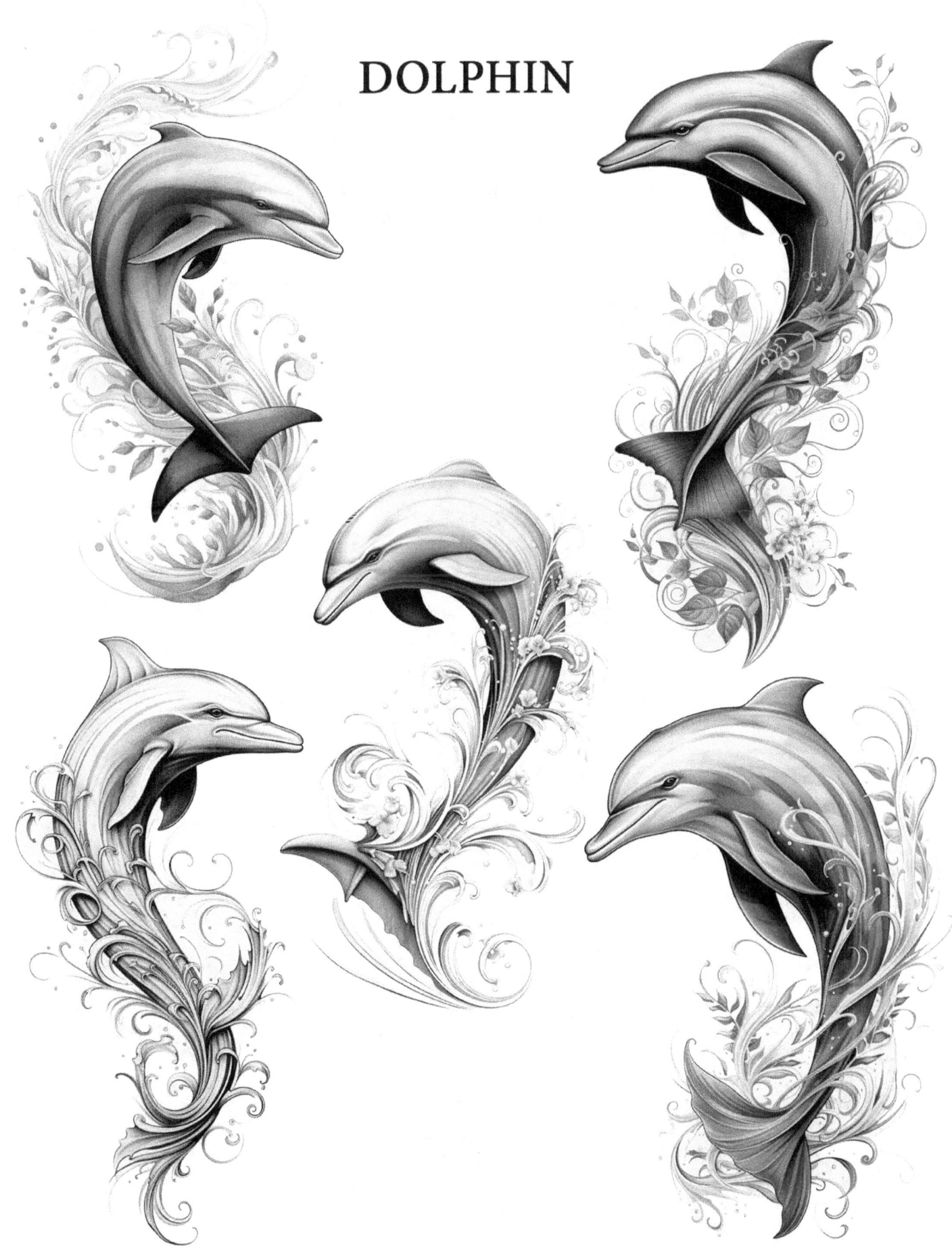

DOVE

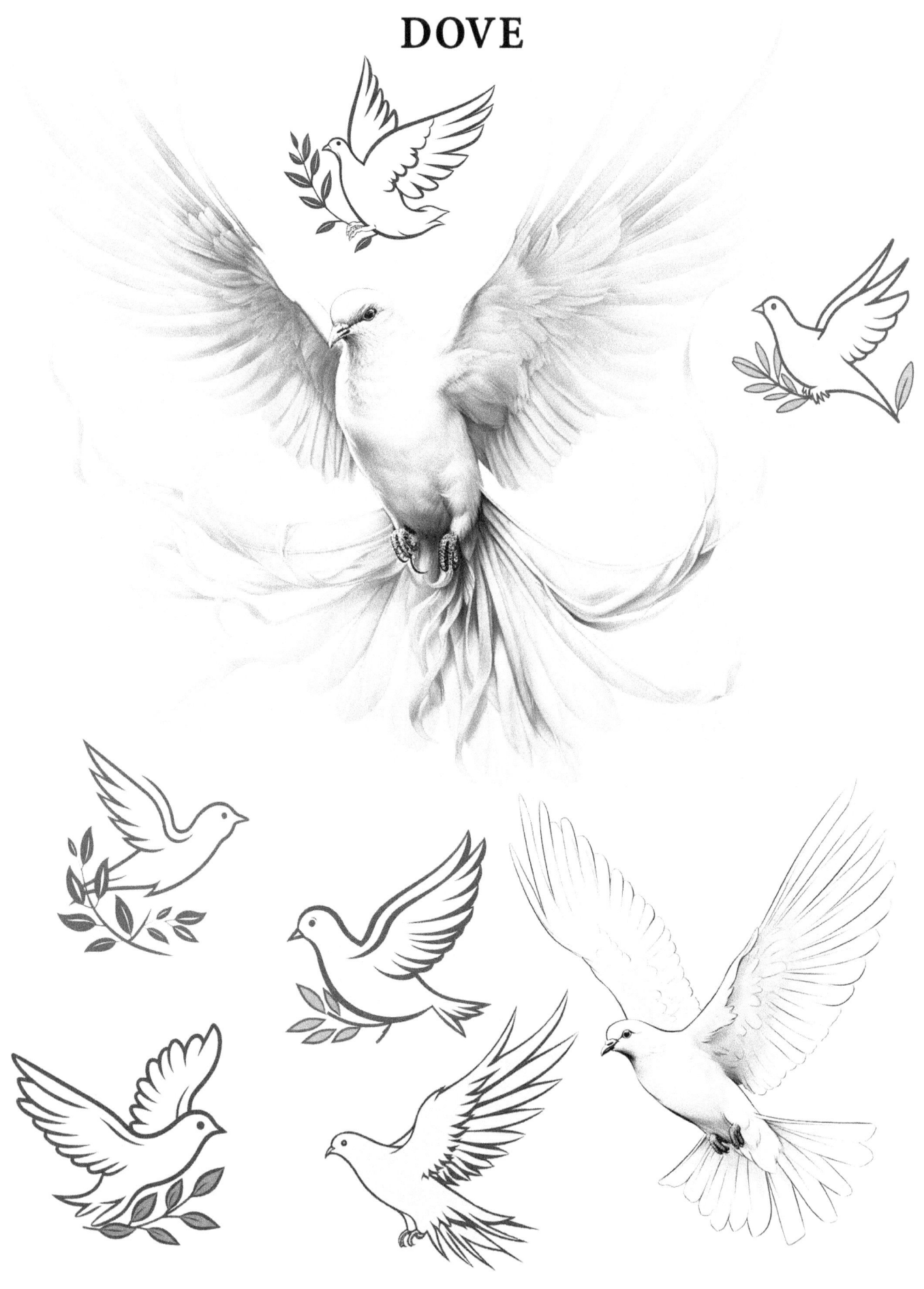

EAGLE

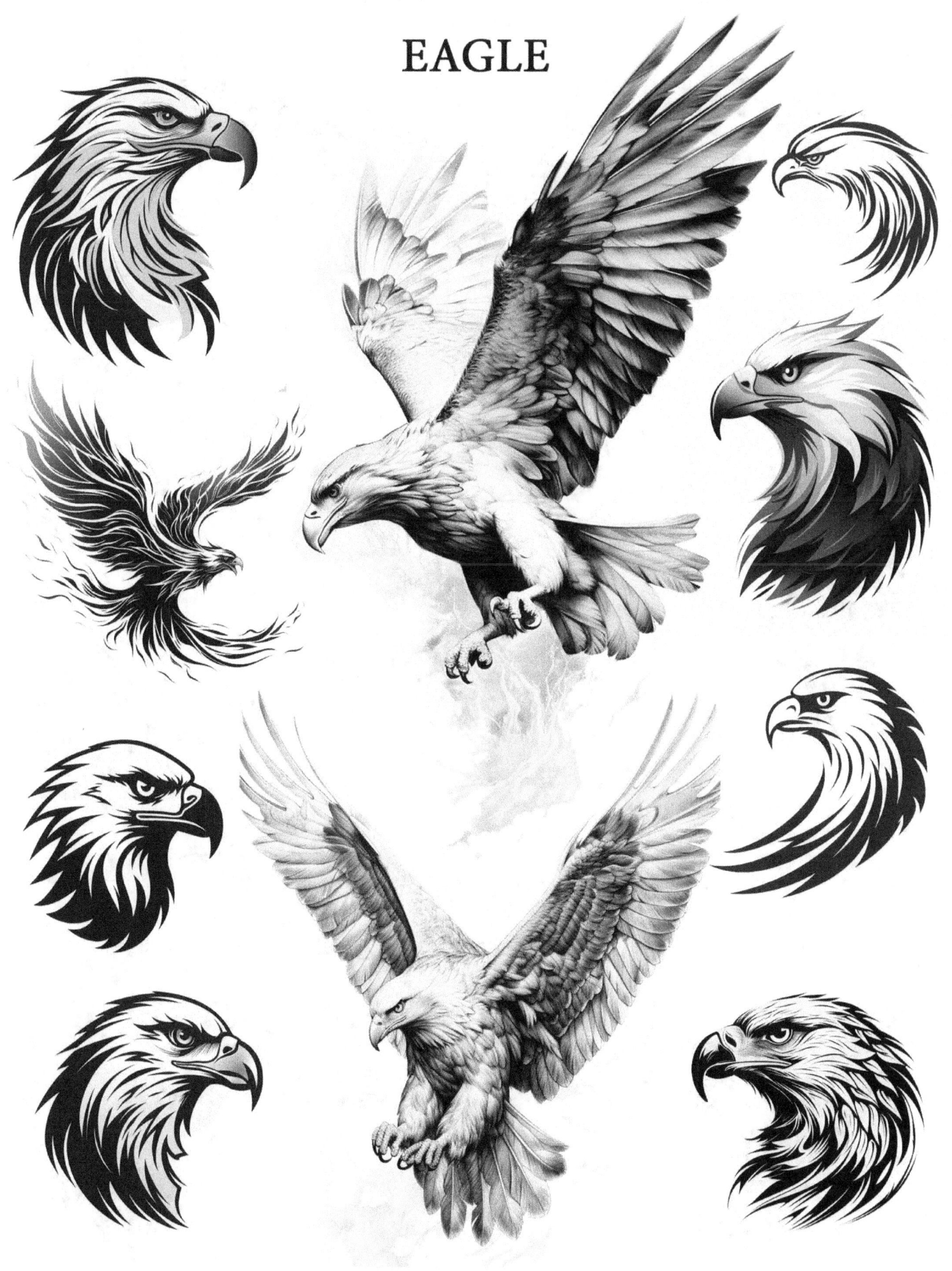

EAGLE

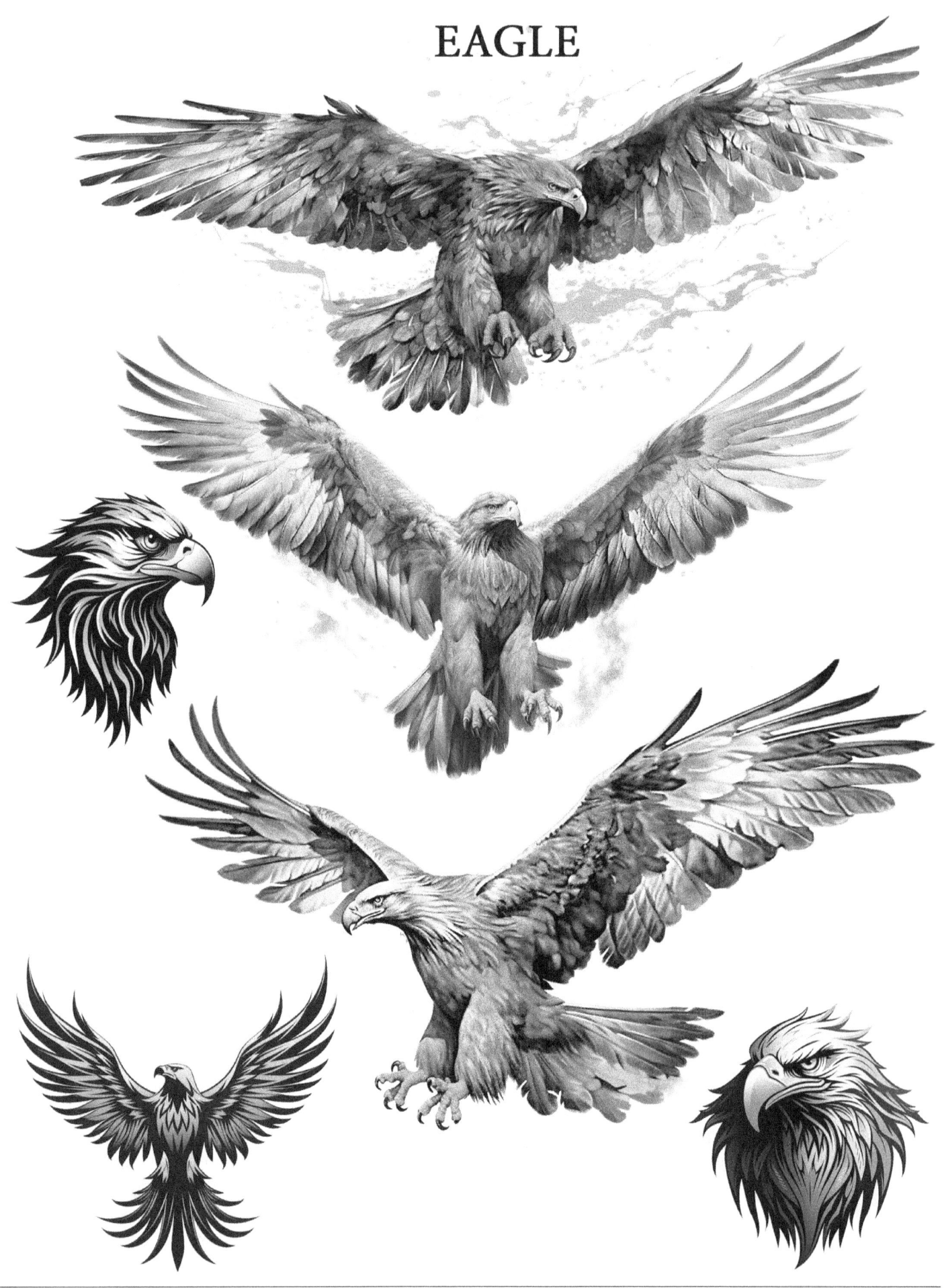

EAGLE

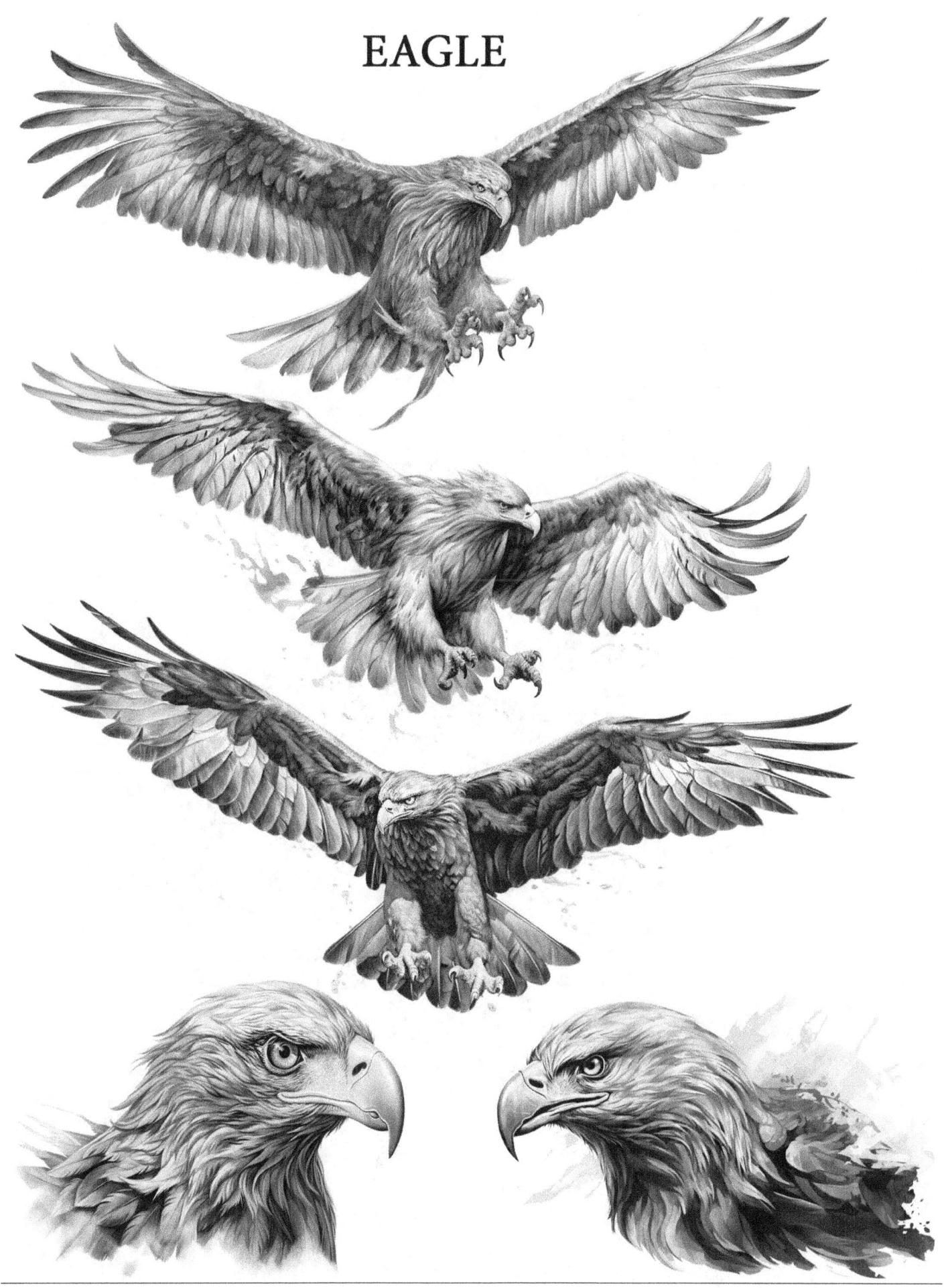

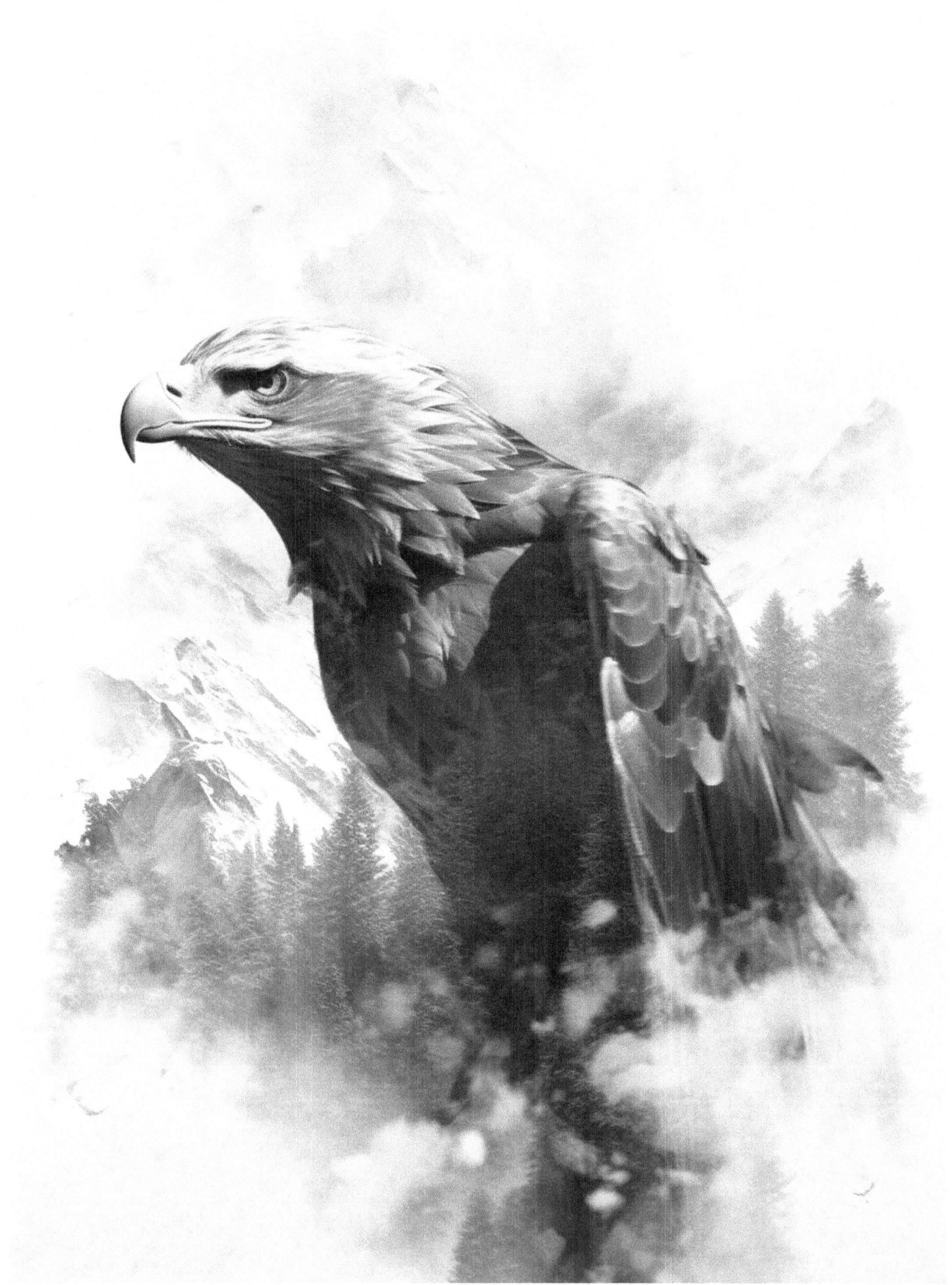

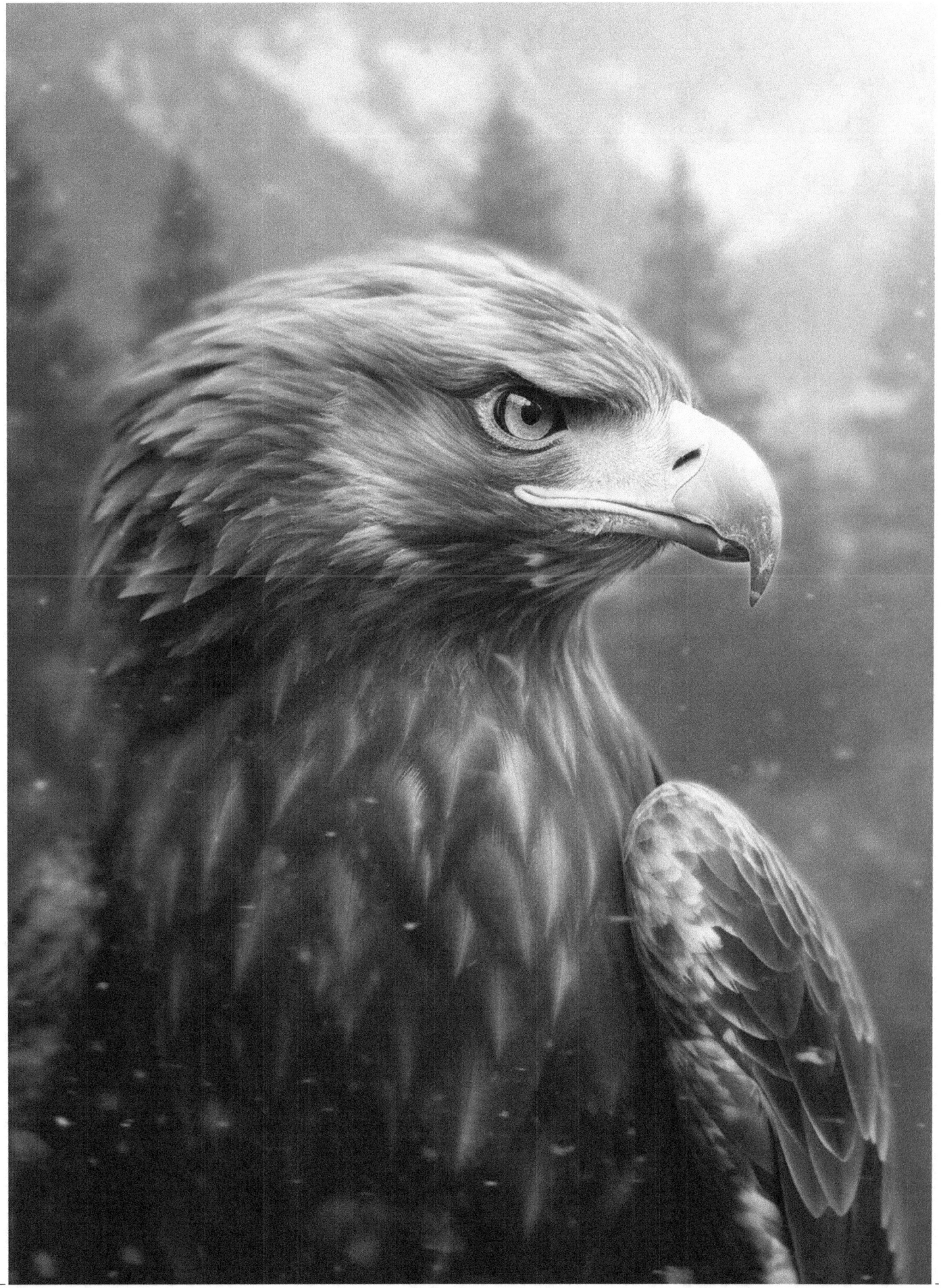

EAGLE

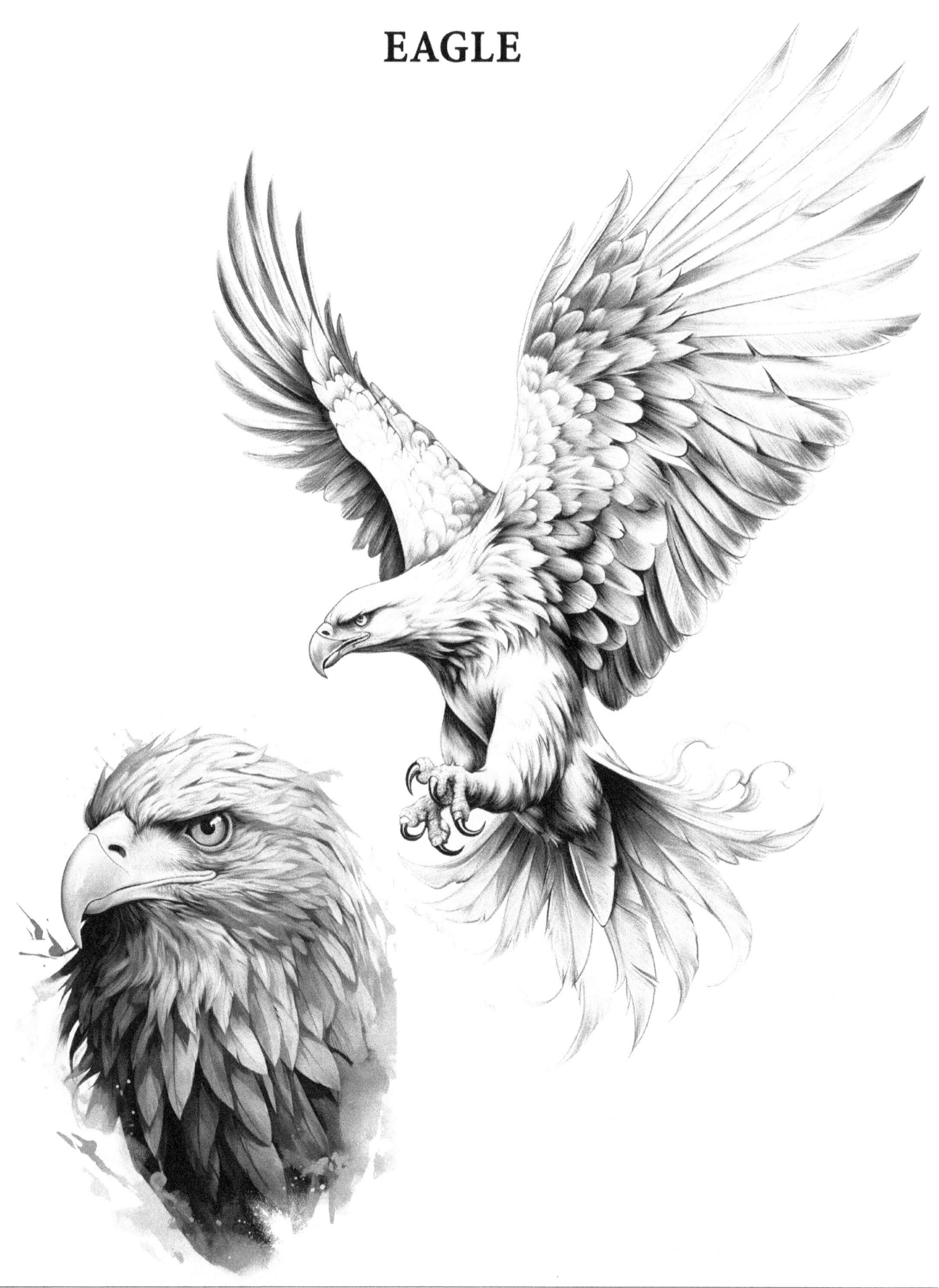

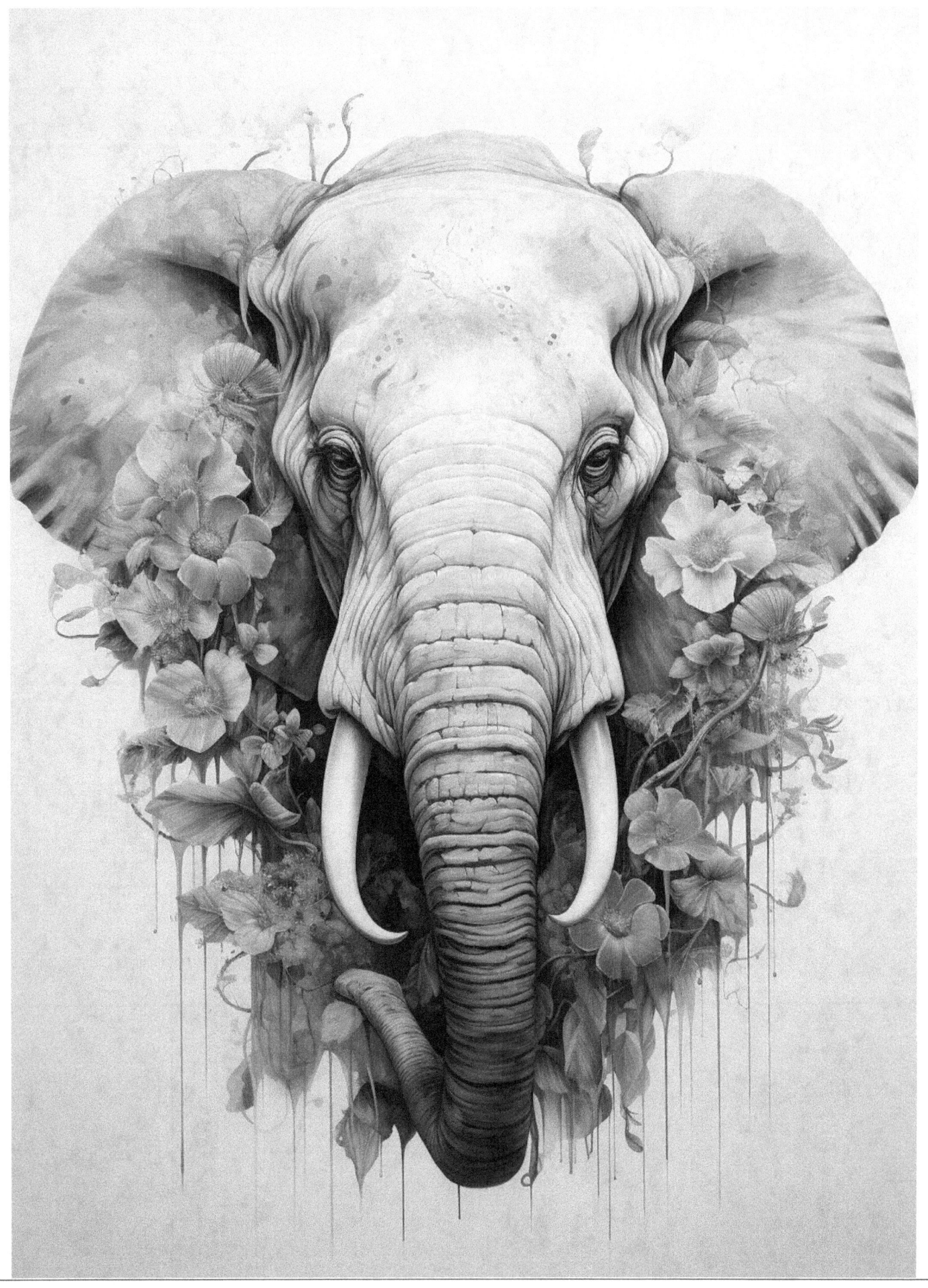

ELEPHANT

FLEUR DE LIS

FLEUR DE LIS

FLEUR DE LIS

FLEUR DE LIS

FOX

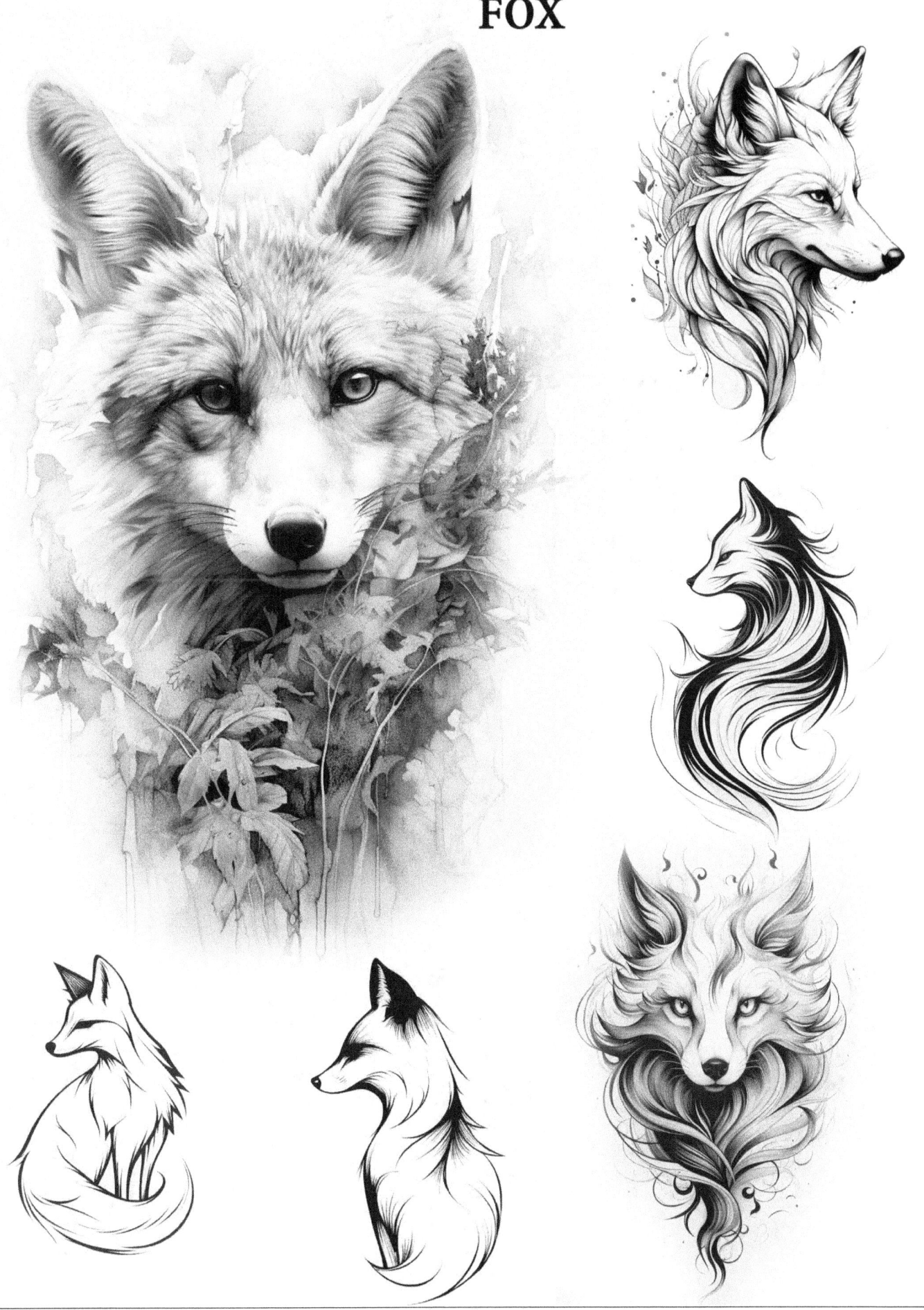

FOX

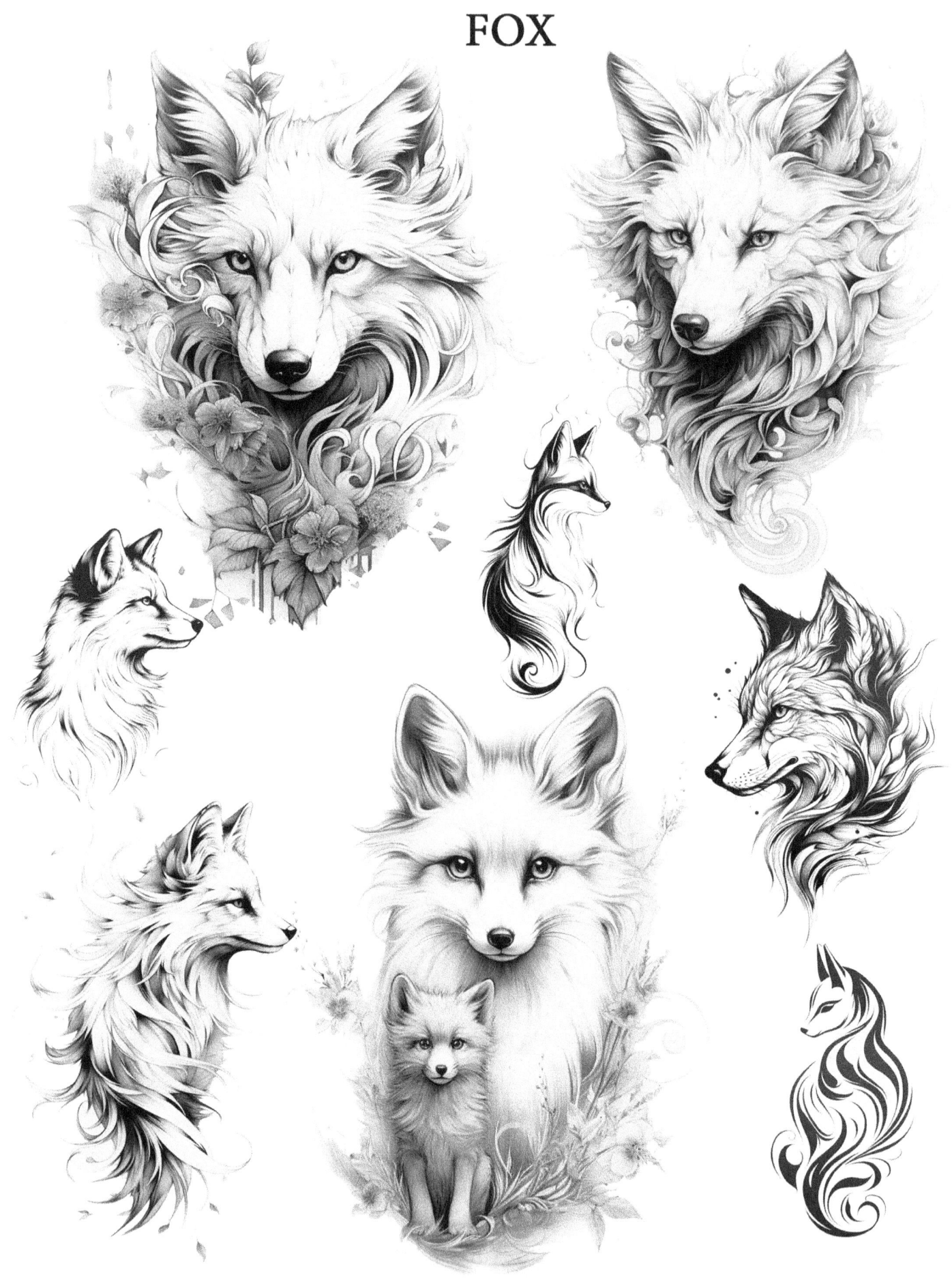

FOX

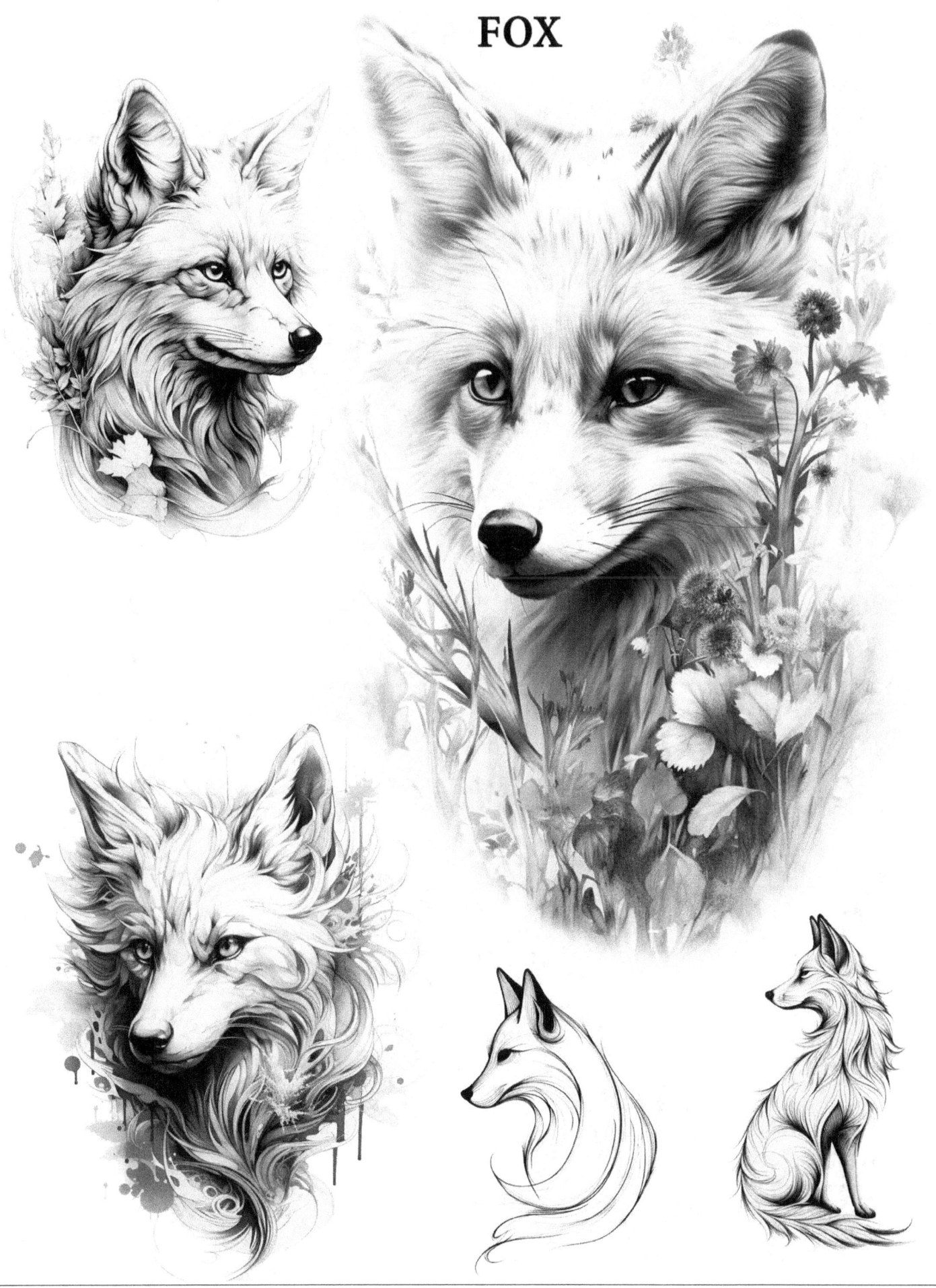

FOX

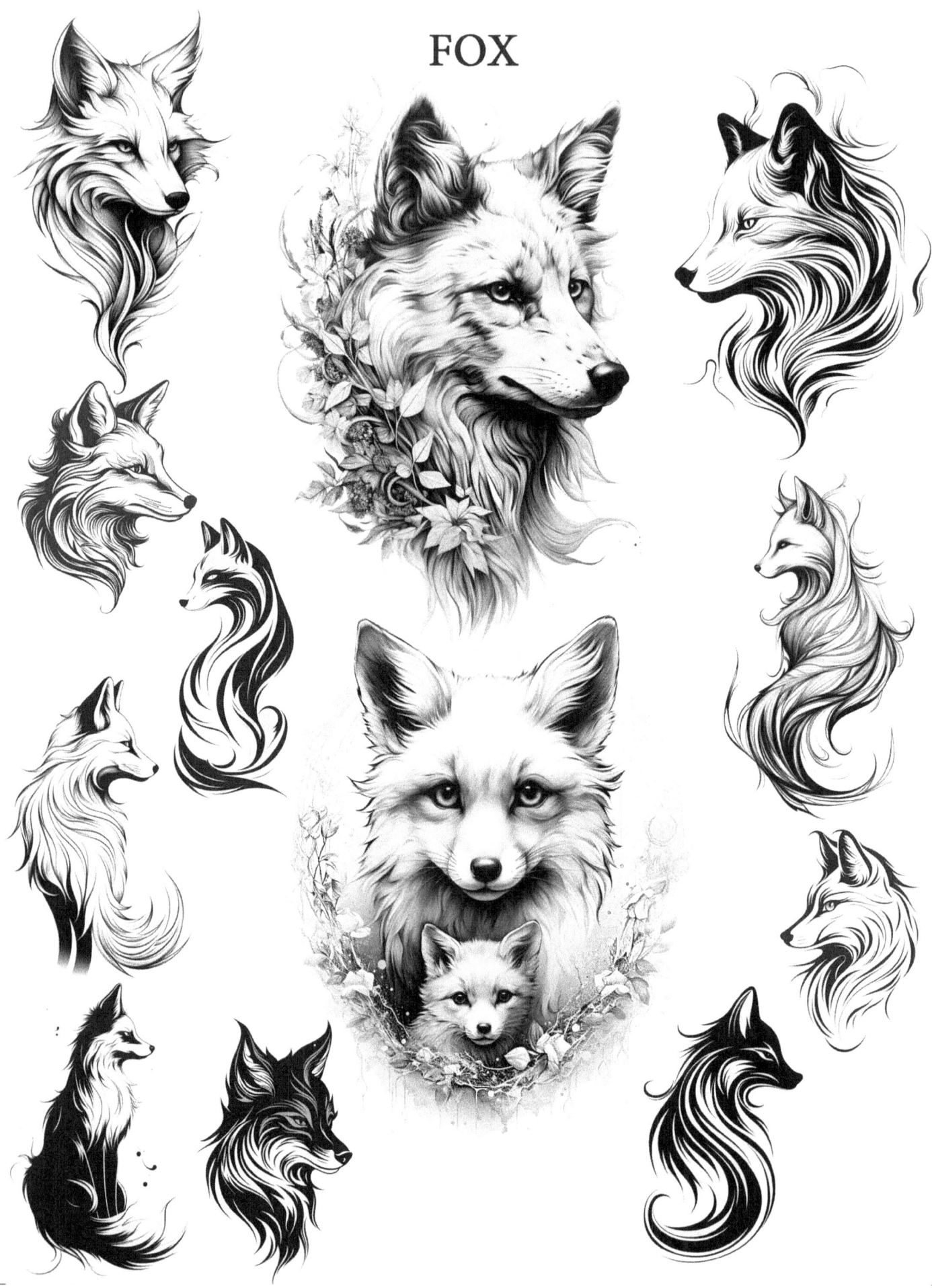

GIRAFFE

HARP

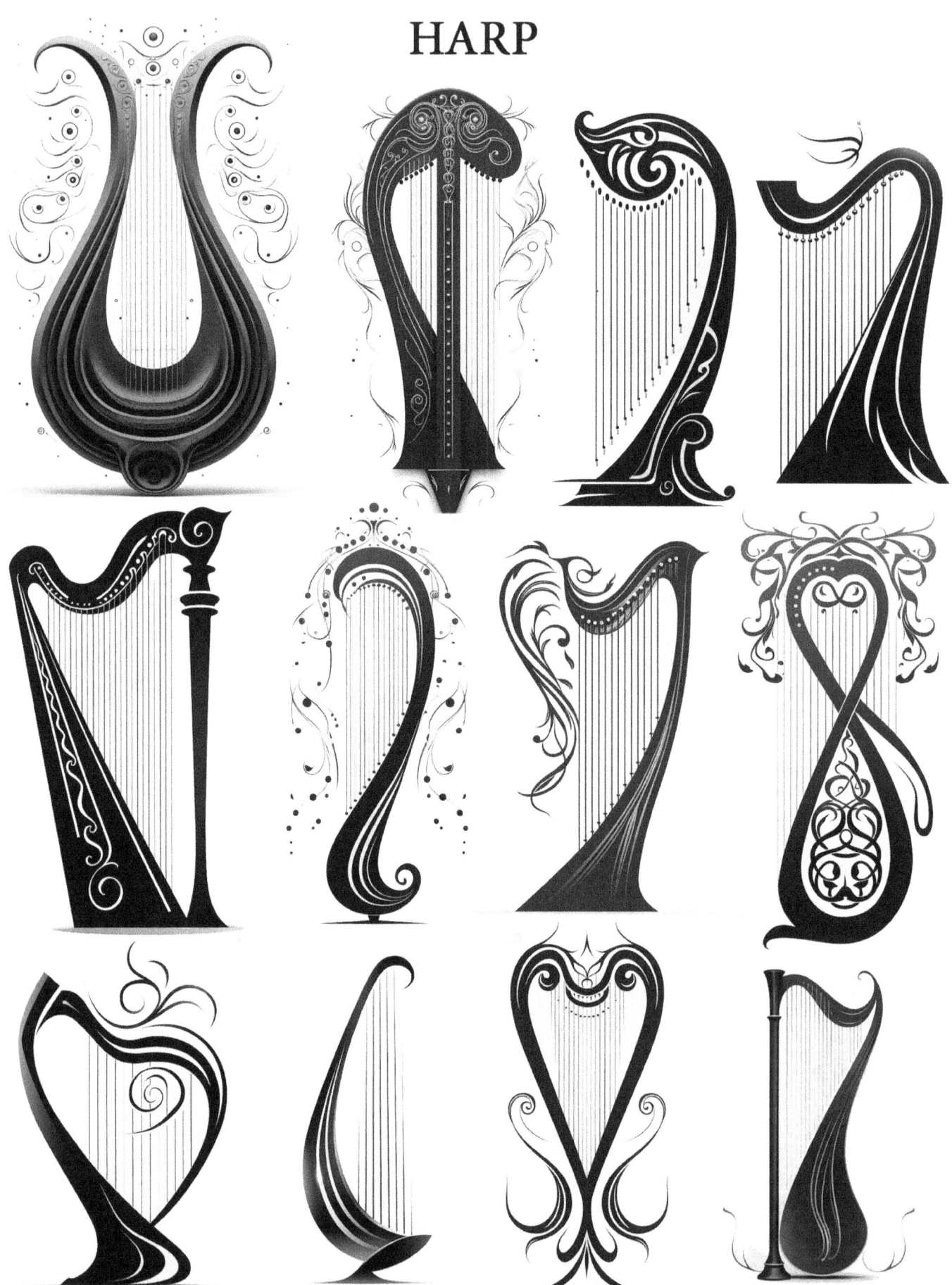

HARP

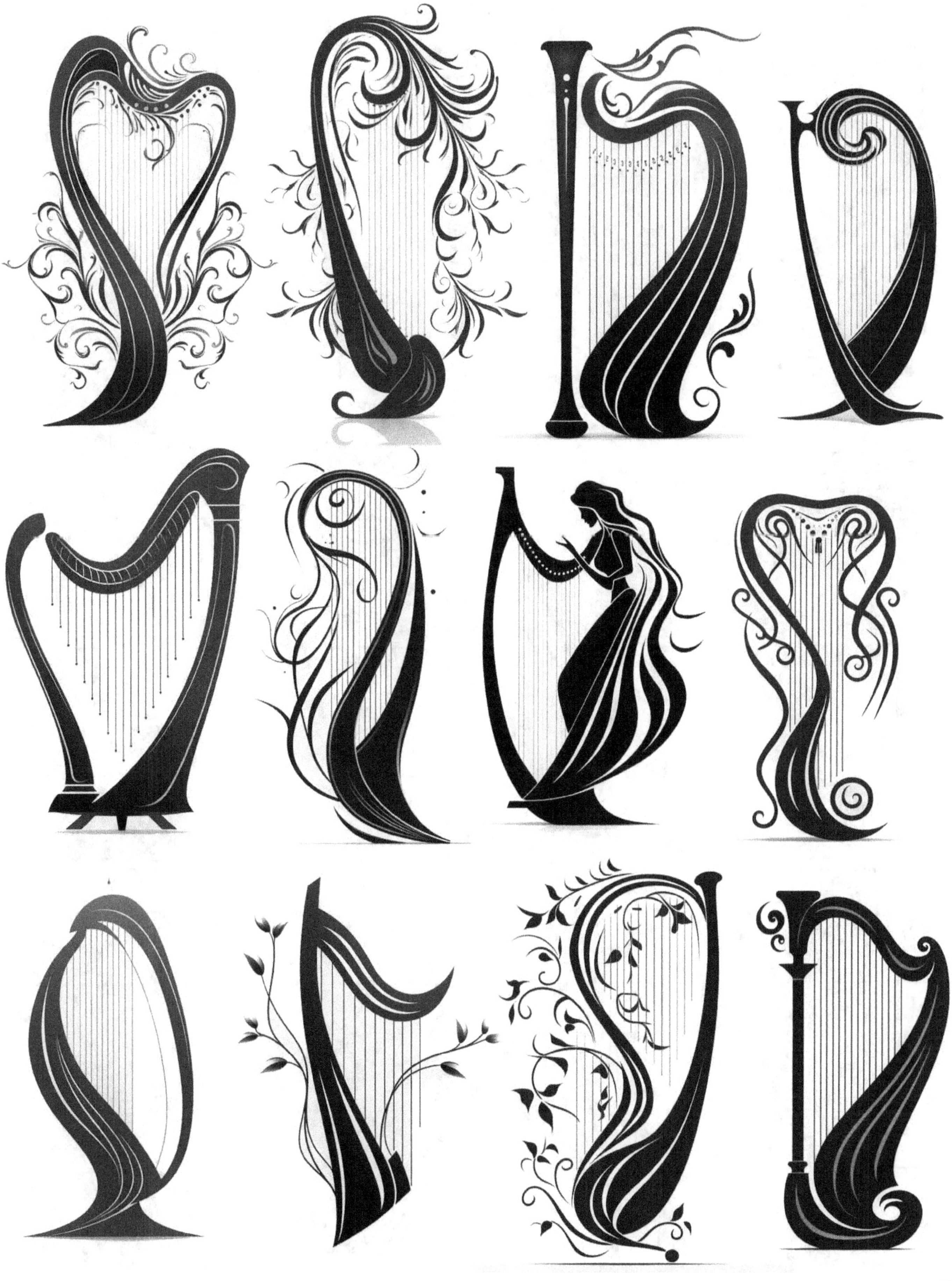

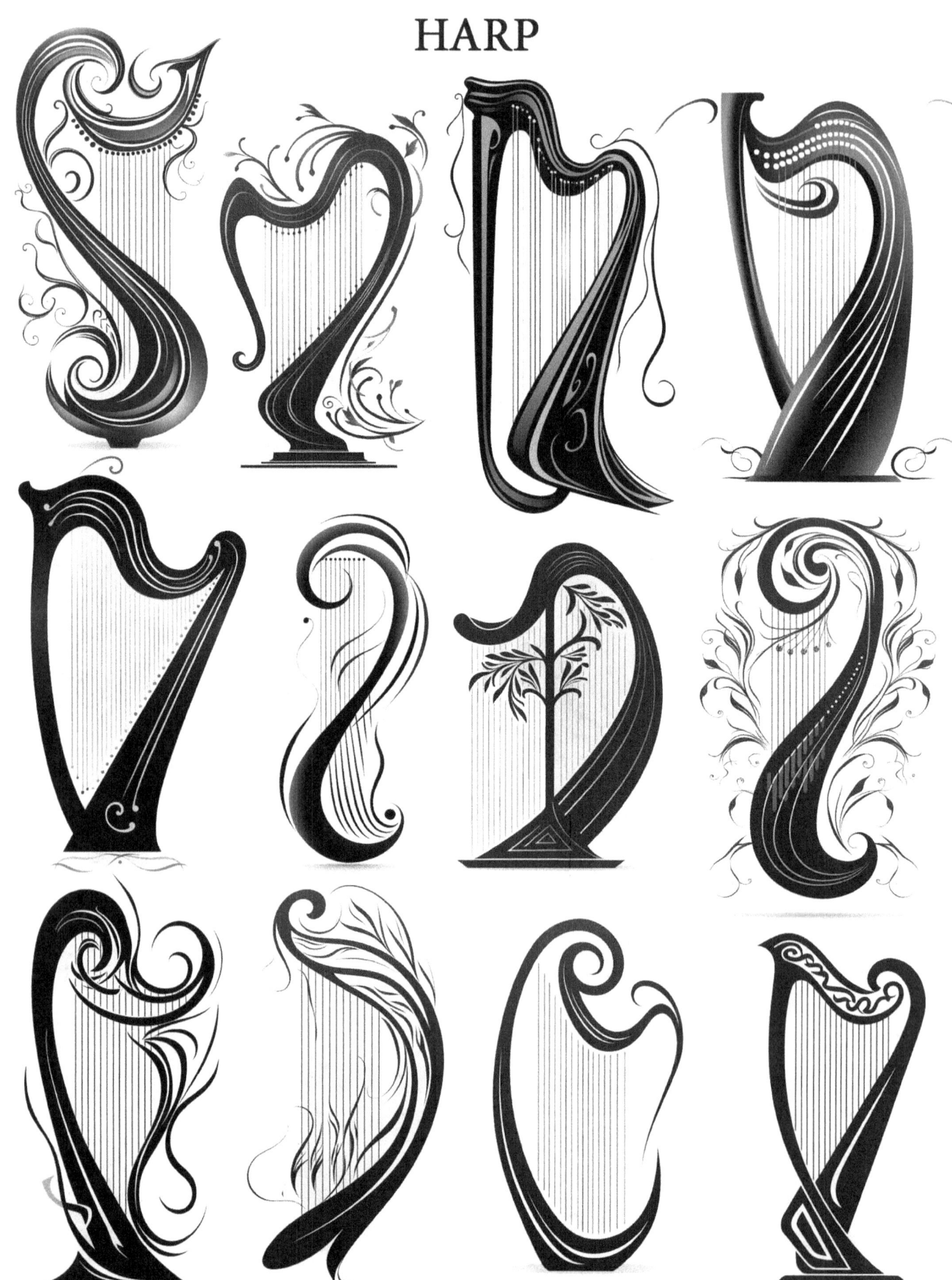

HEARTS

HEARTS

HEARTS

HORSE

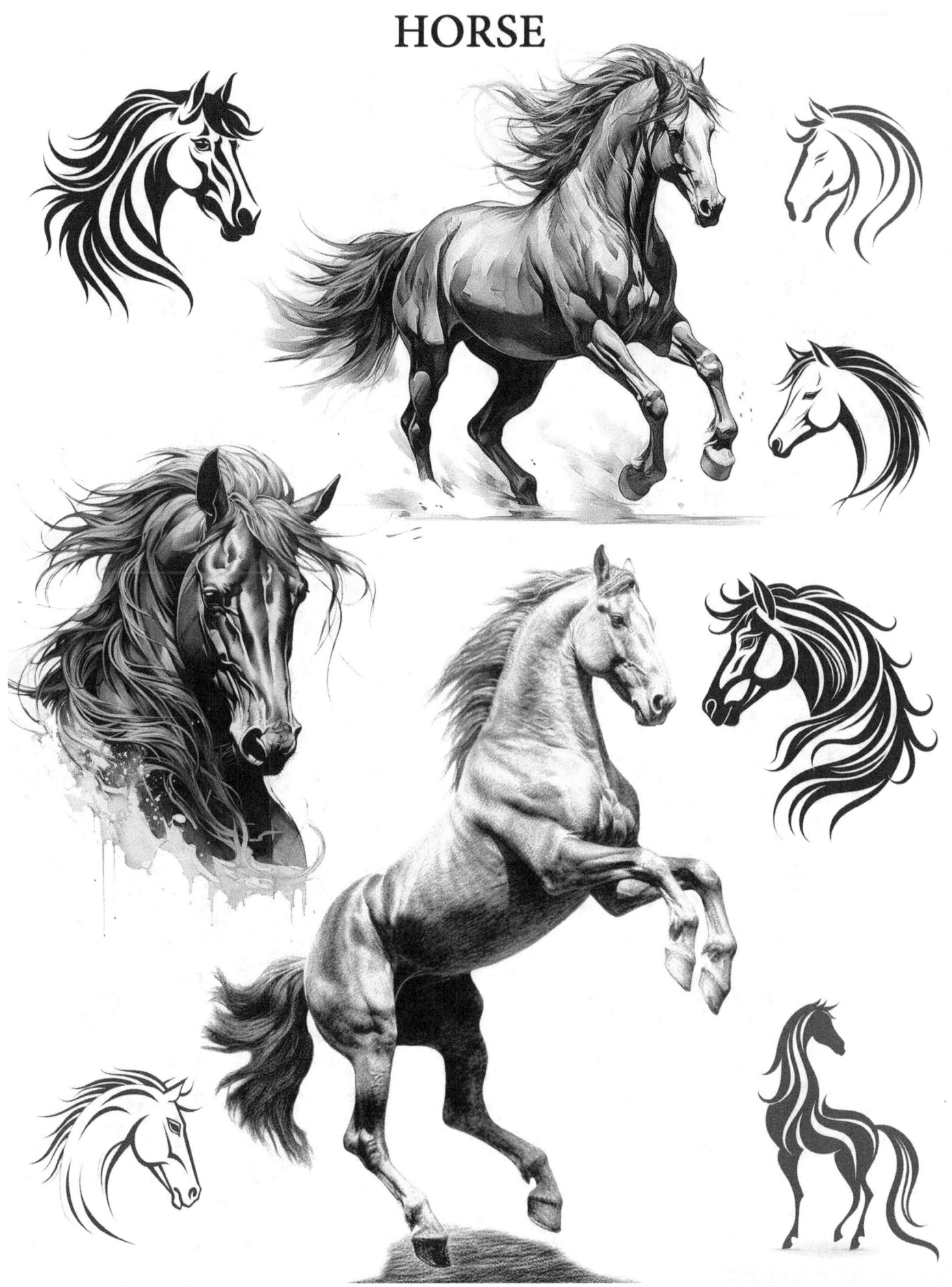

HORSE

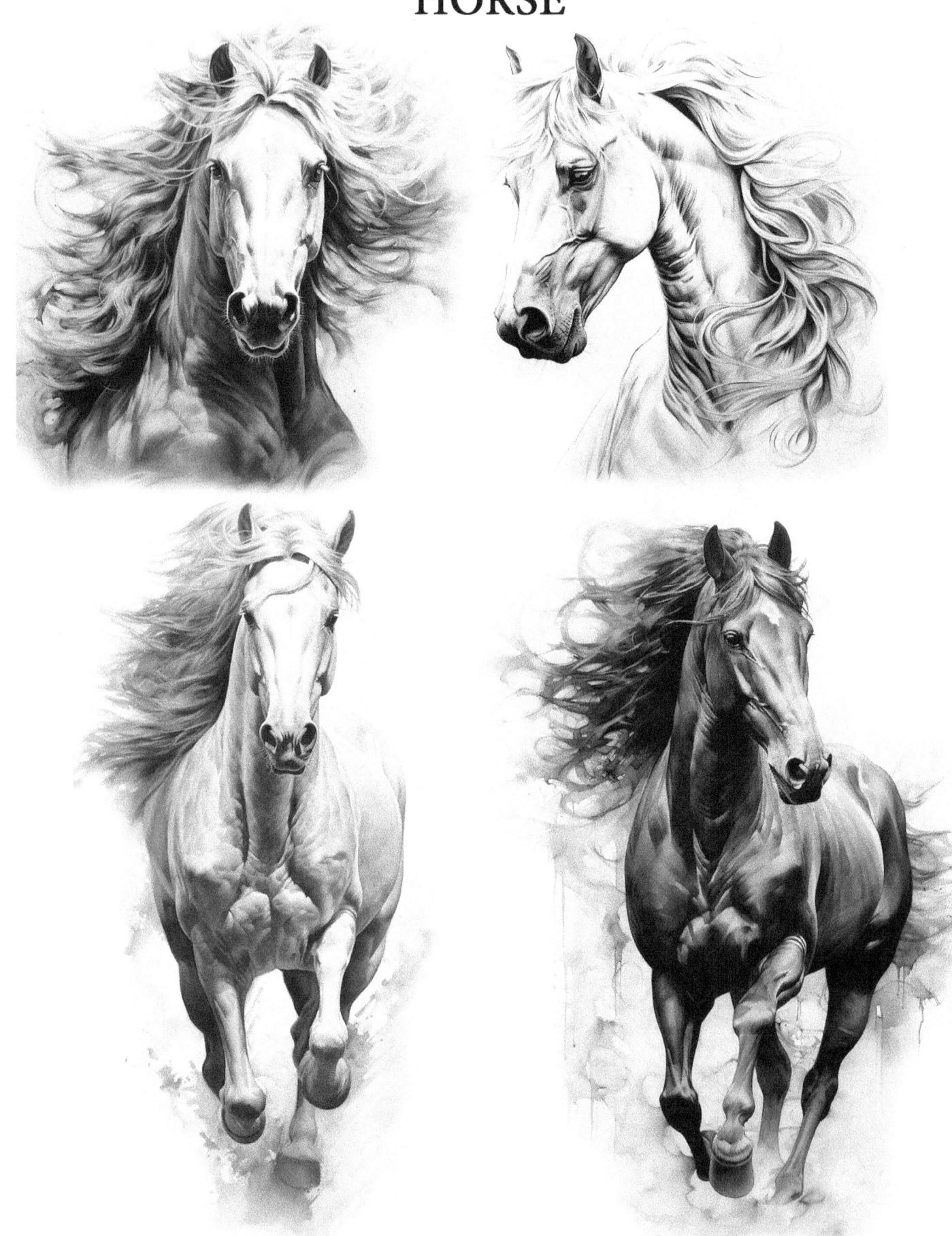

HORSE

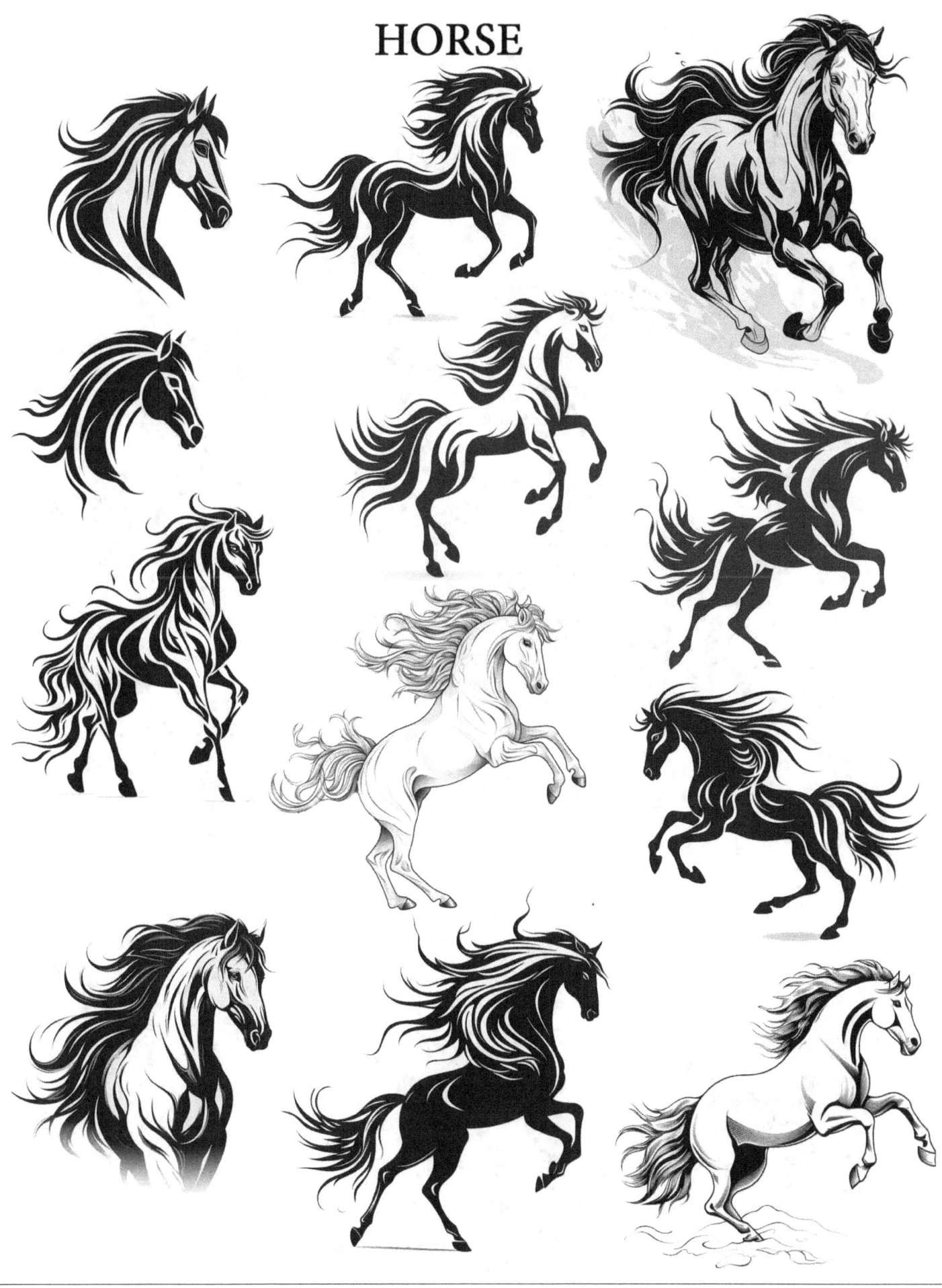

HORSE - PEGASUS

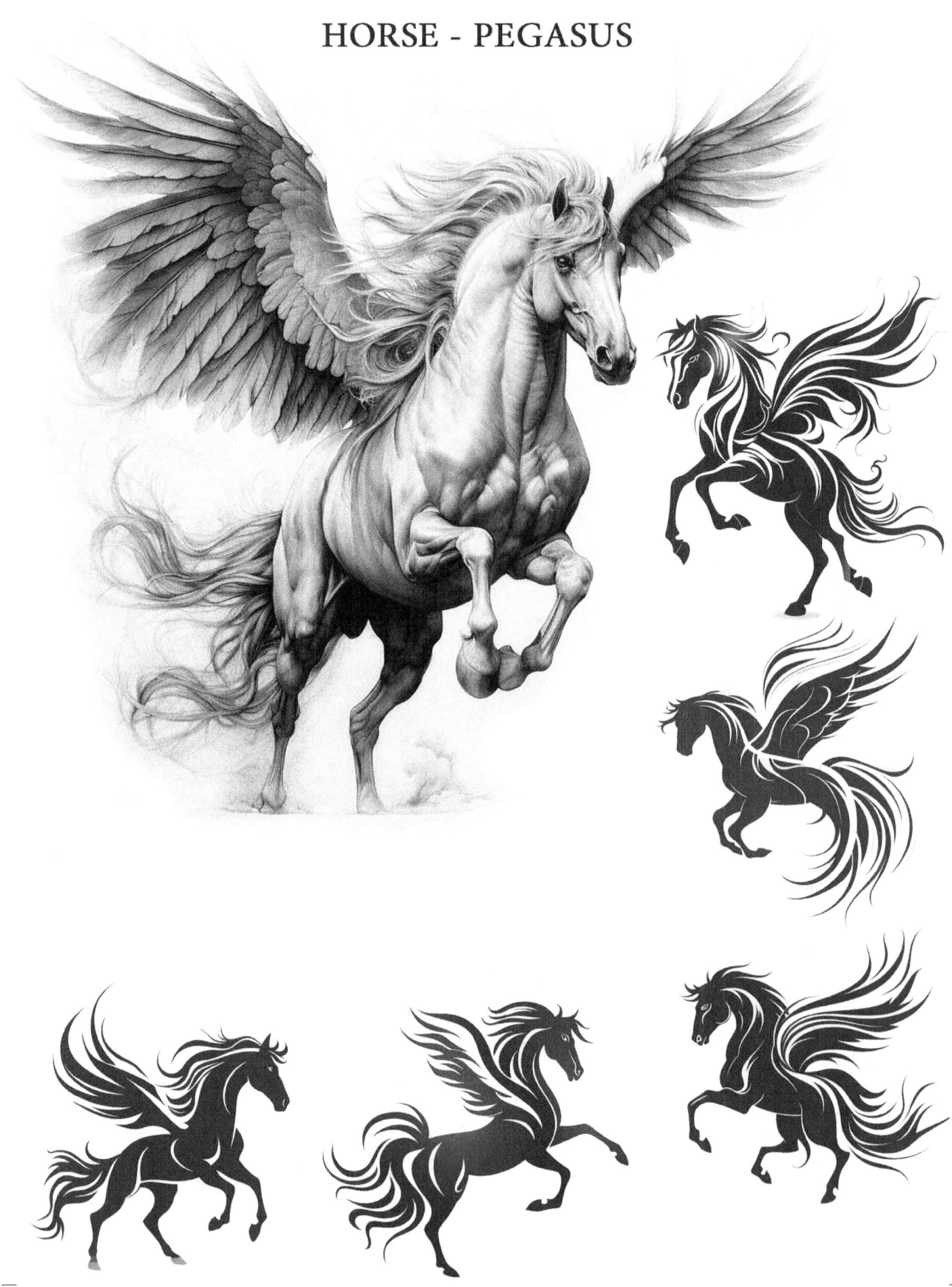

HUMMINGBIRD

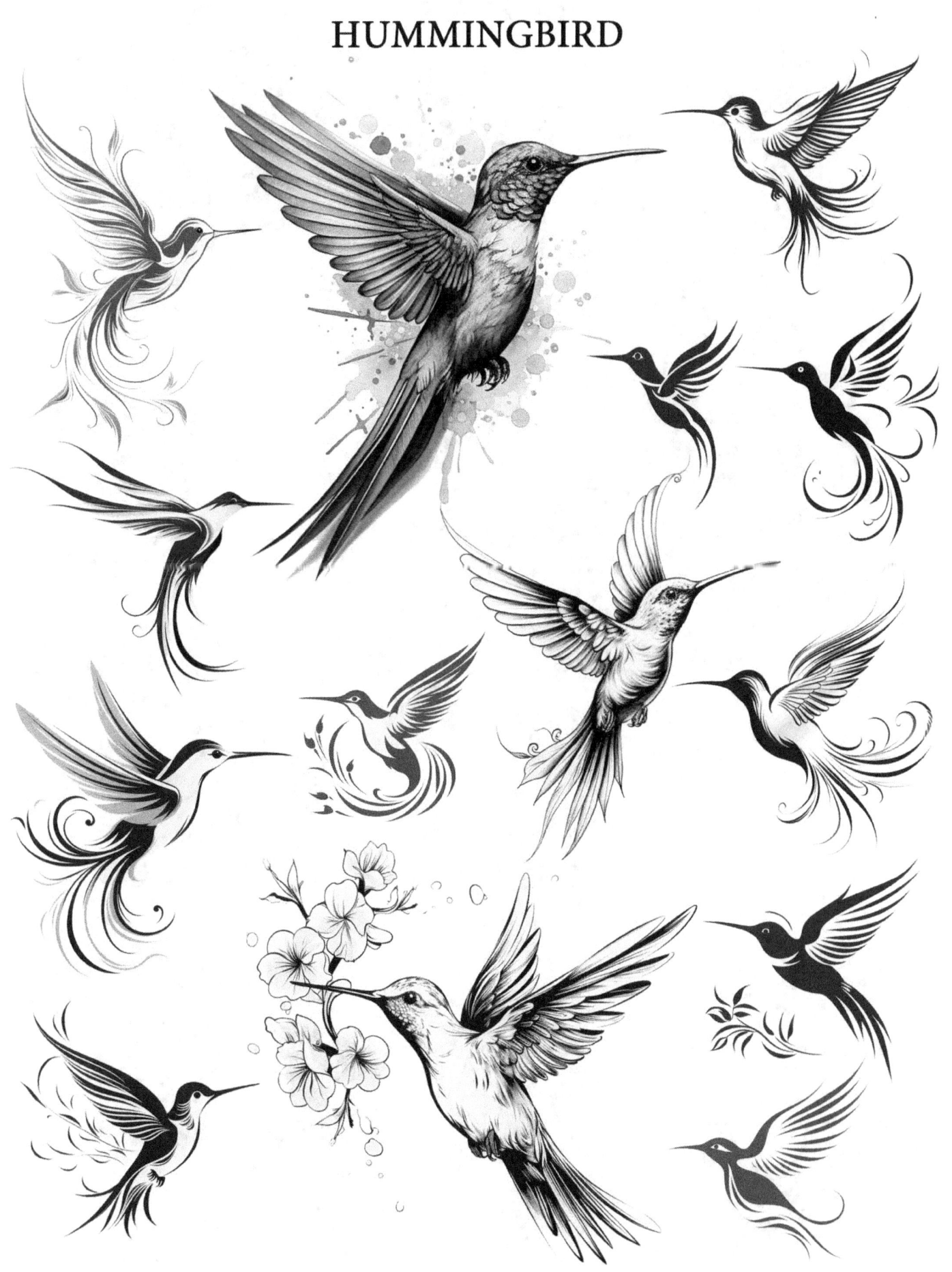

JAGUAR

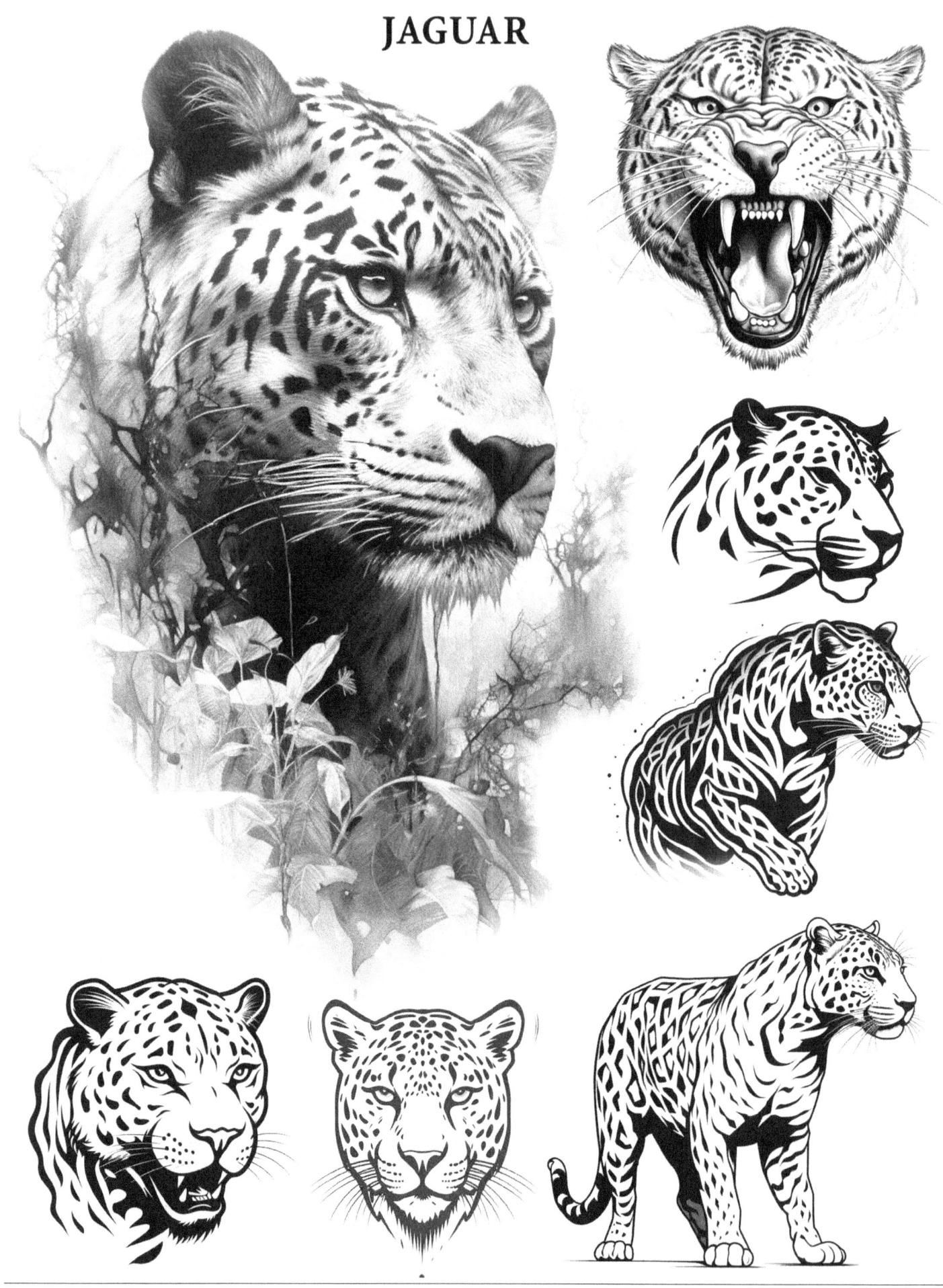

JAGUAR

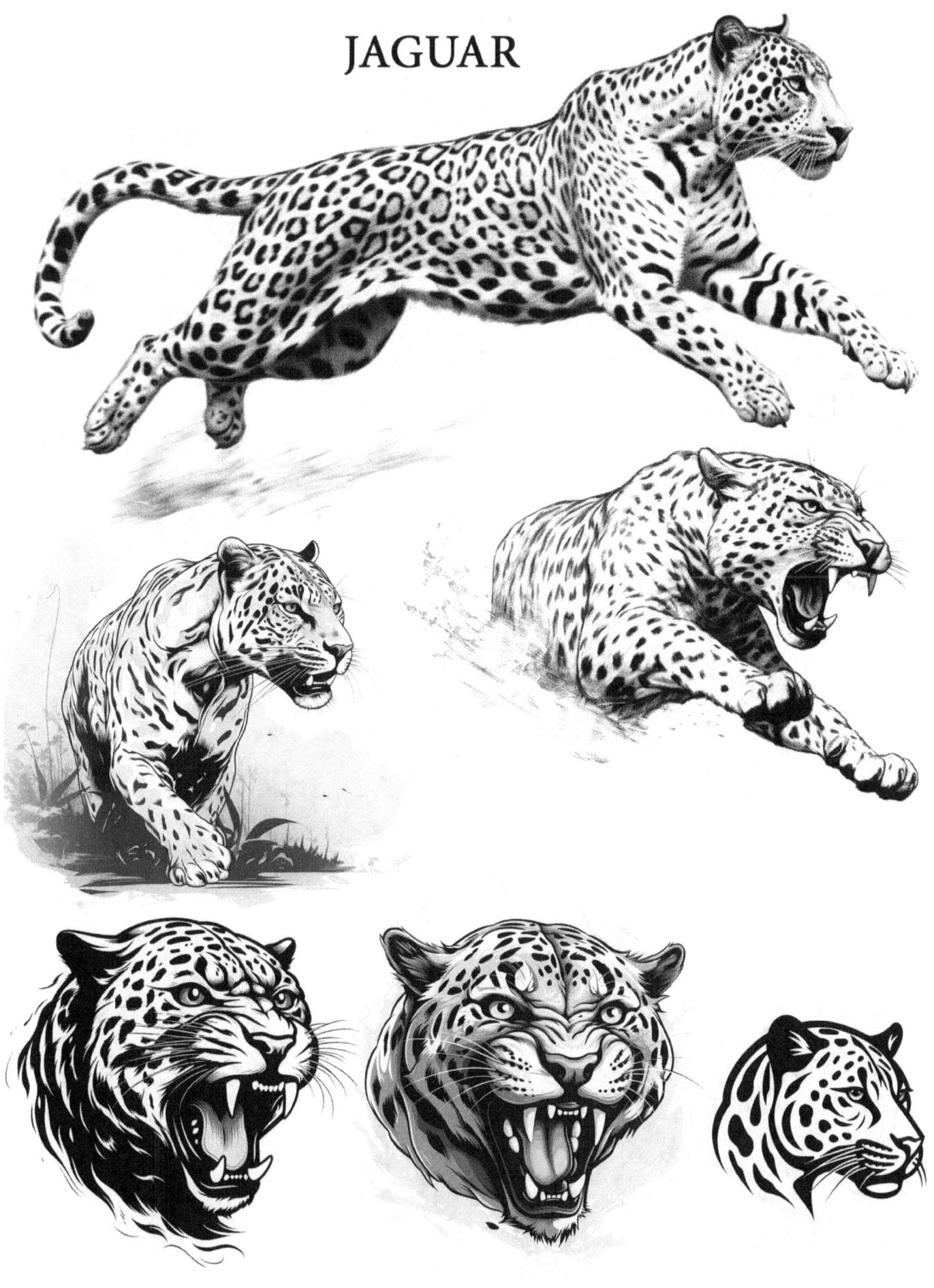

JAGUAR

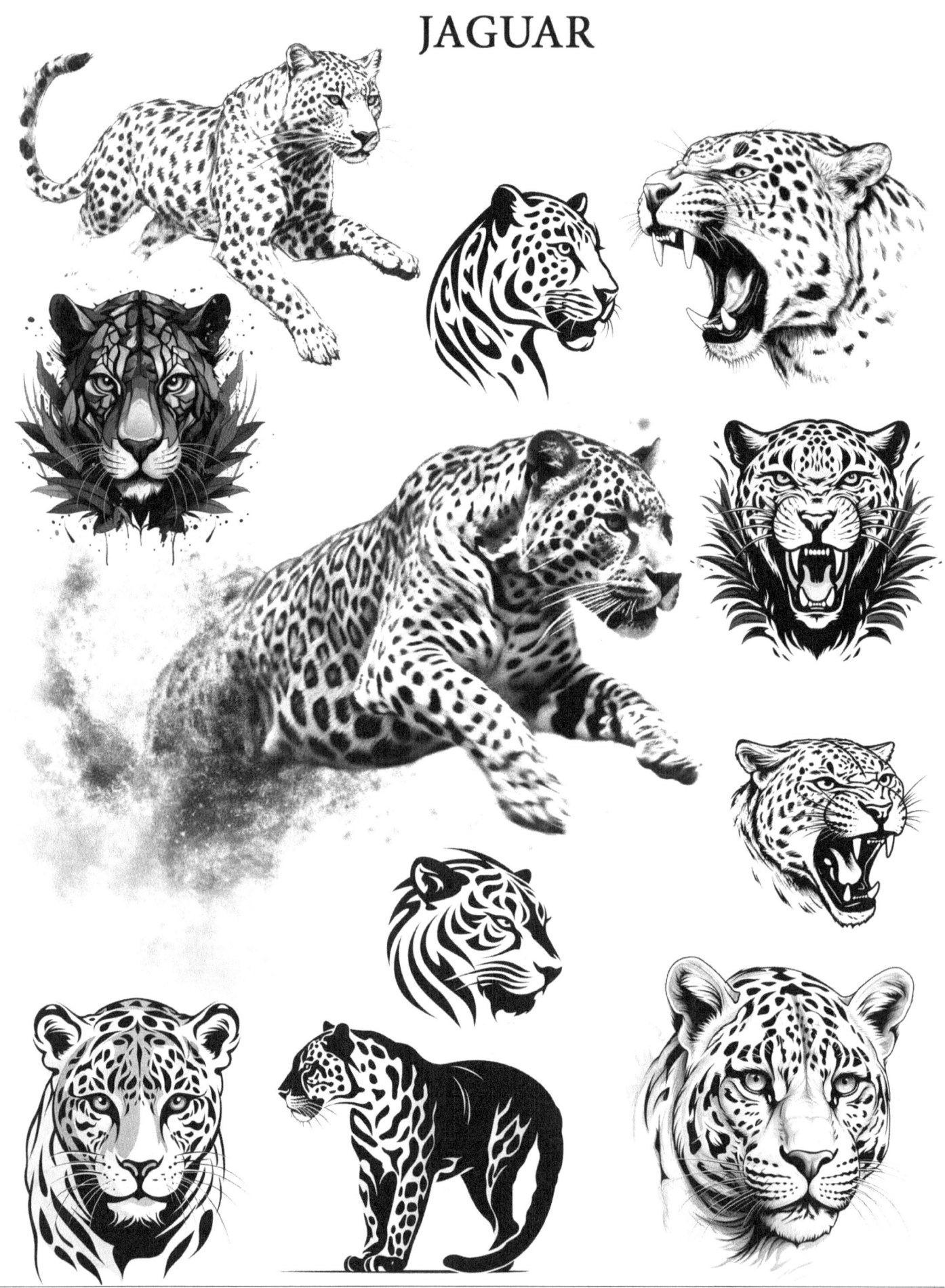

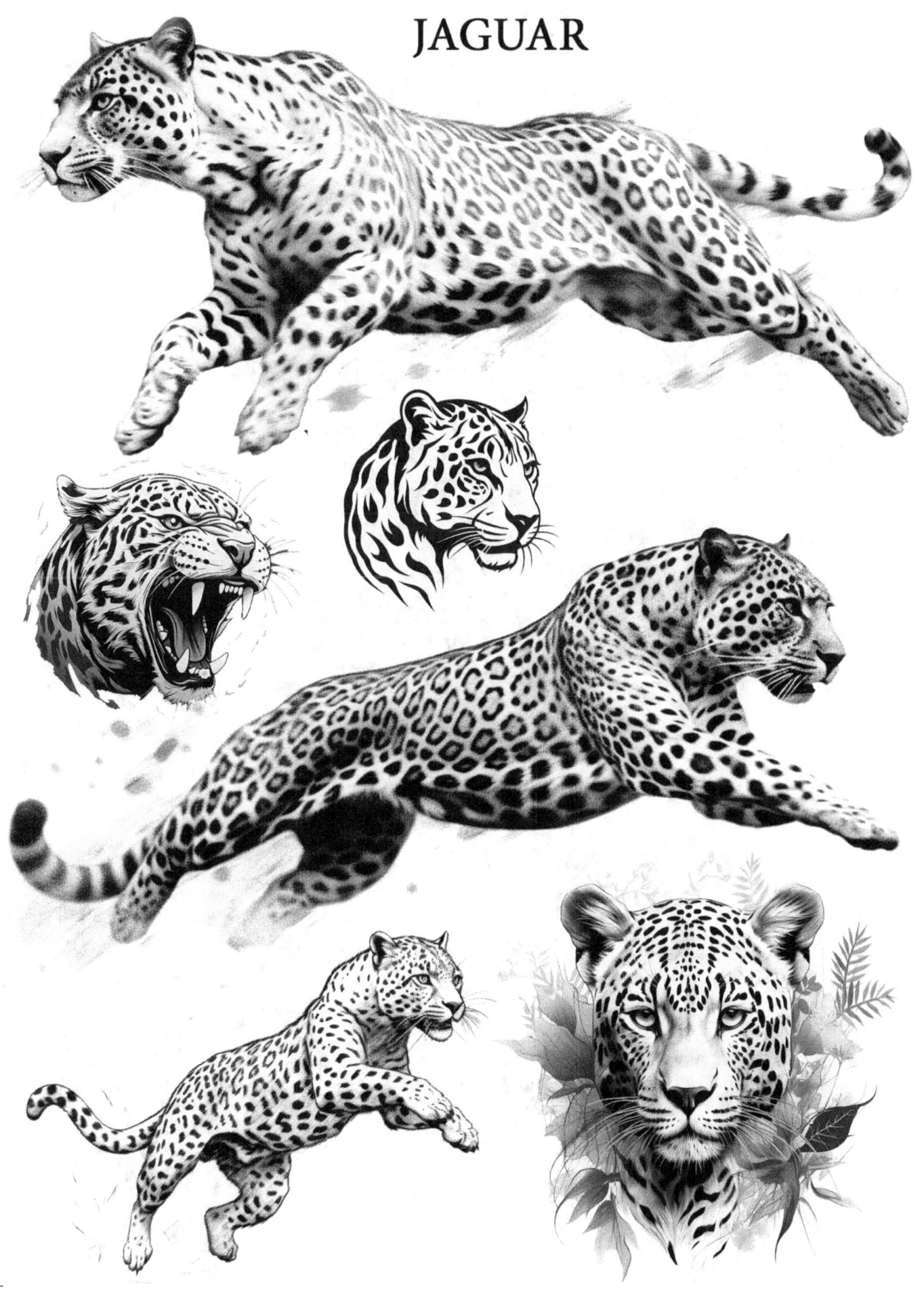

JAGUAR

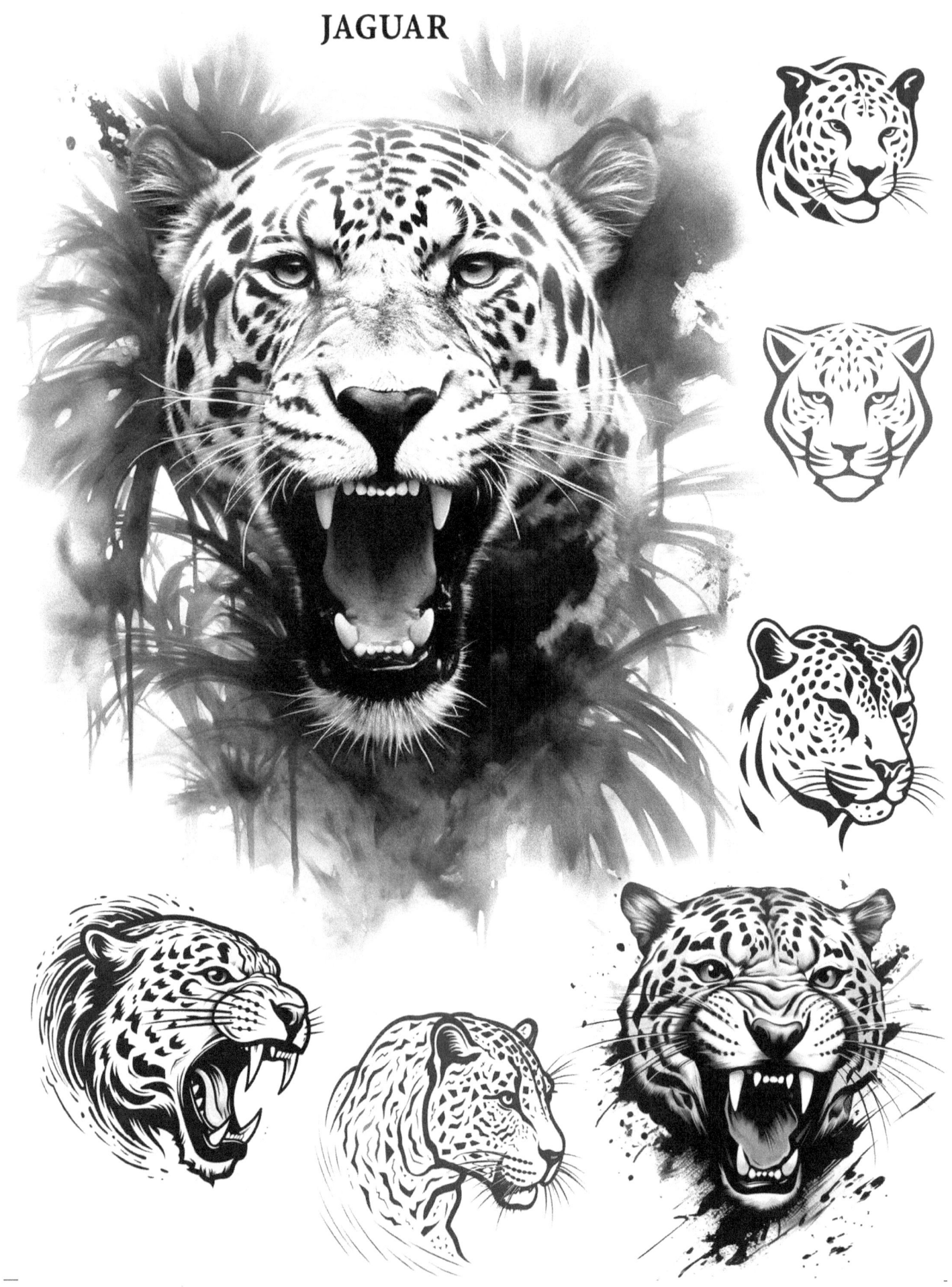

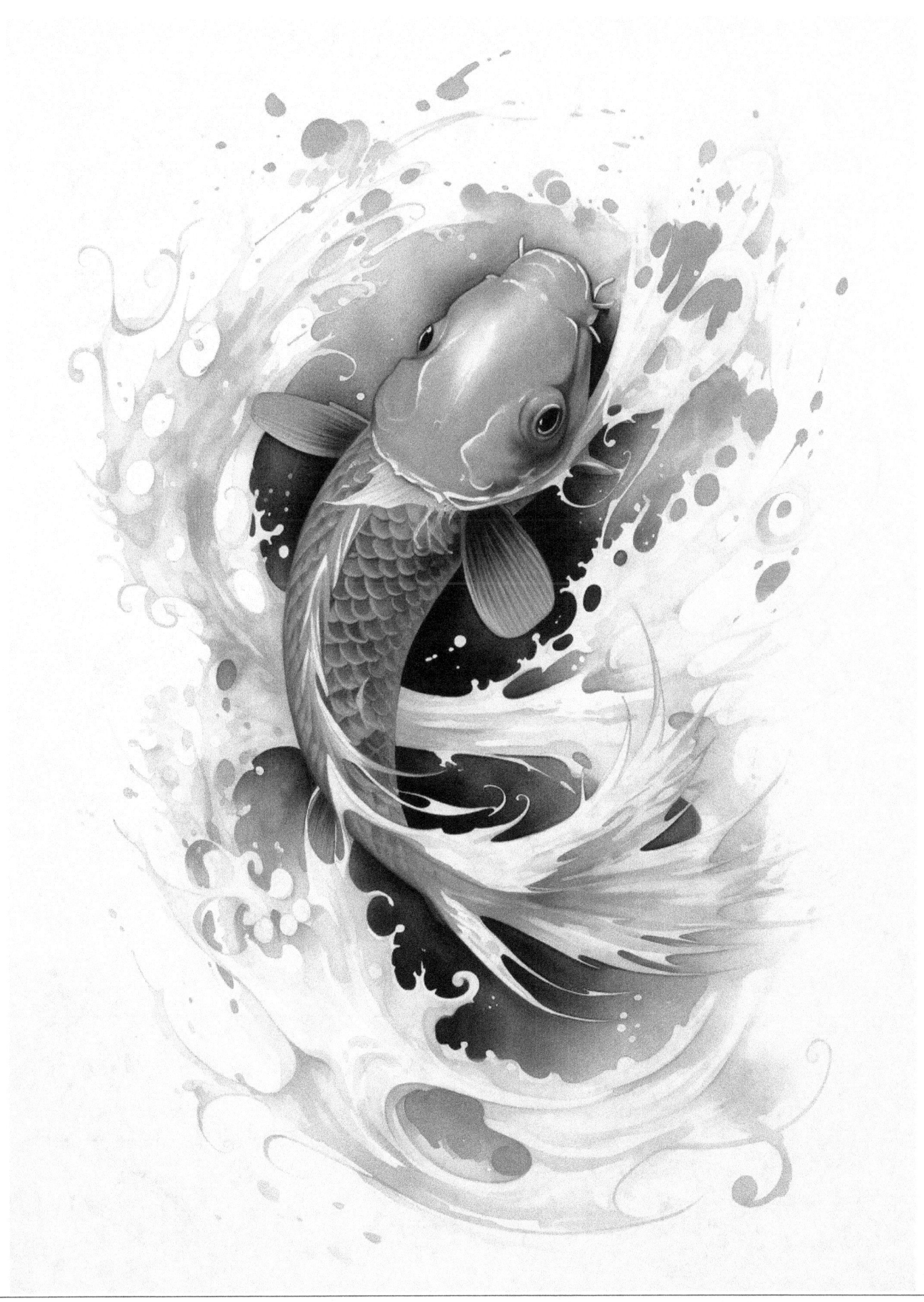

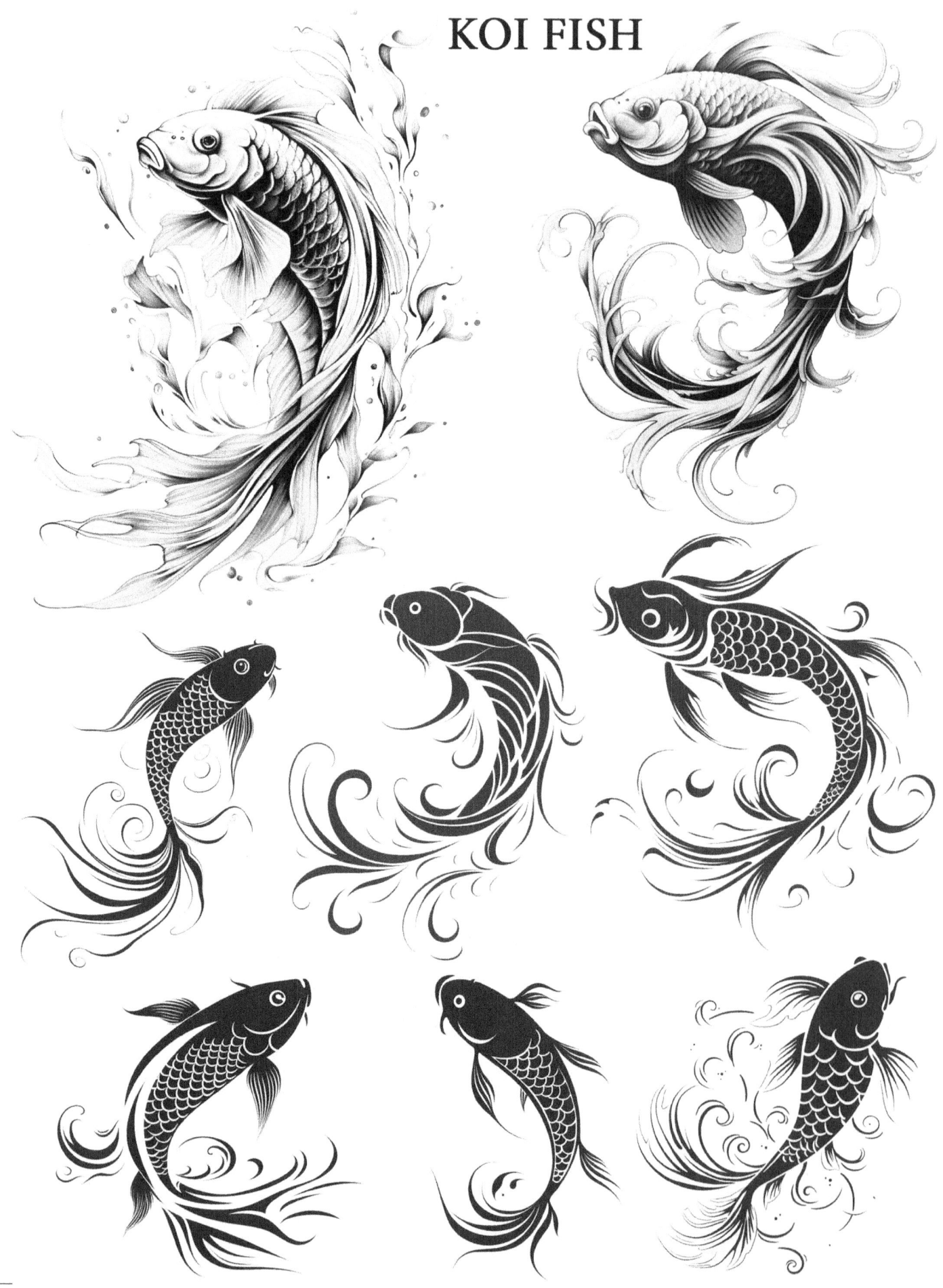

KOI FISH

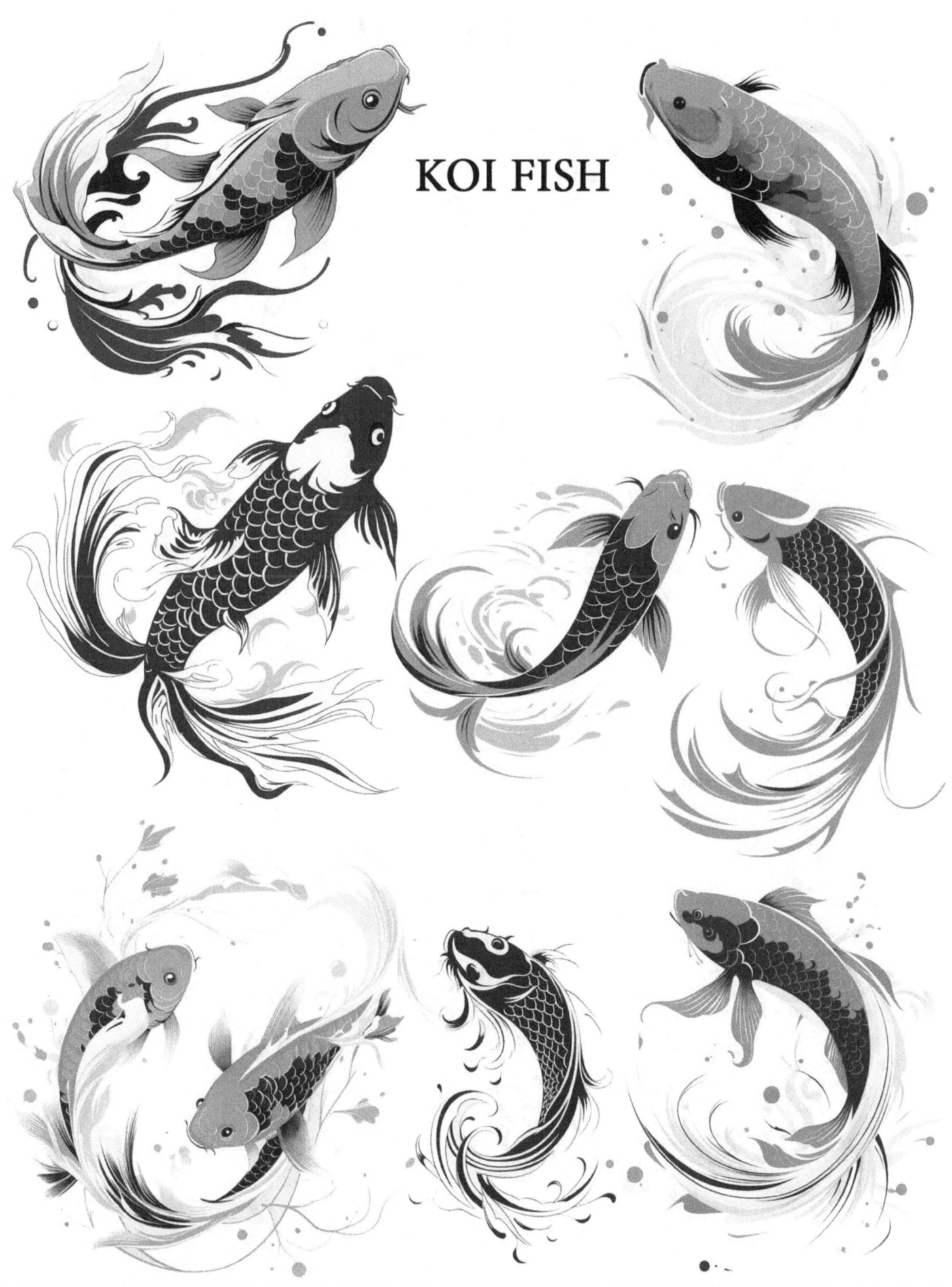

LAUREL

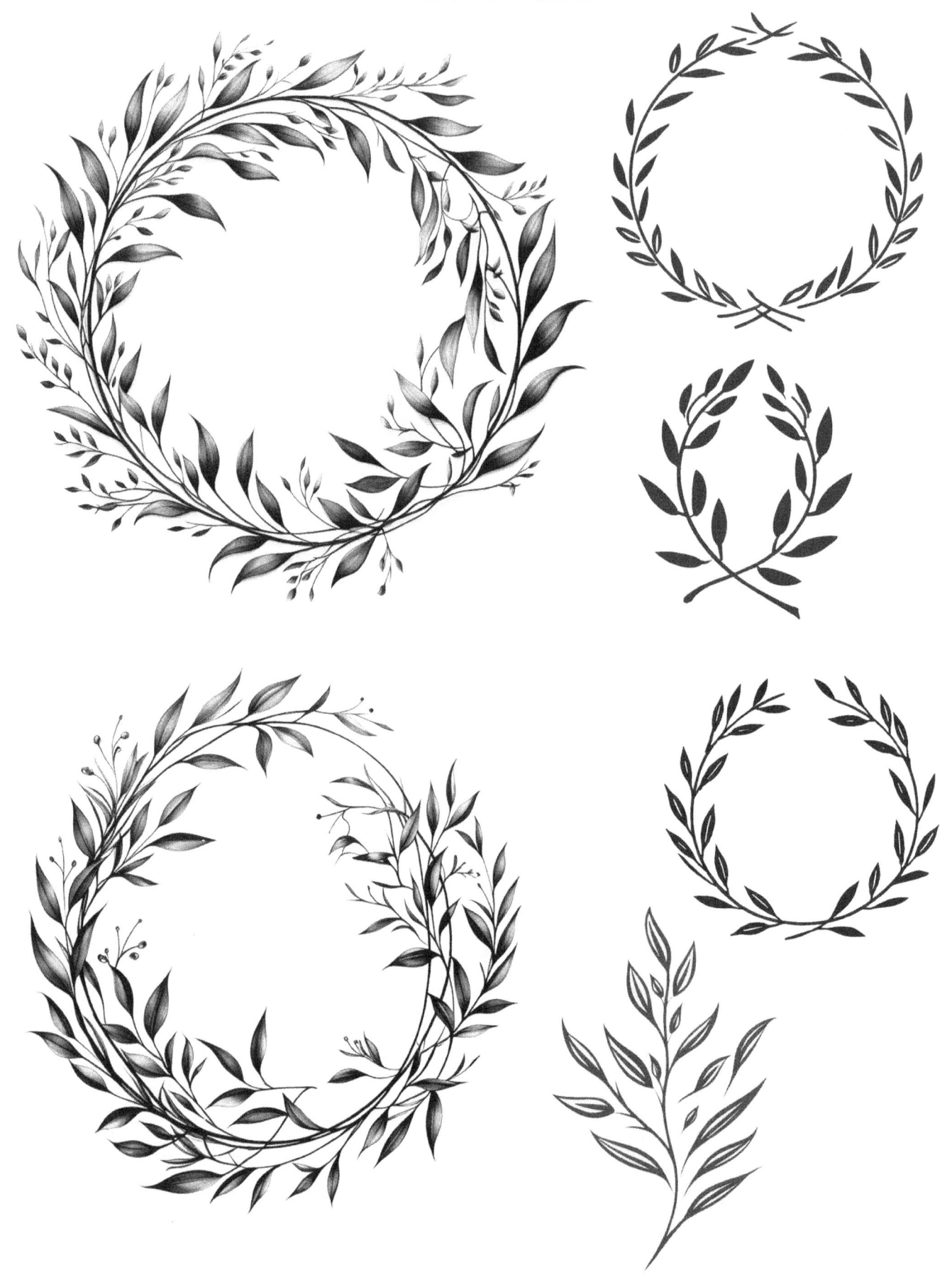

LAUREL

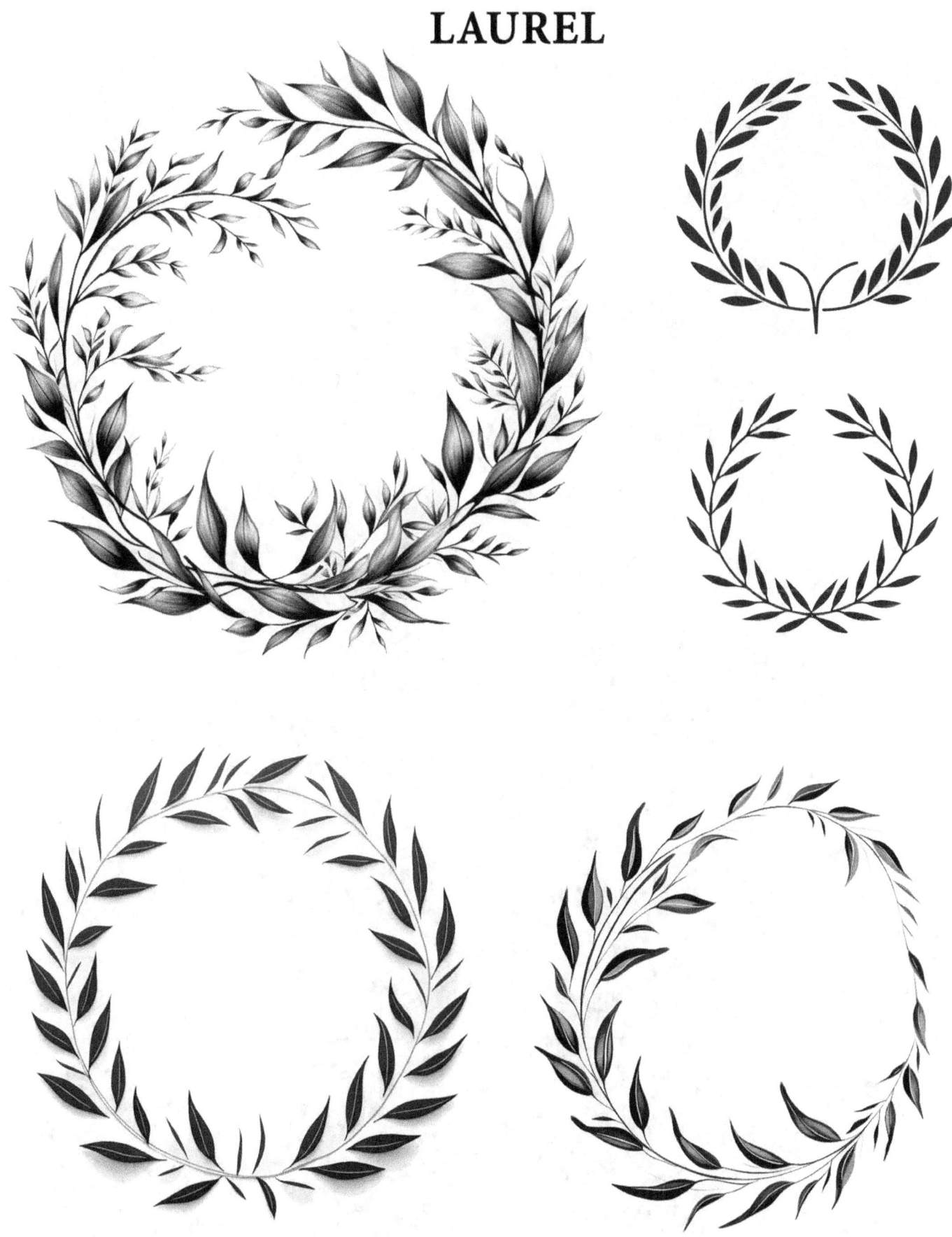

LEOPARD

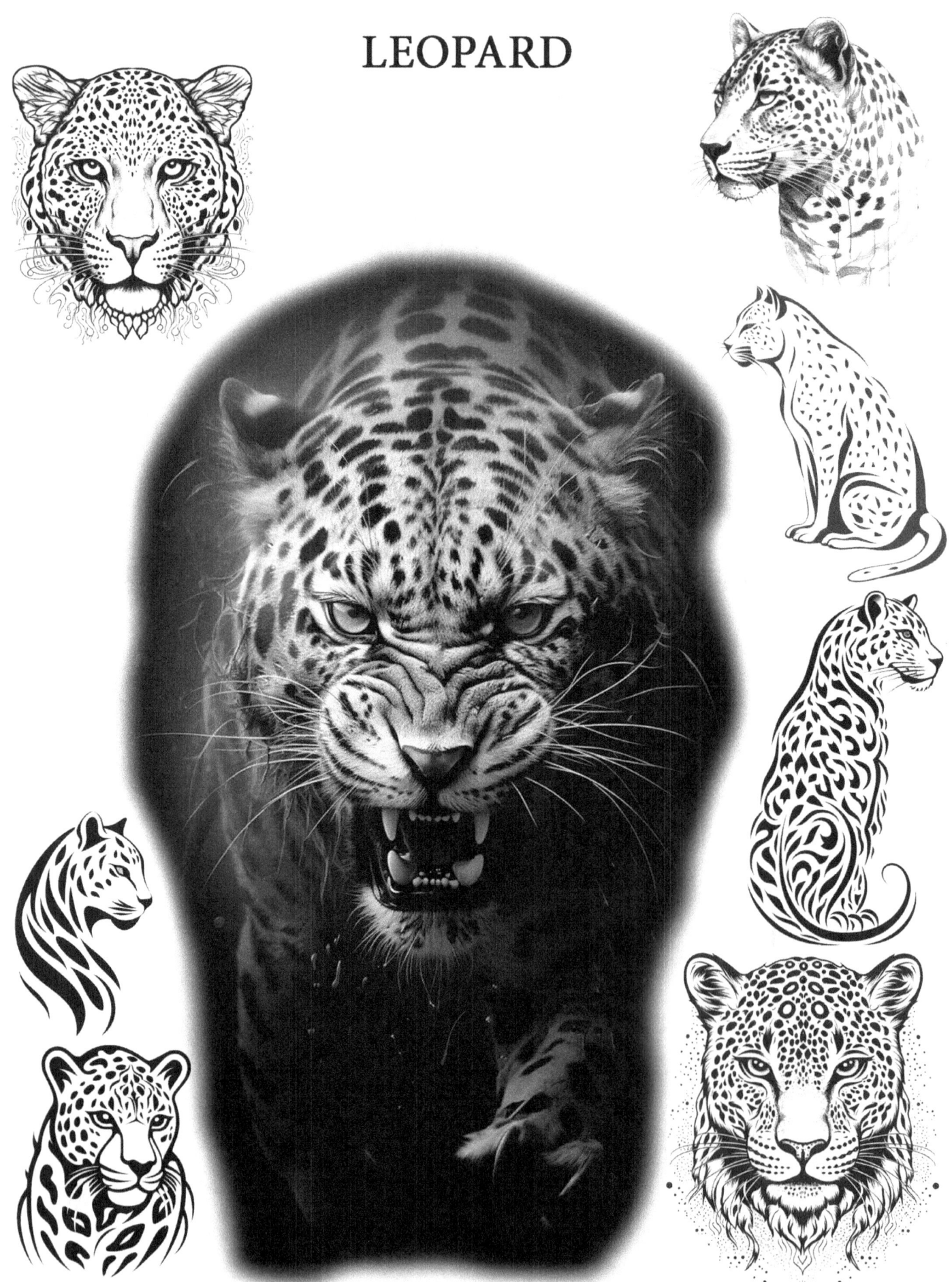

LEOPARD

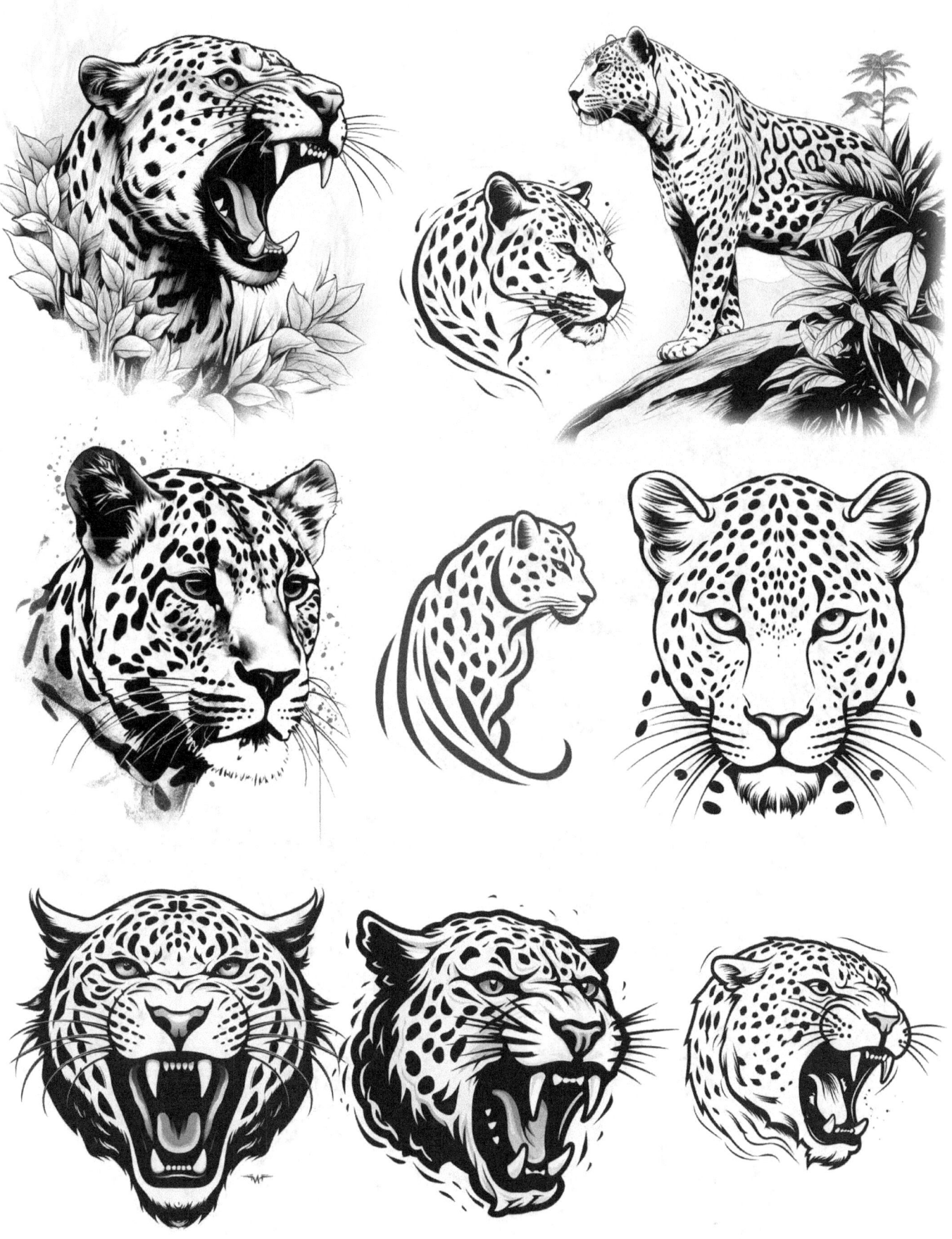

LEOPARD

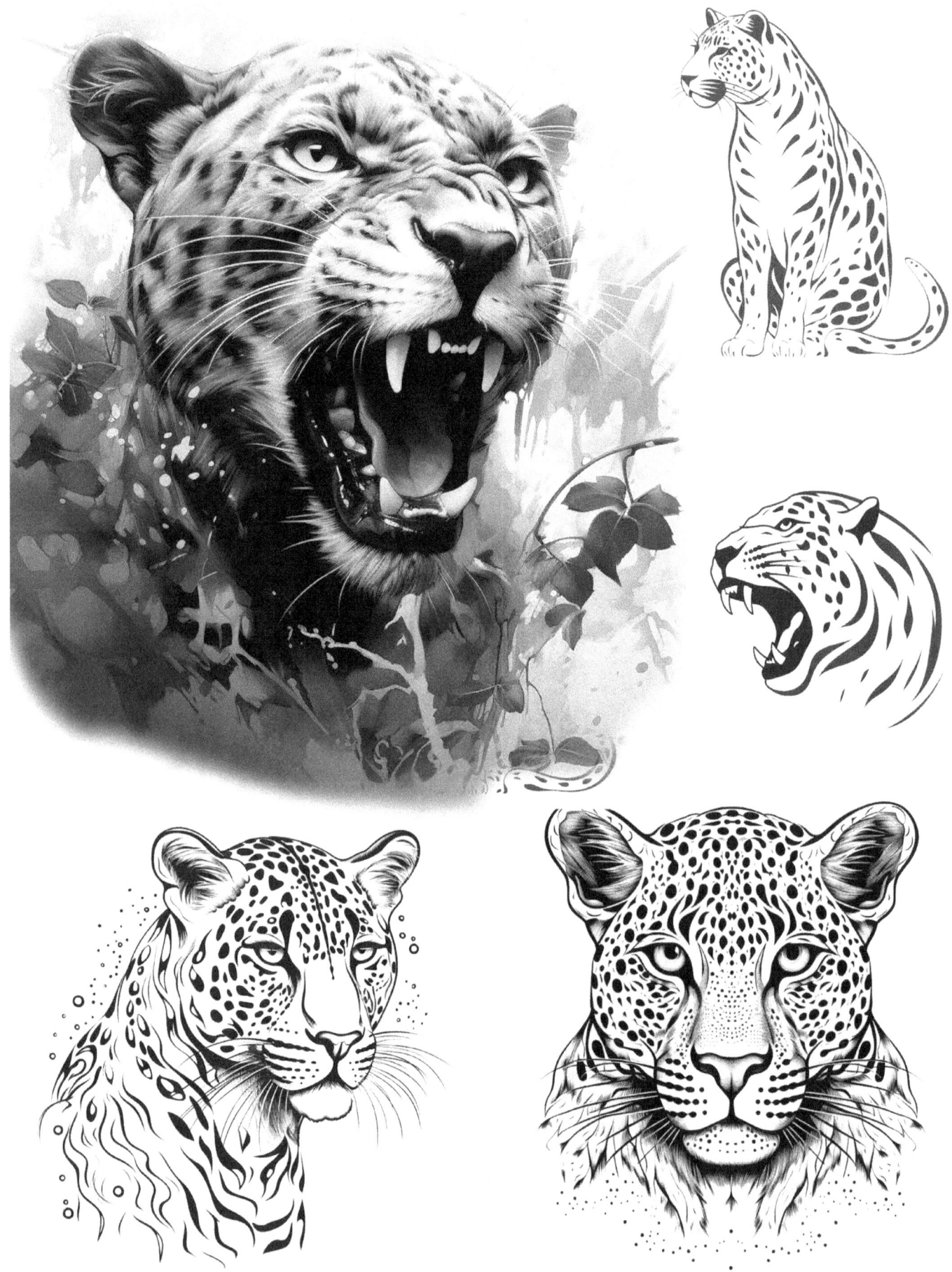

LEOPARD

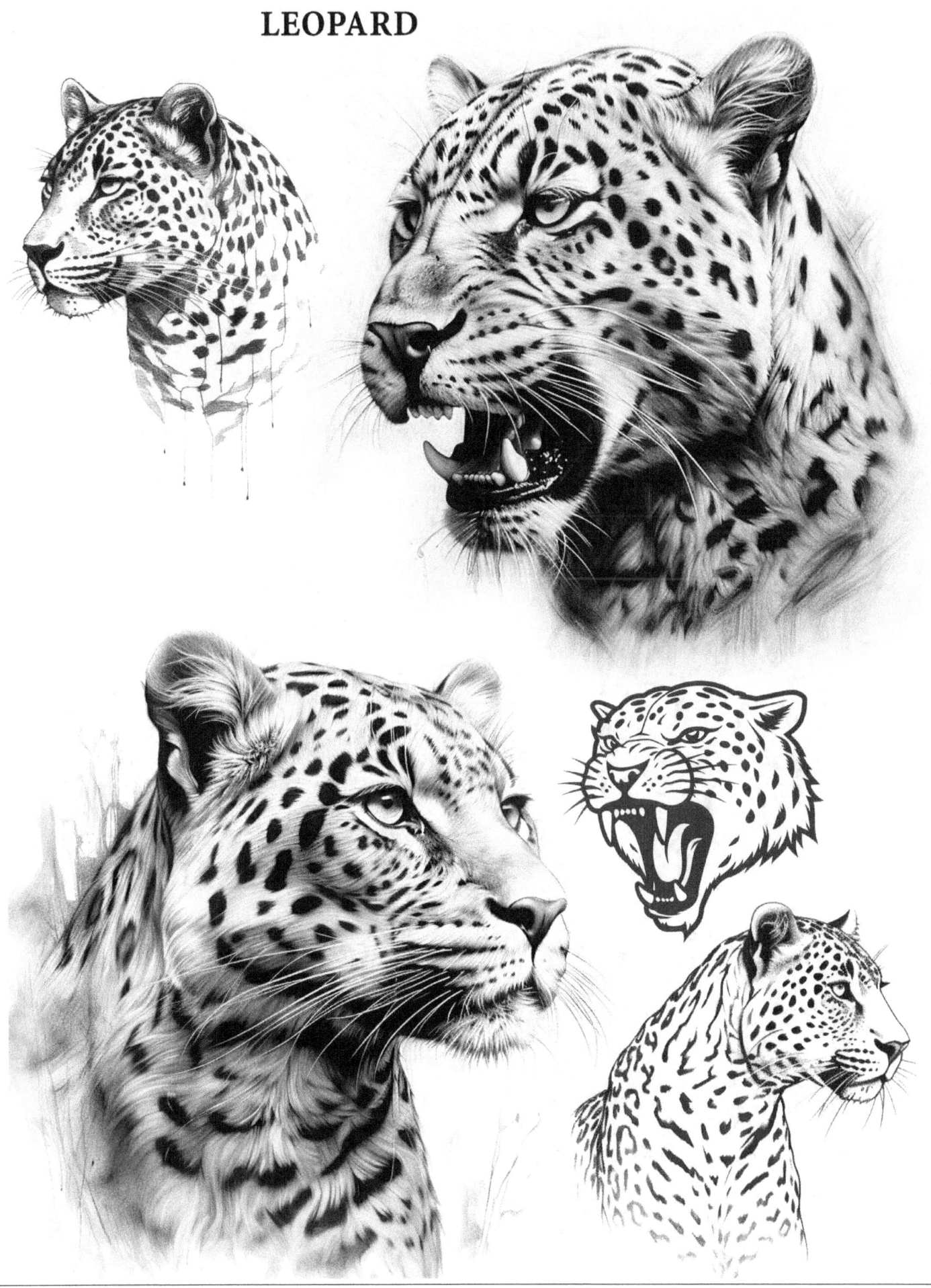

LEOPARD

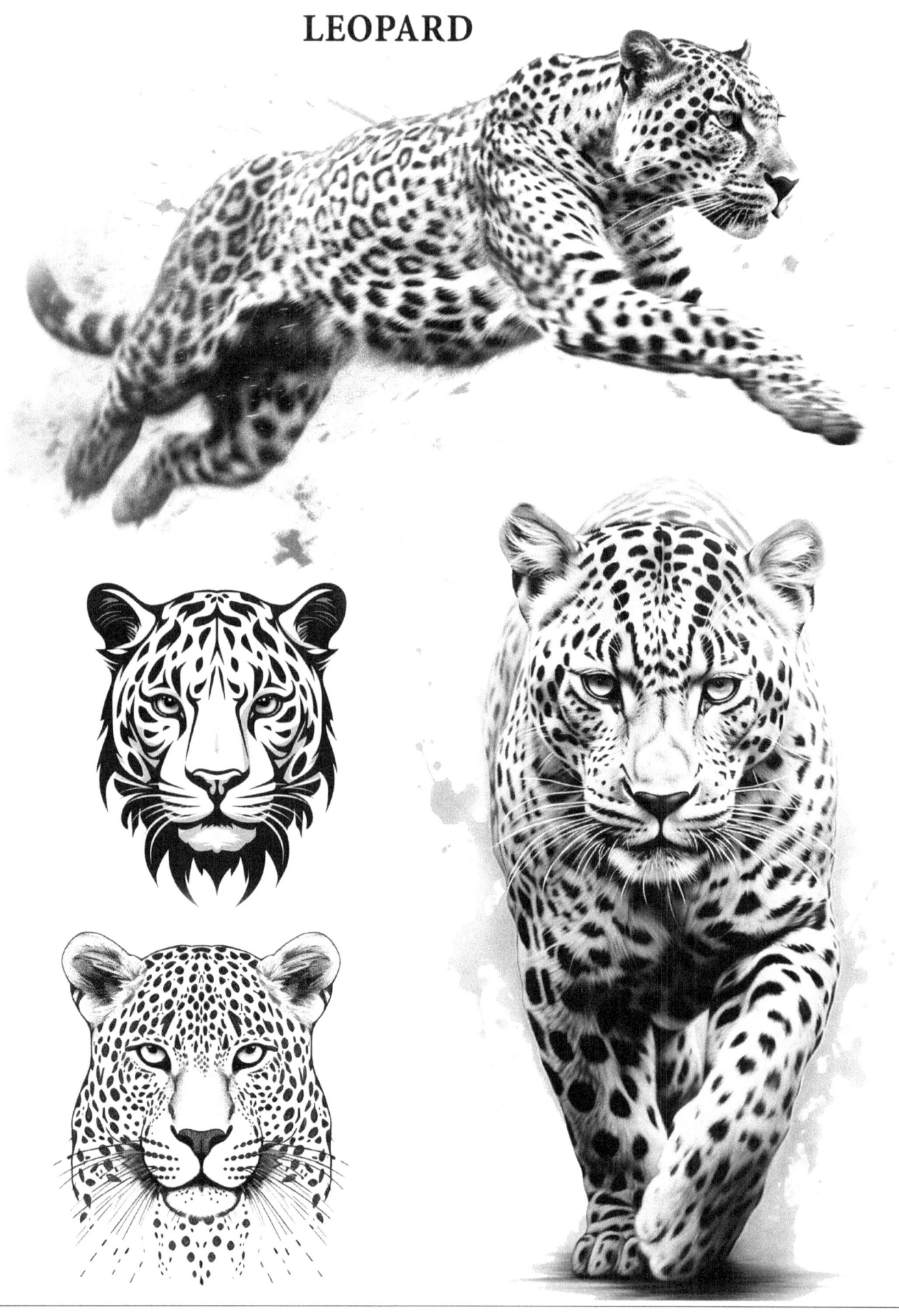

LION

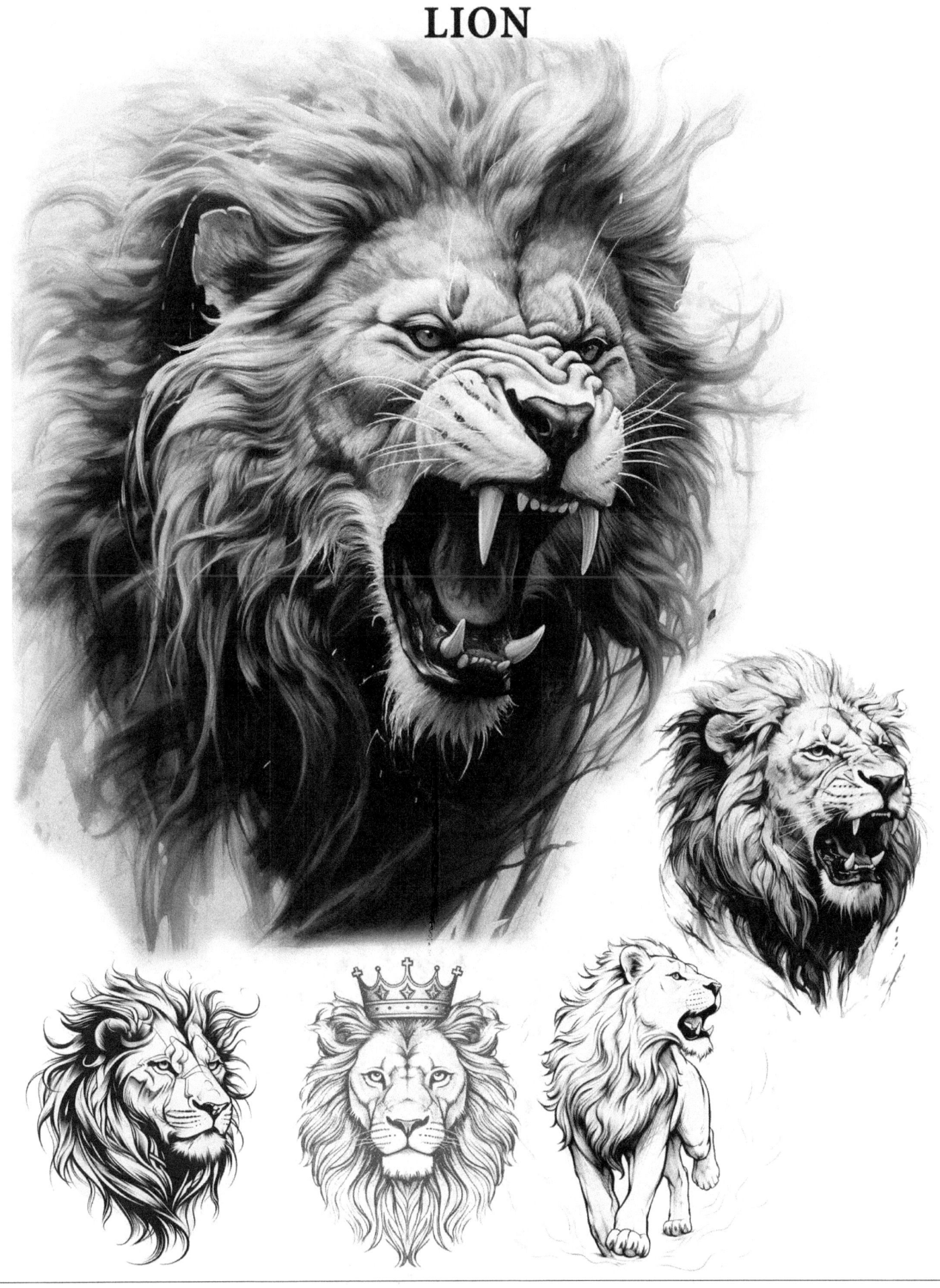

LION

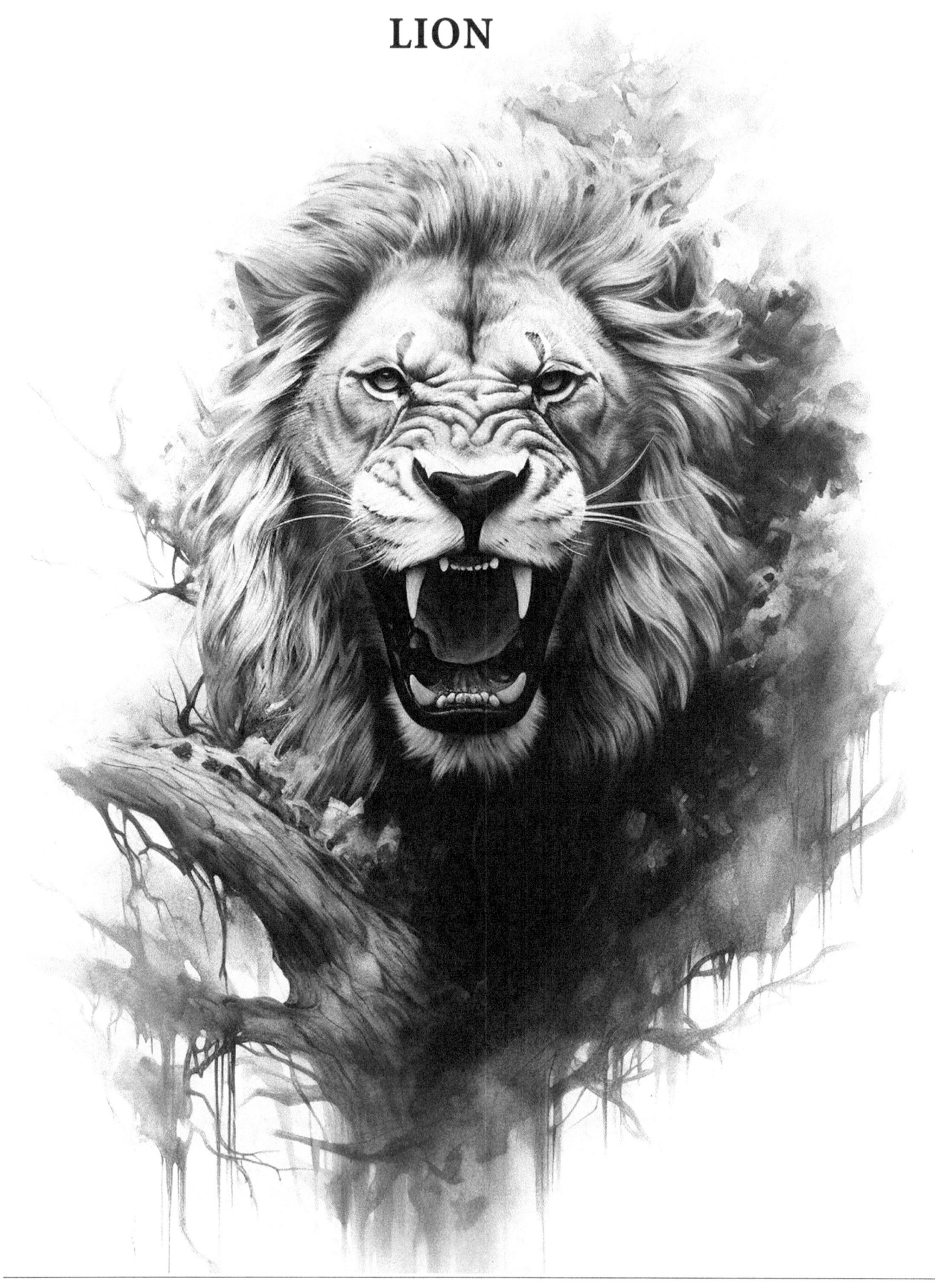

LION

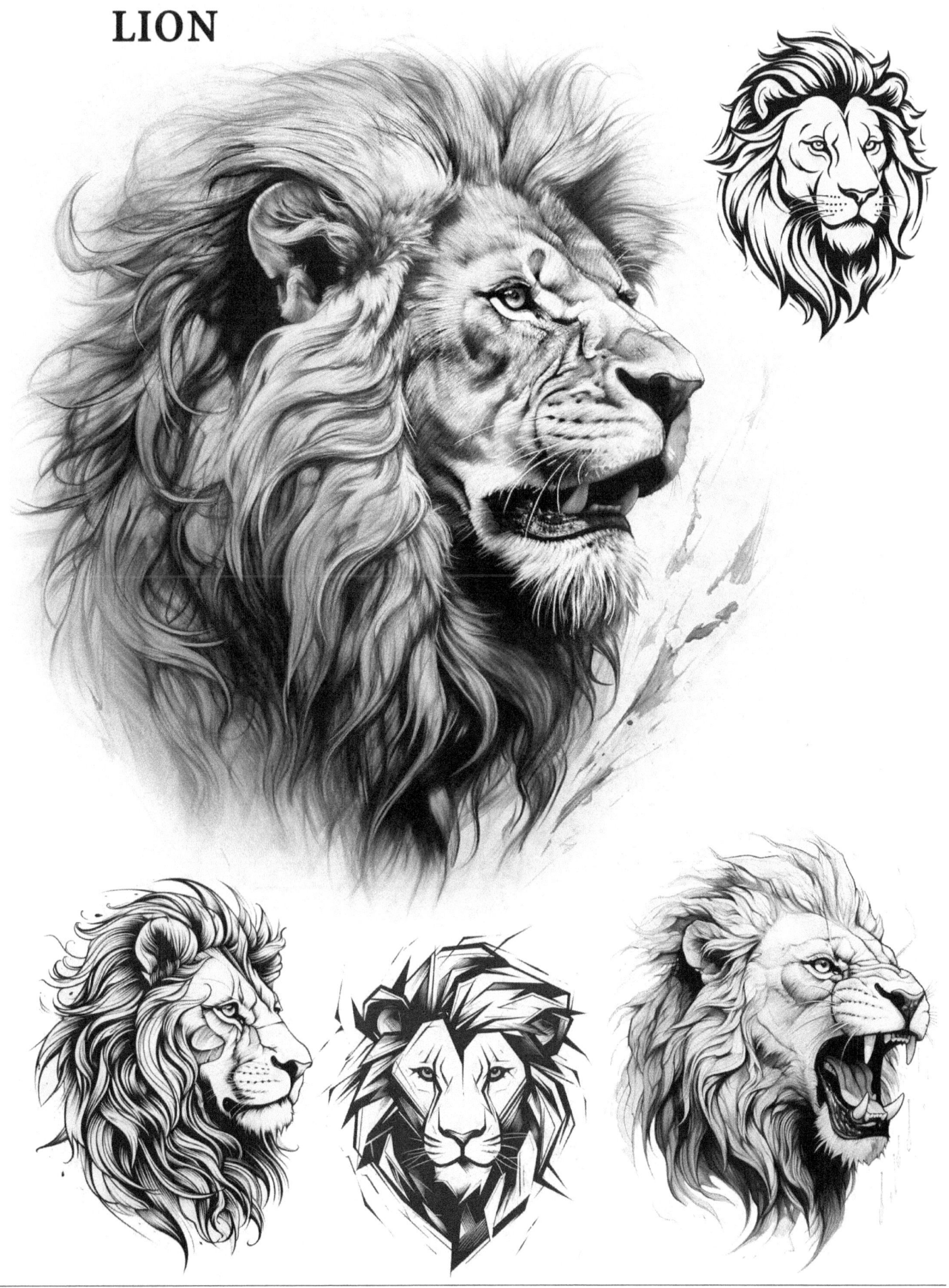

LION

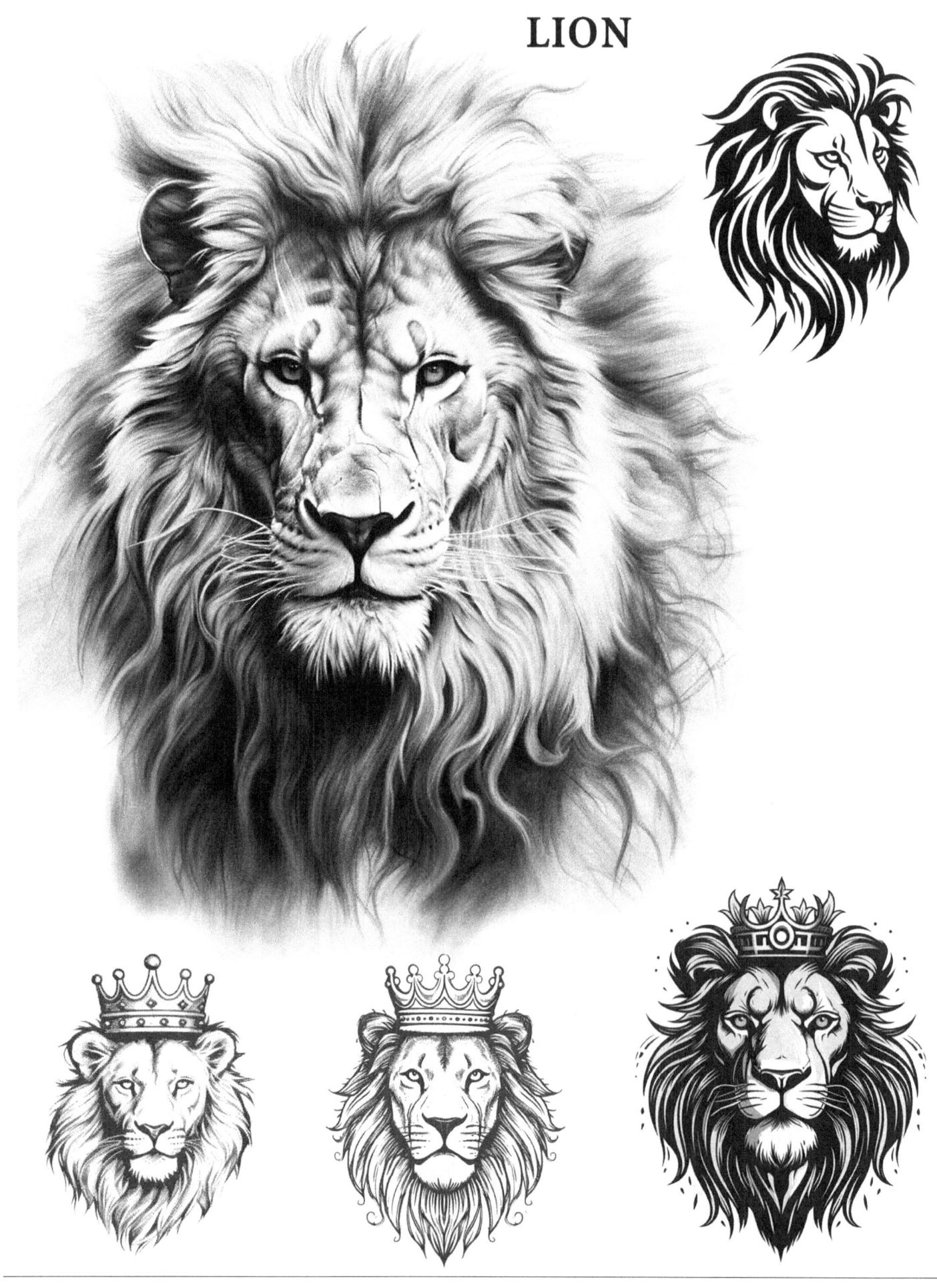

LION

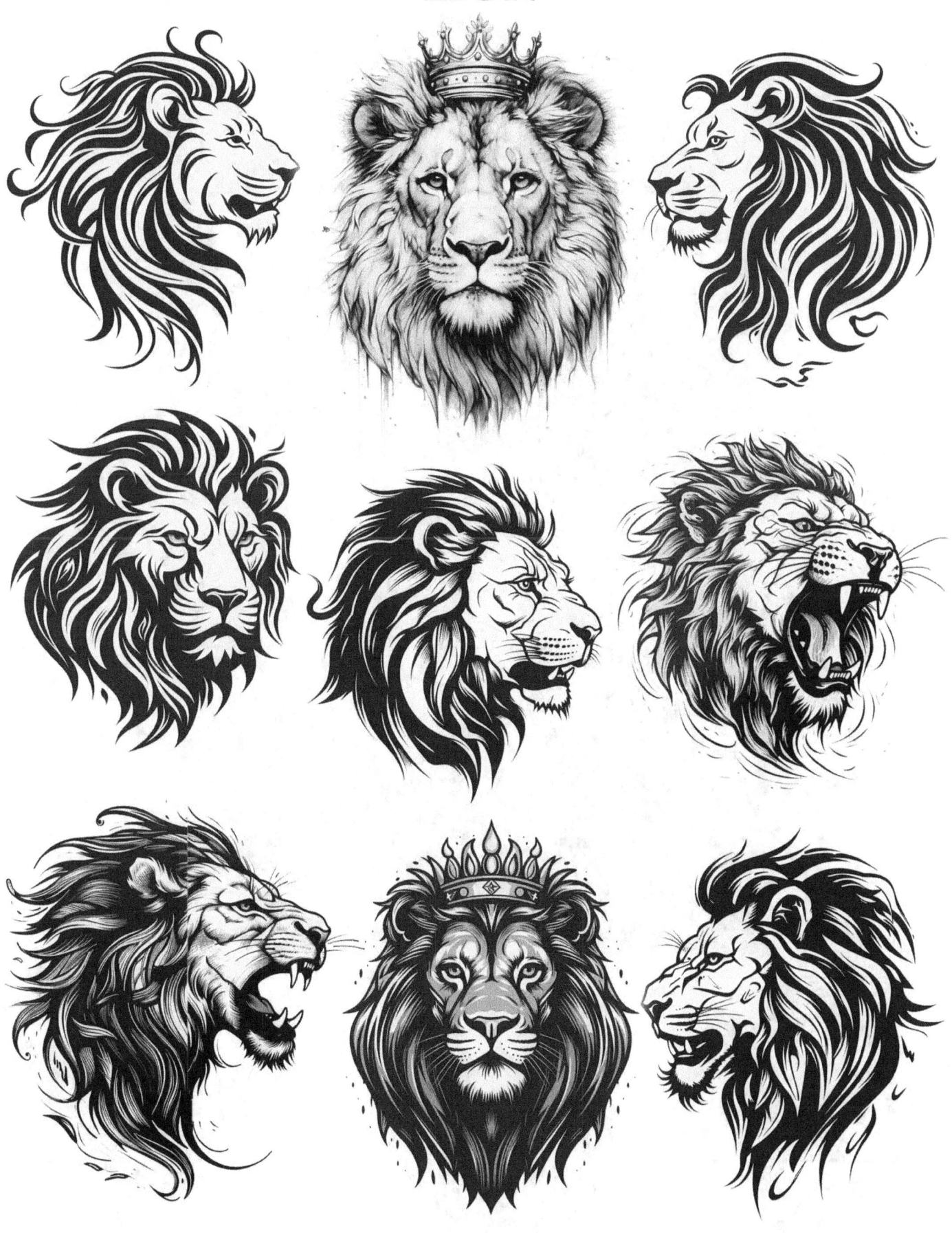

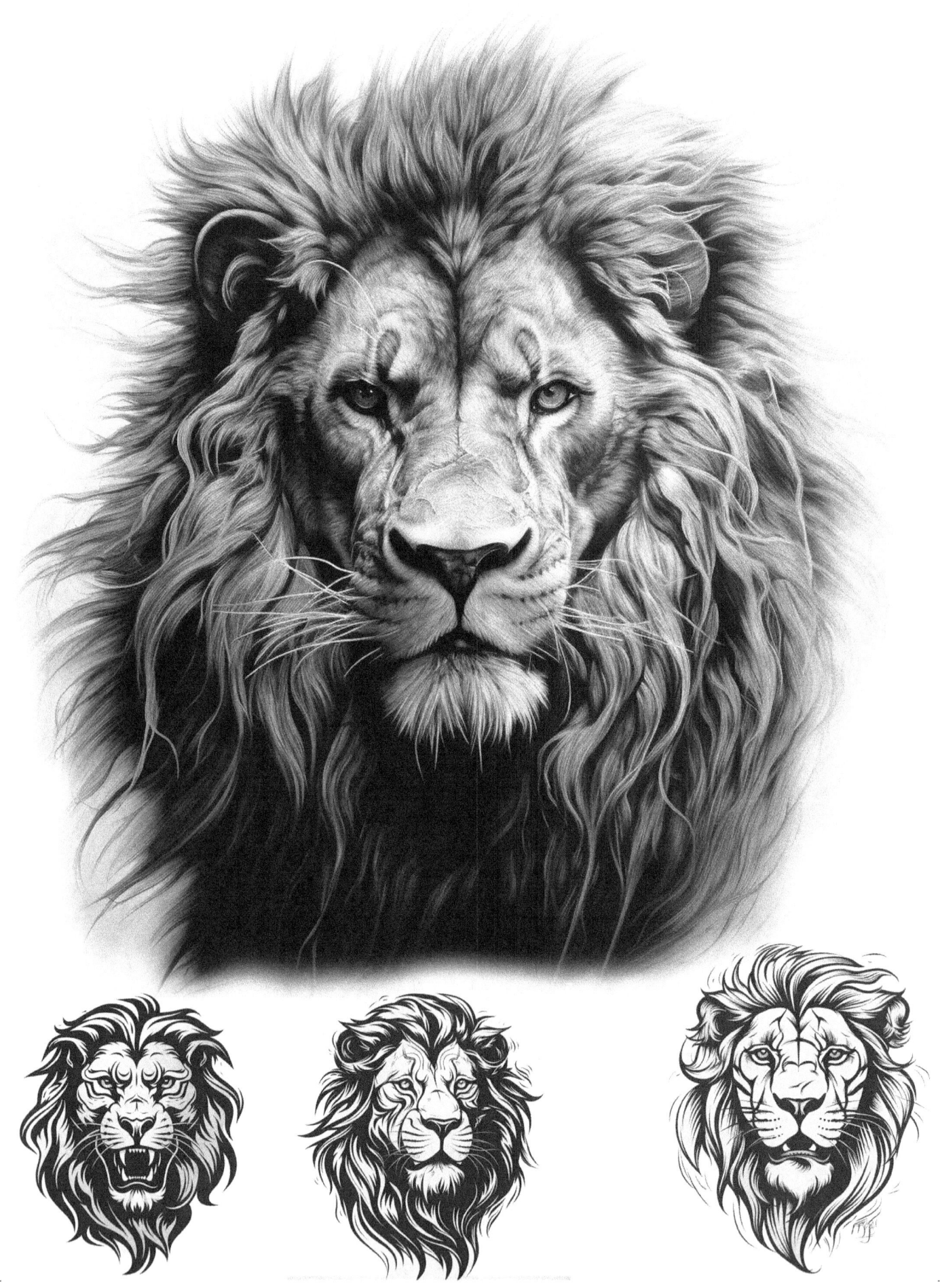

LION

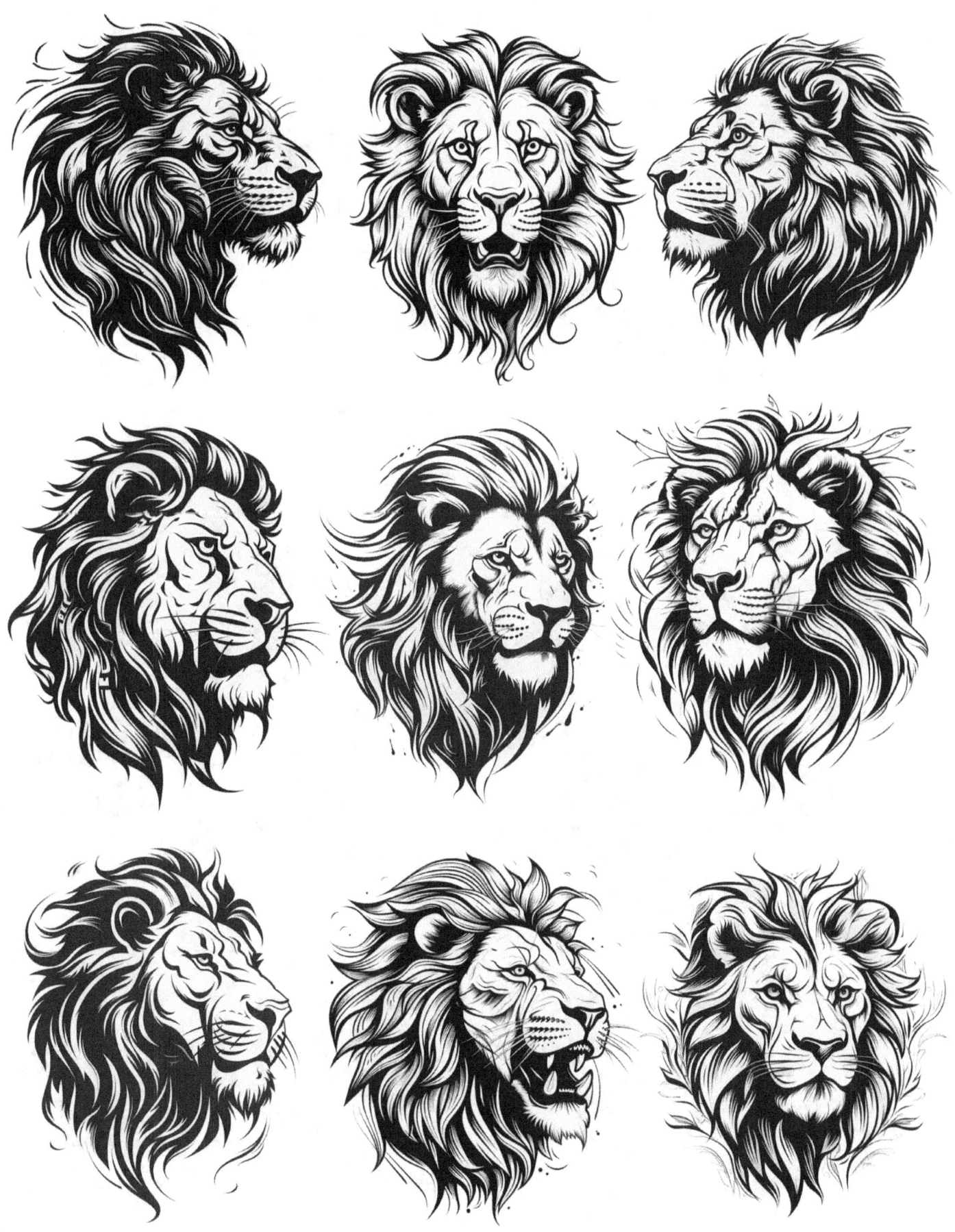

LION

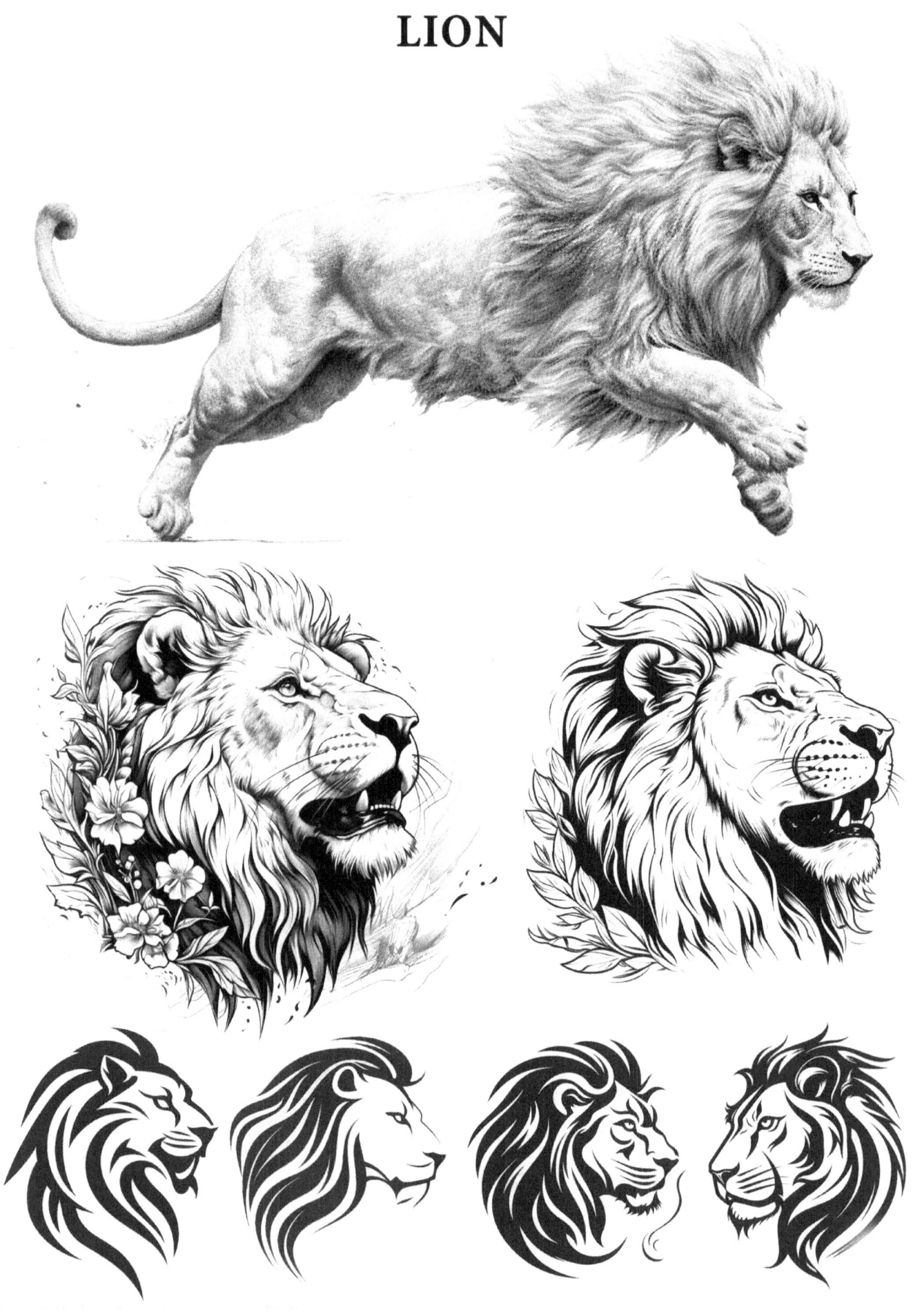

LOTUS

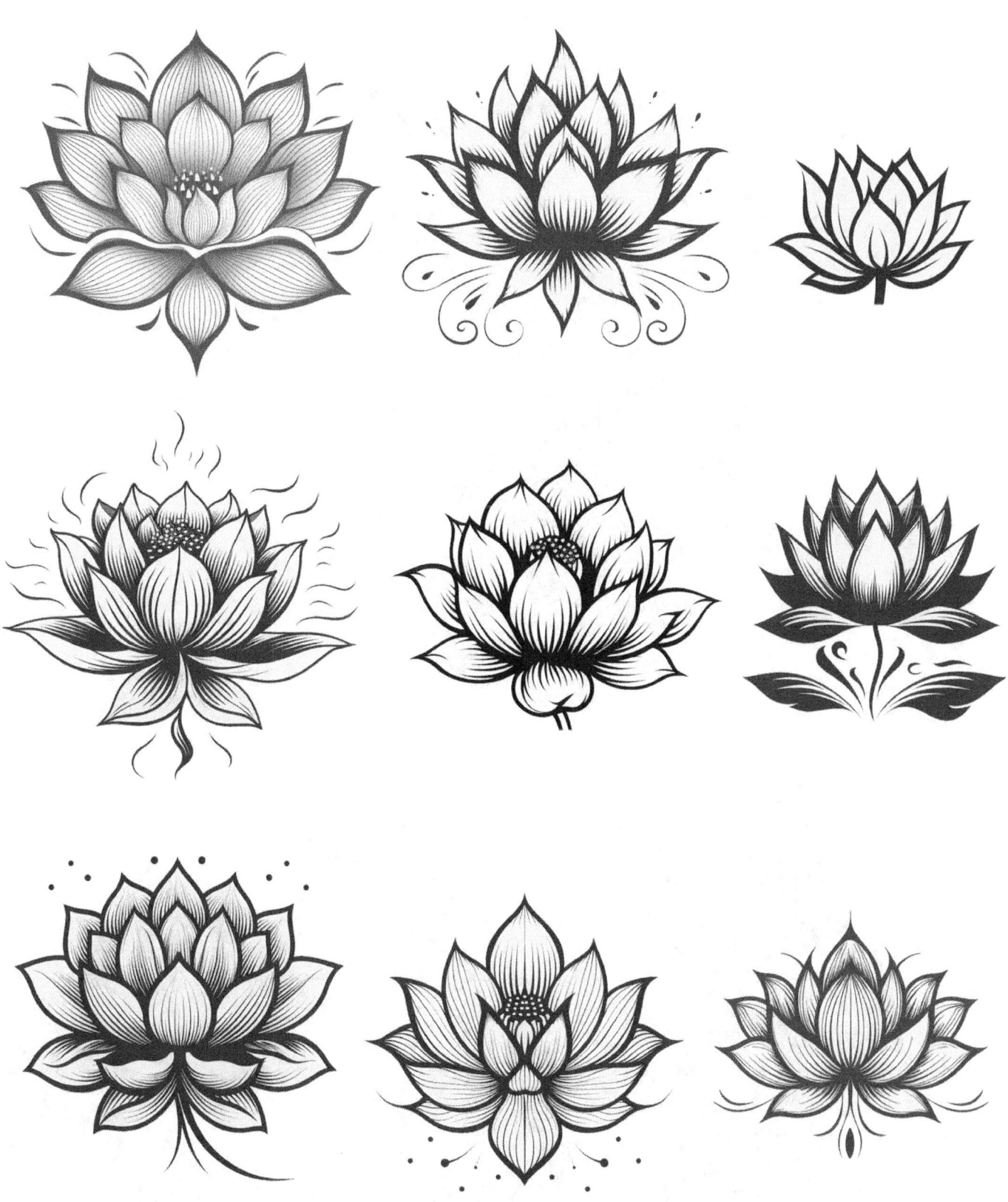

LYNX

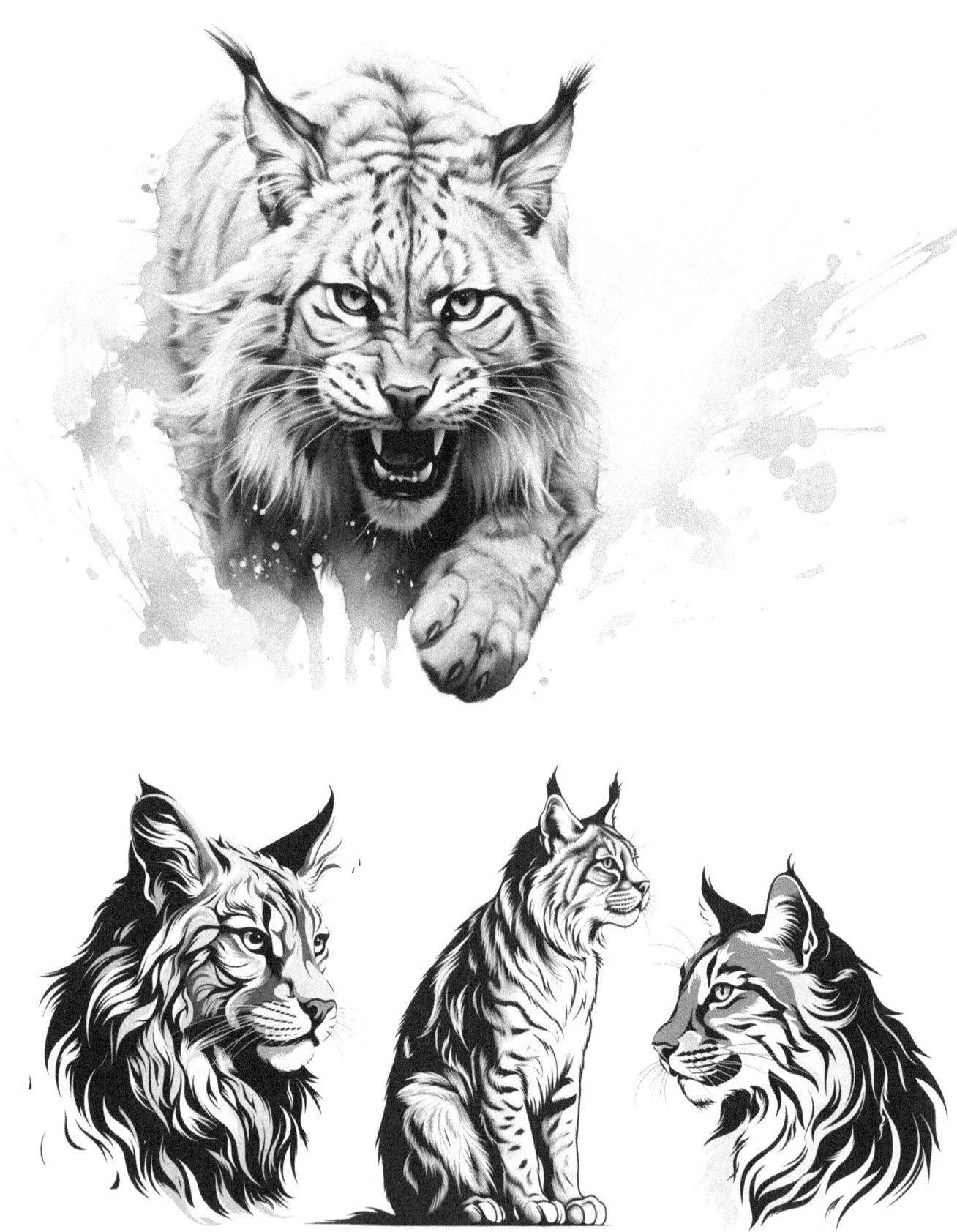

LYNX

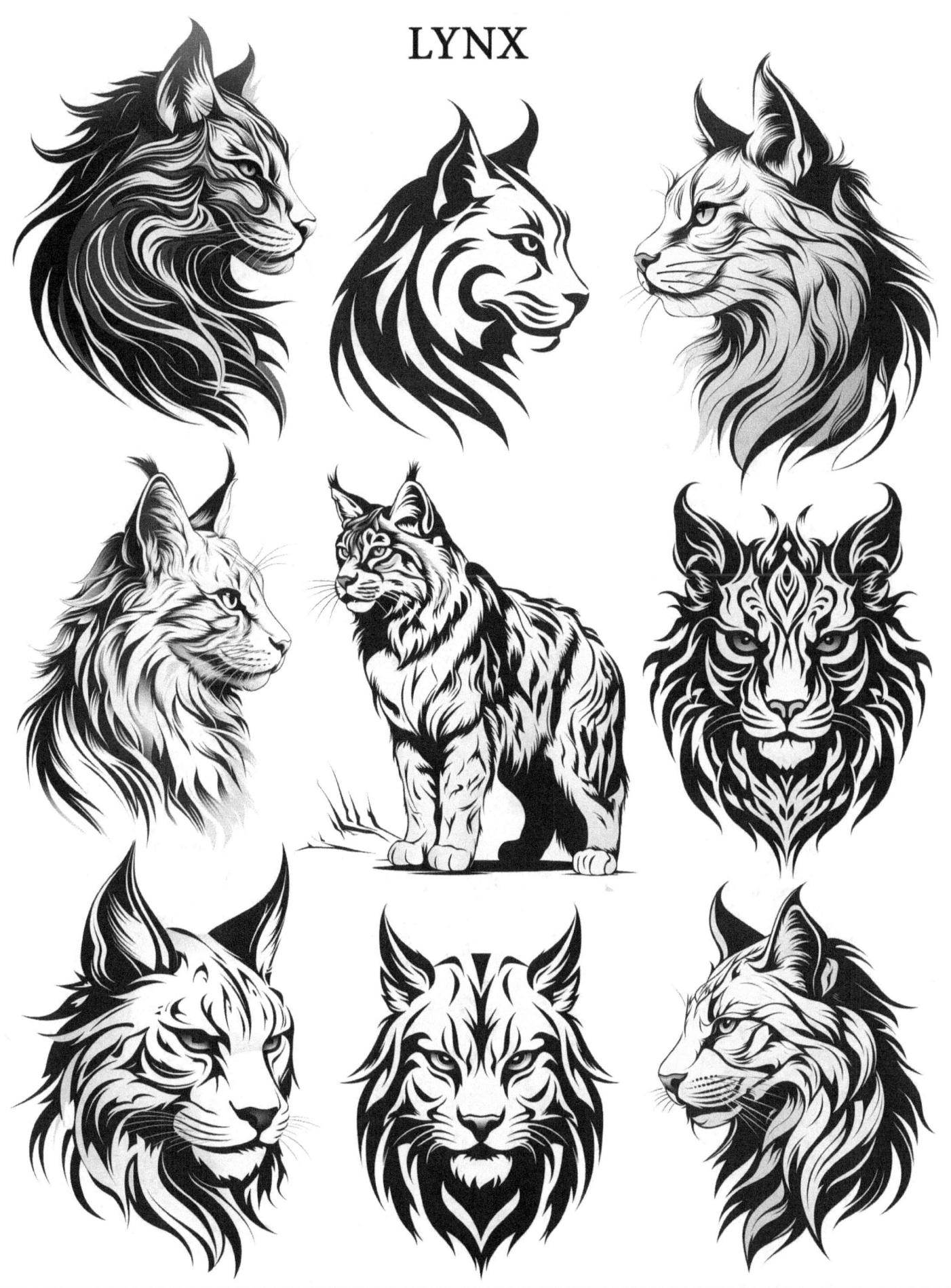

MERMAID

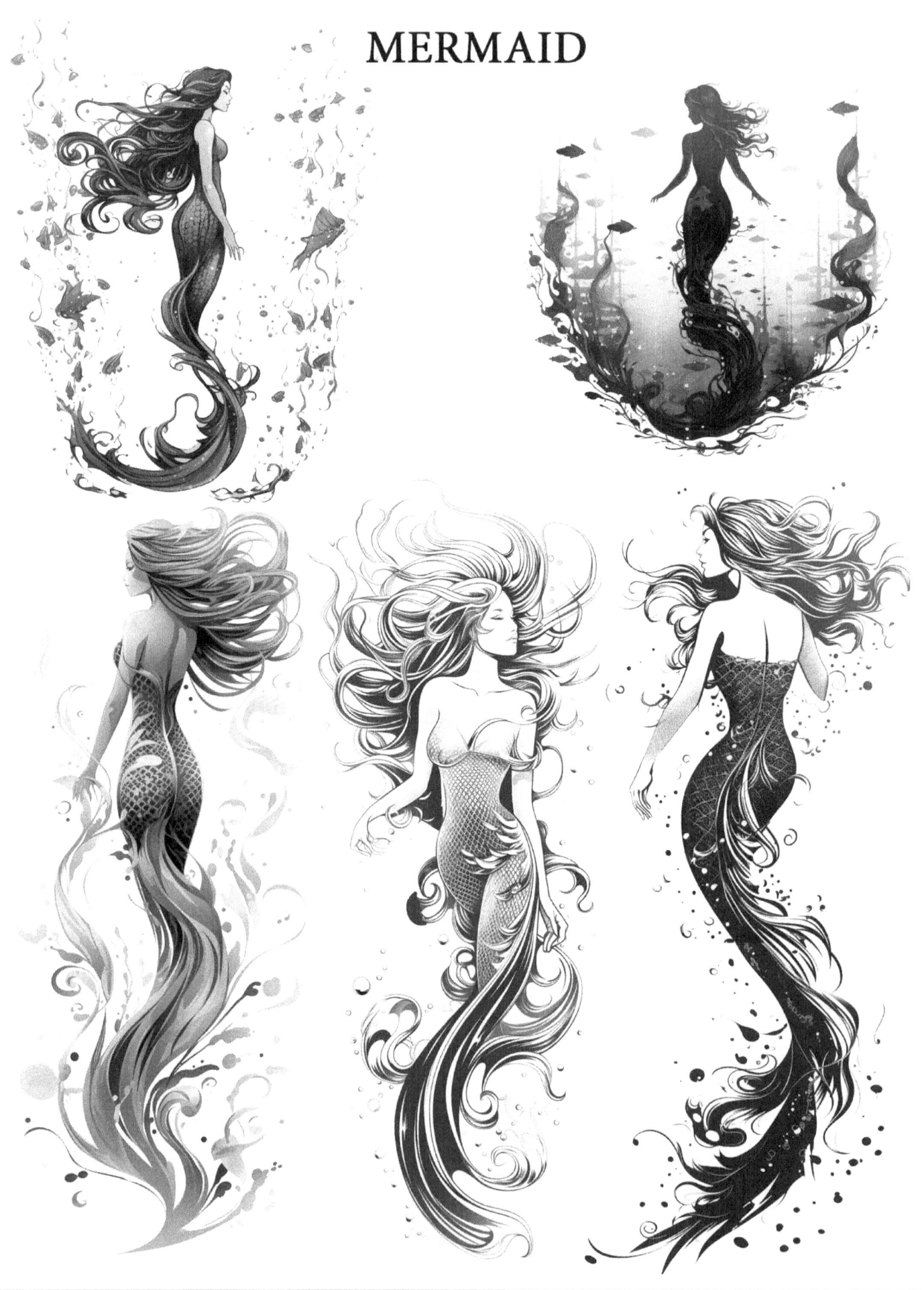

MERMAID

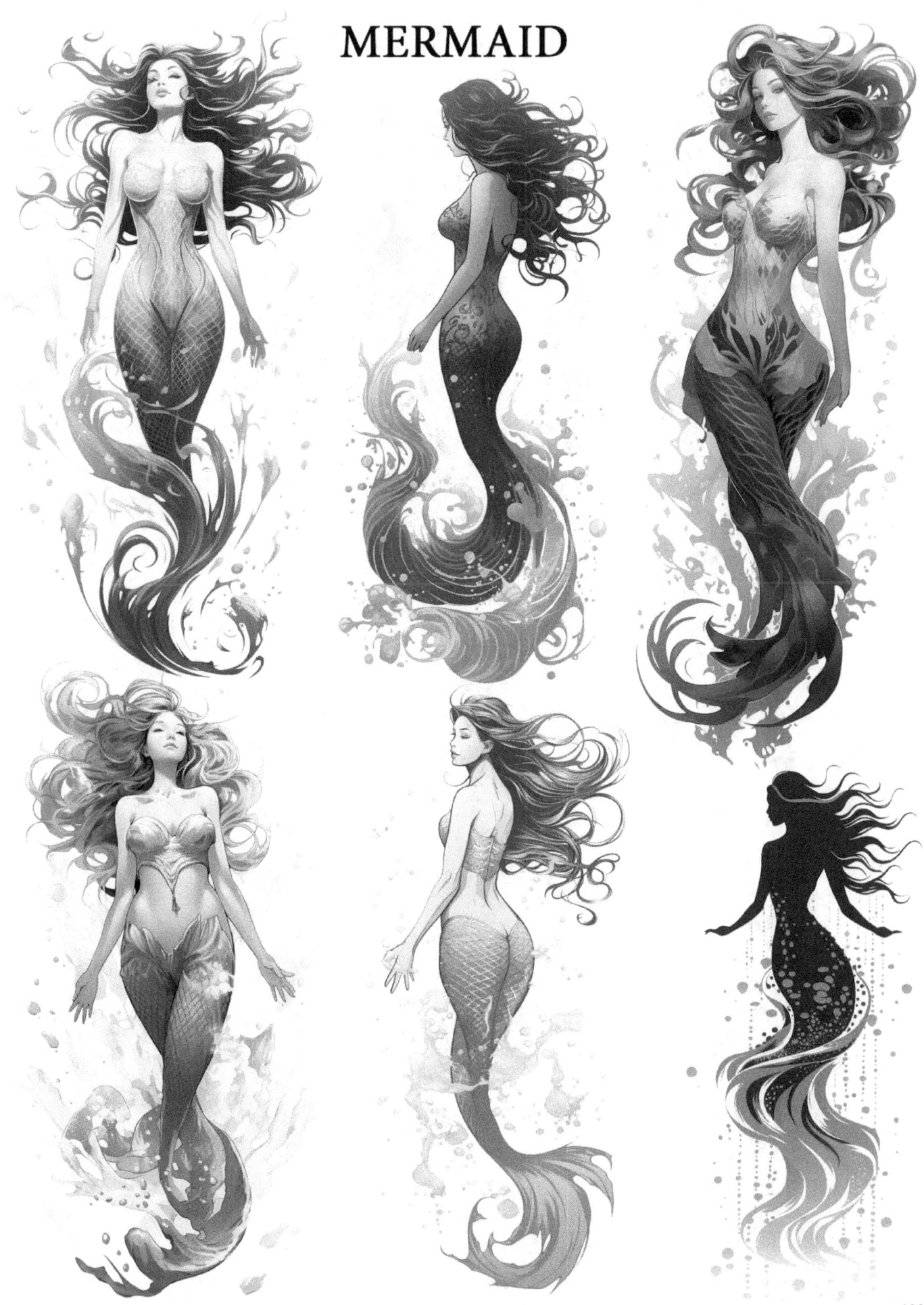

MERMAID

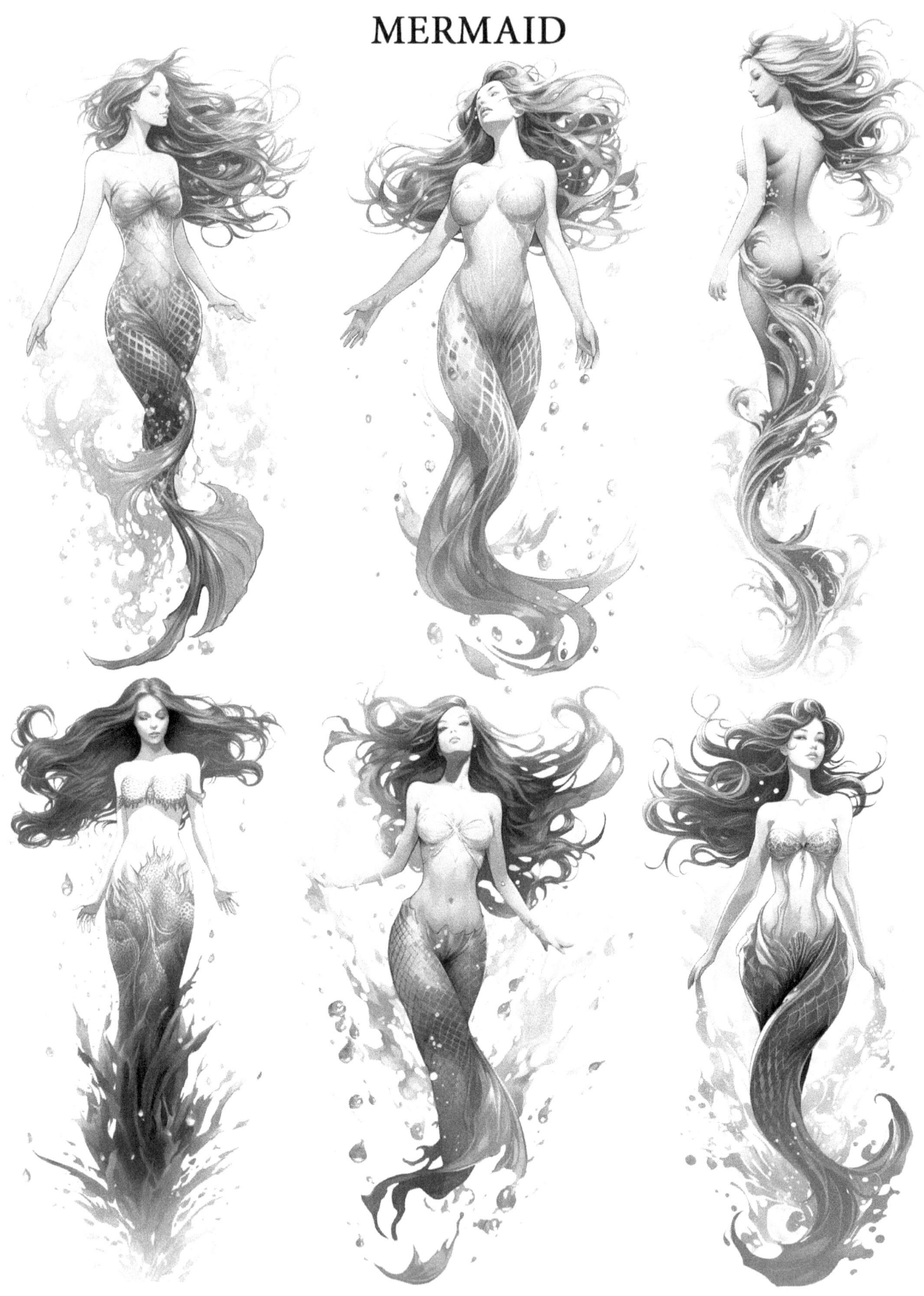

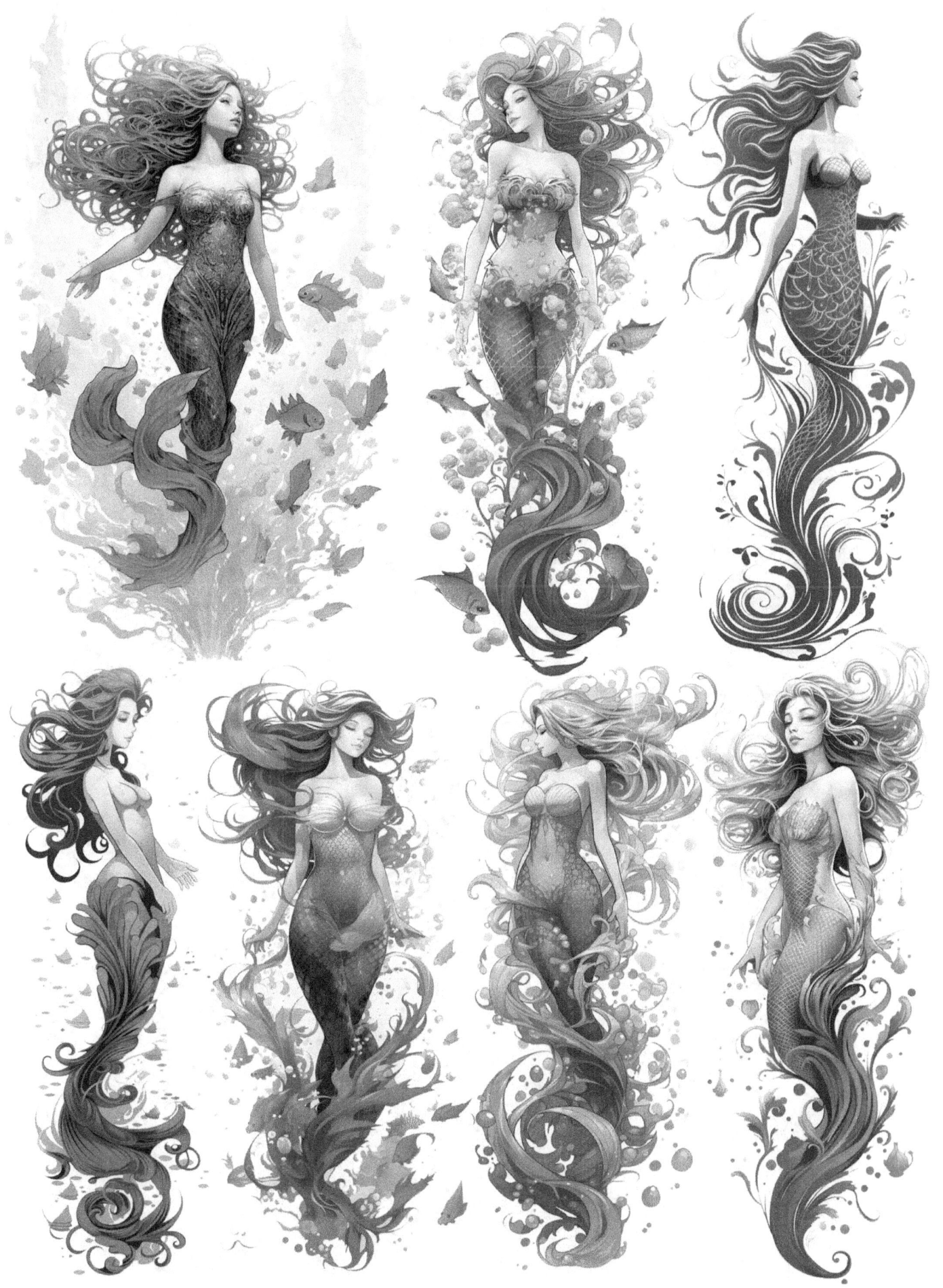

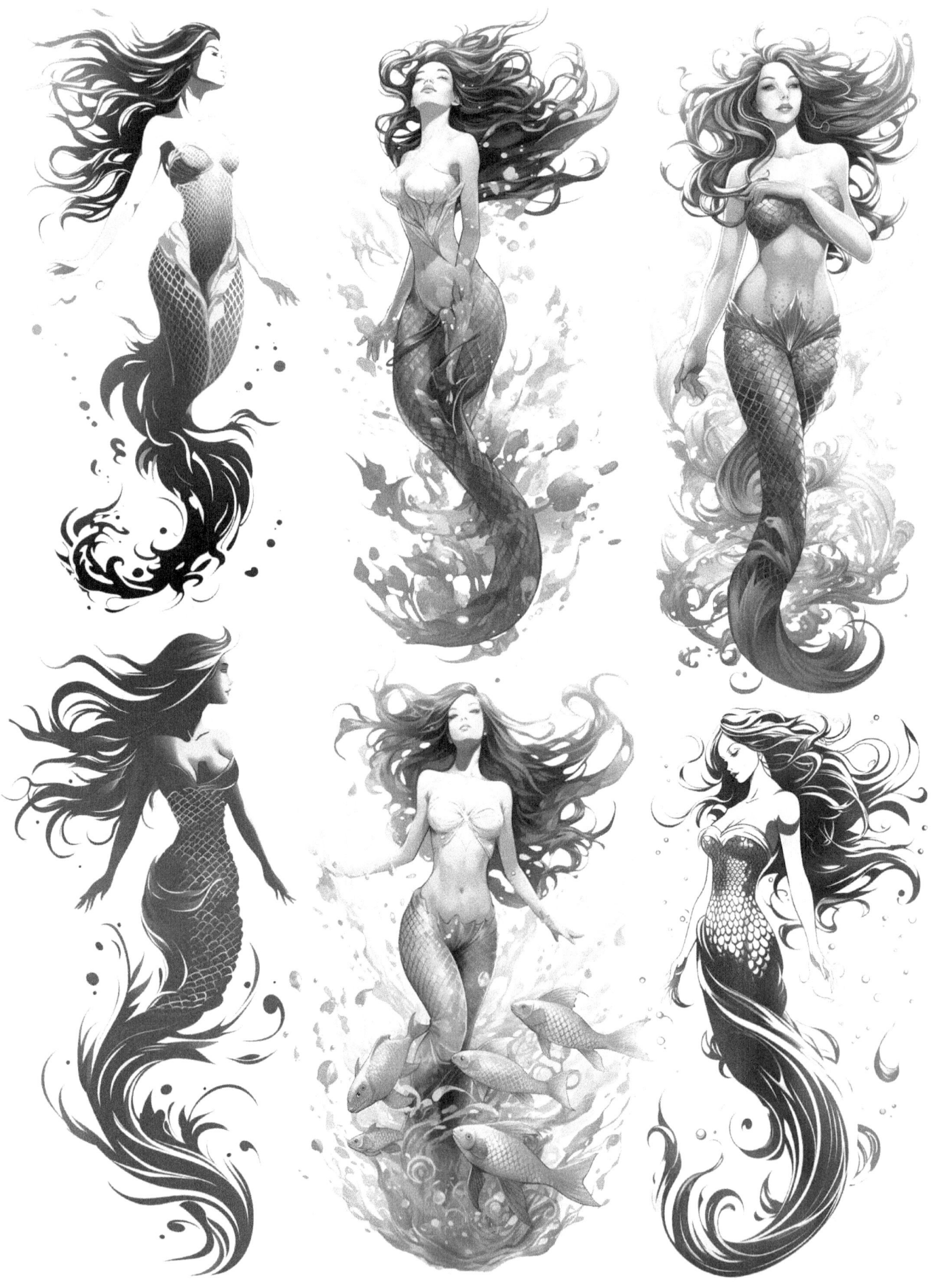

OWL

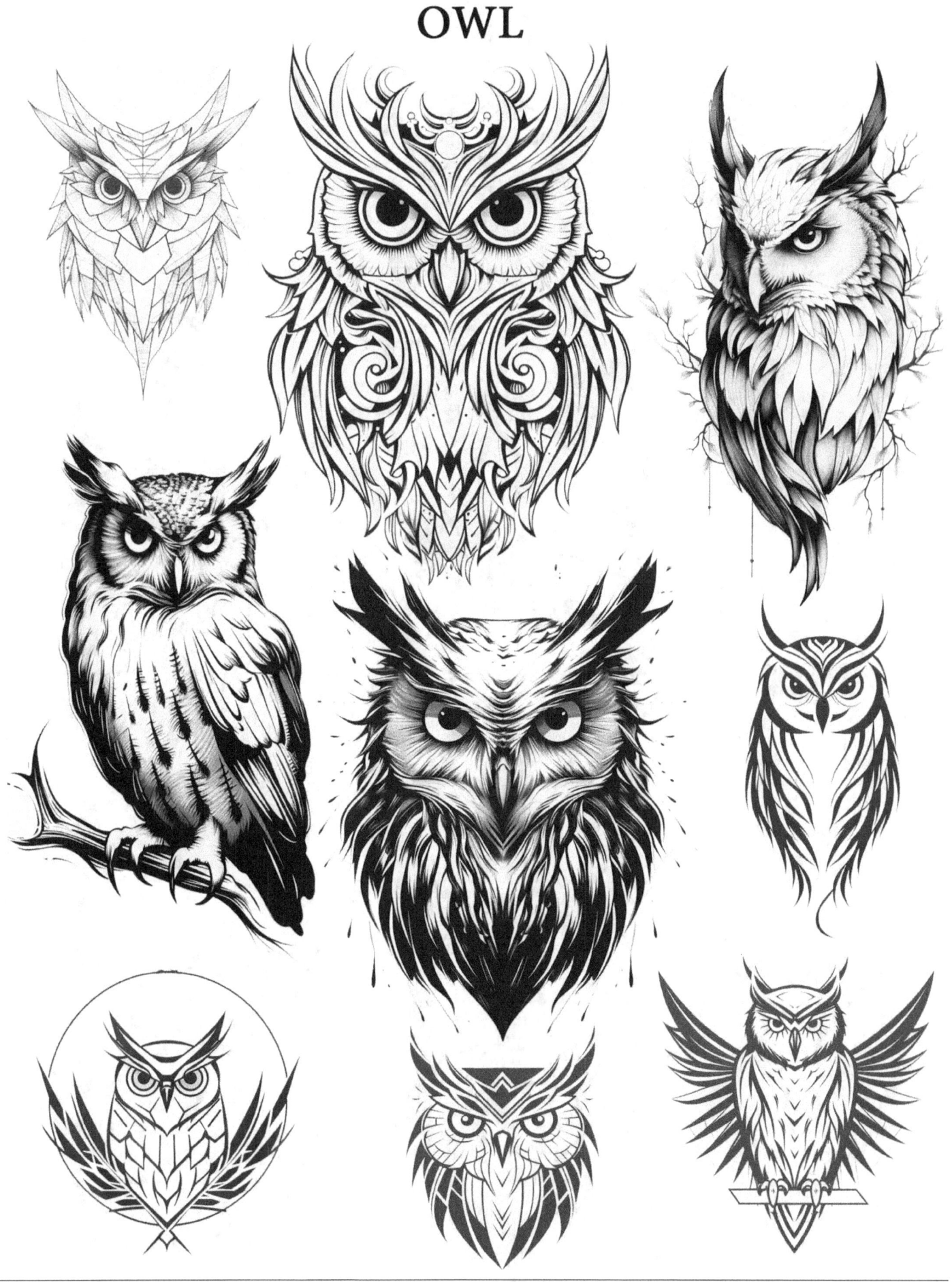

OWL

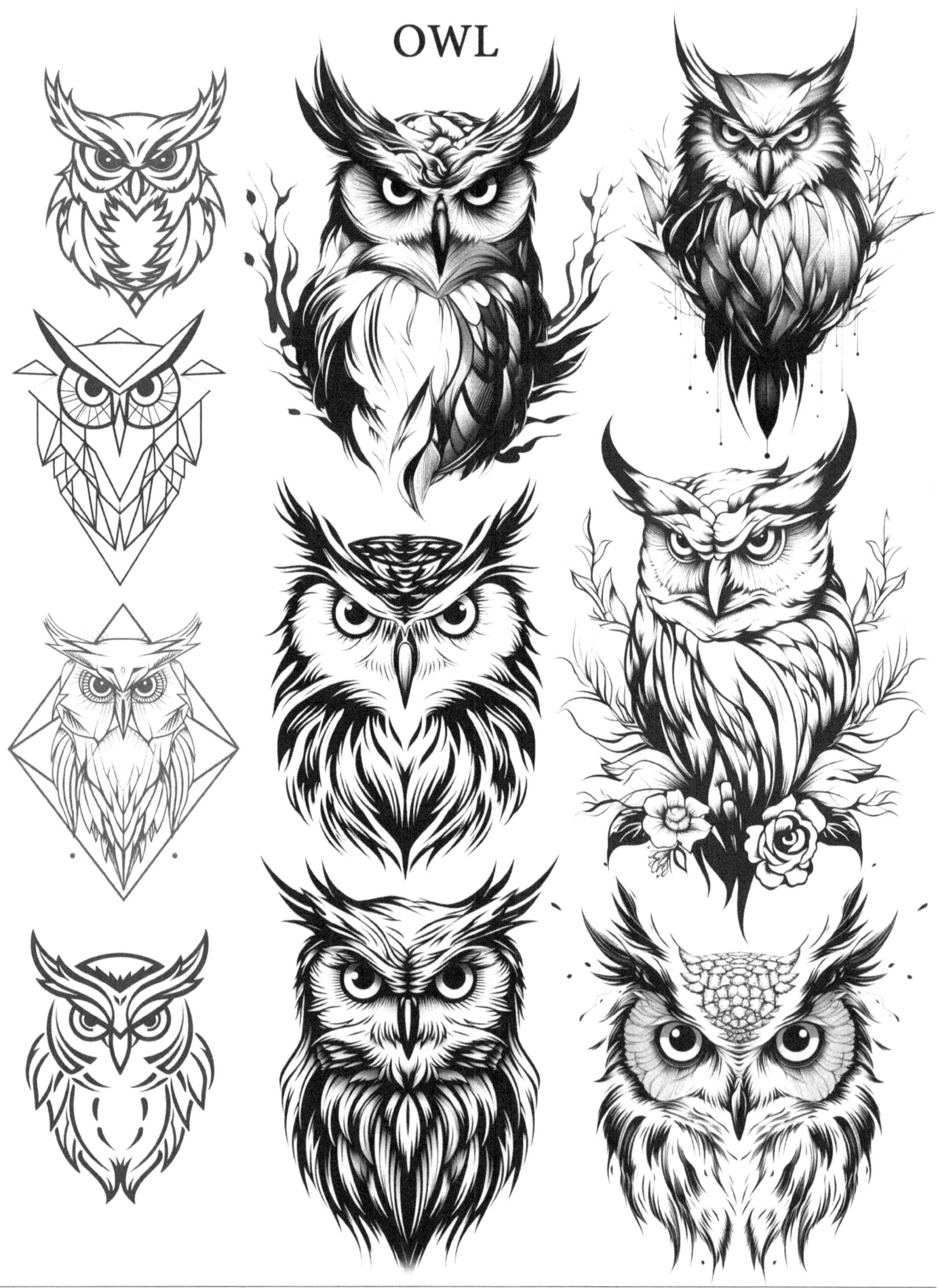

PANTHER

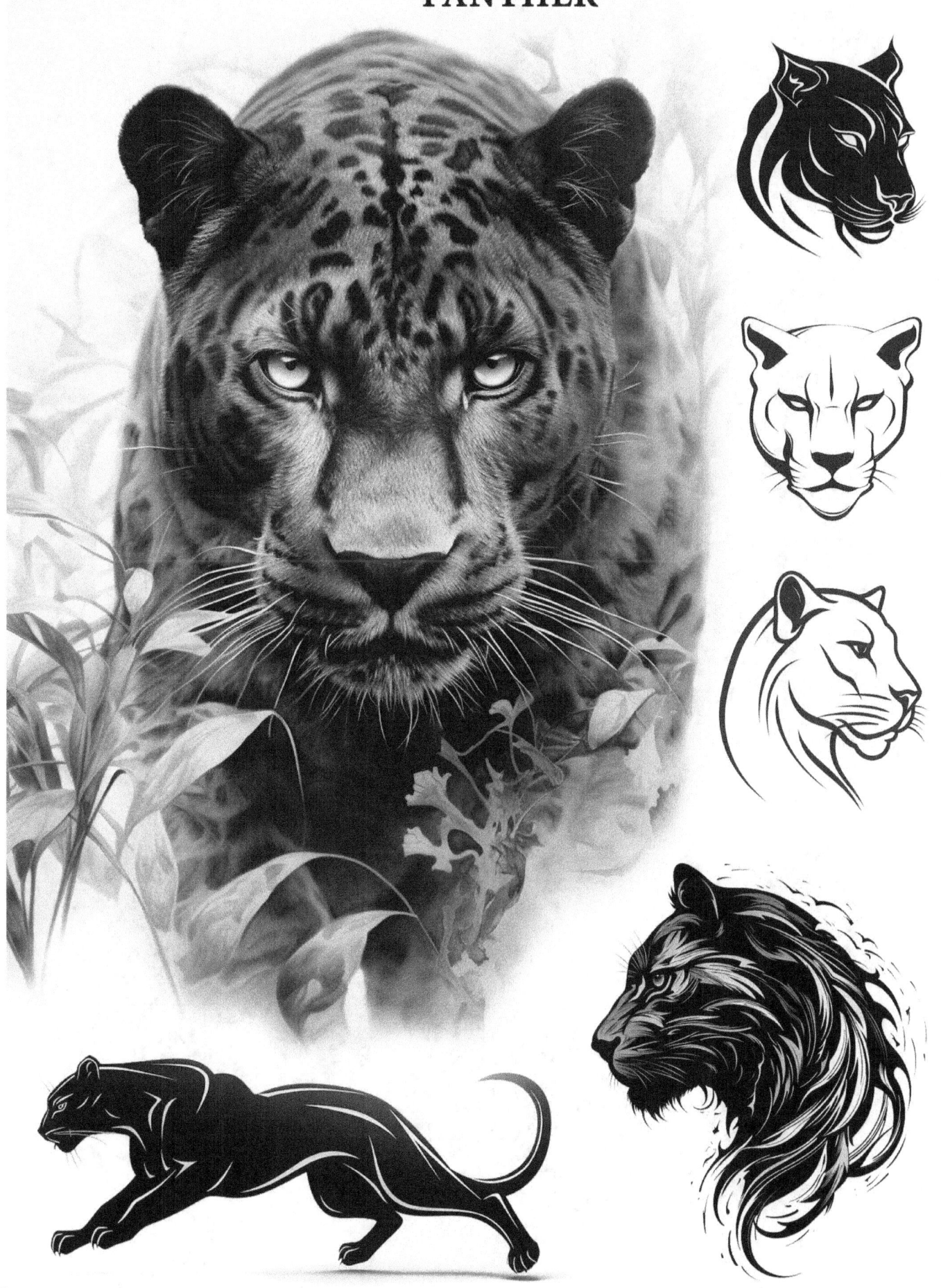

PANTHER

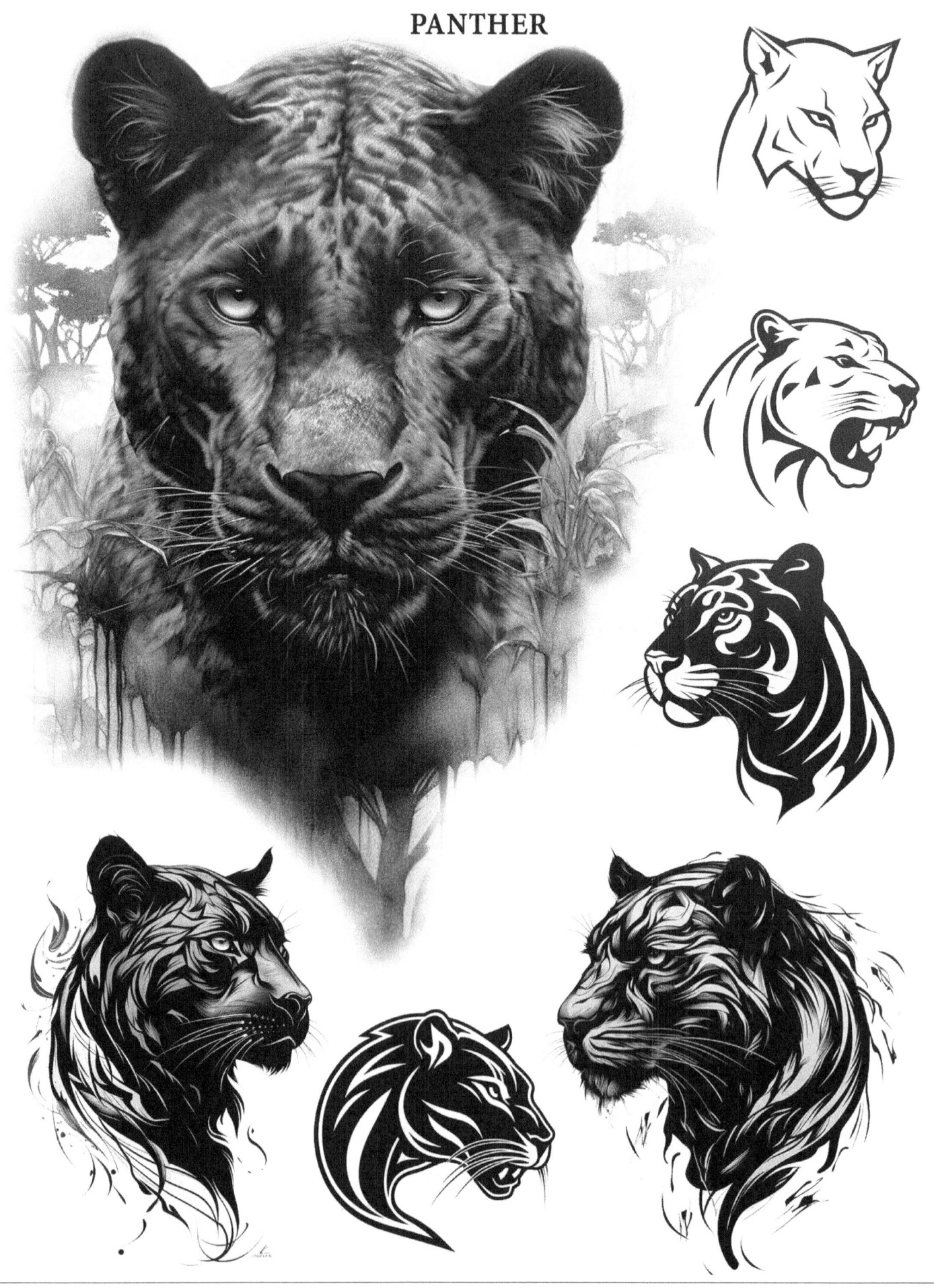

PANTHER

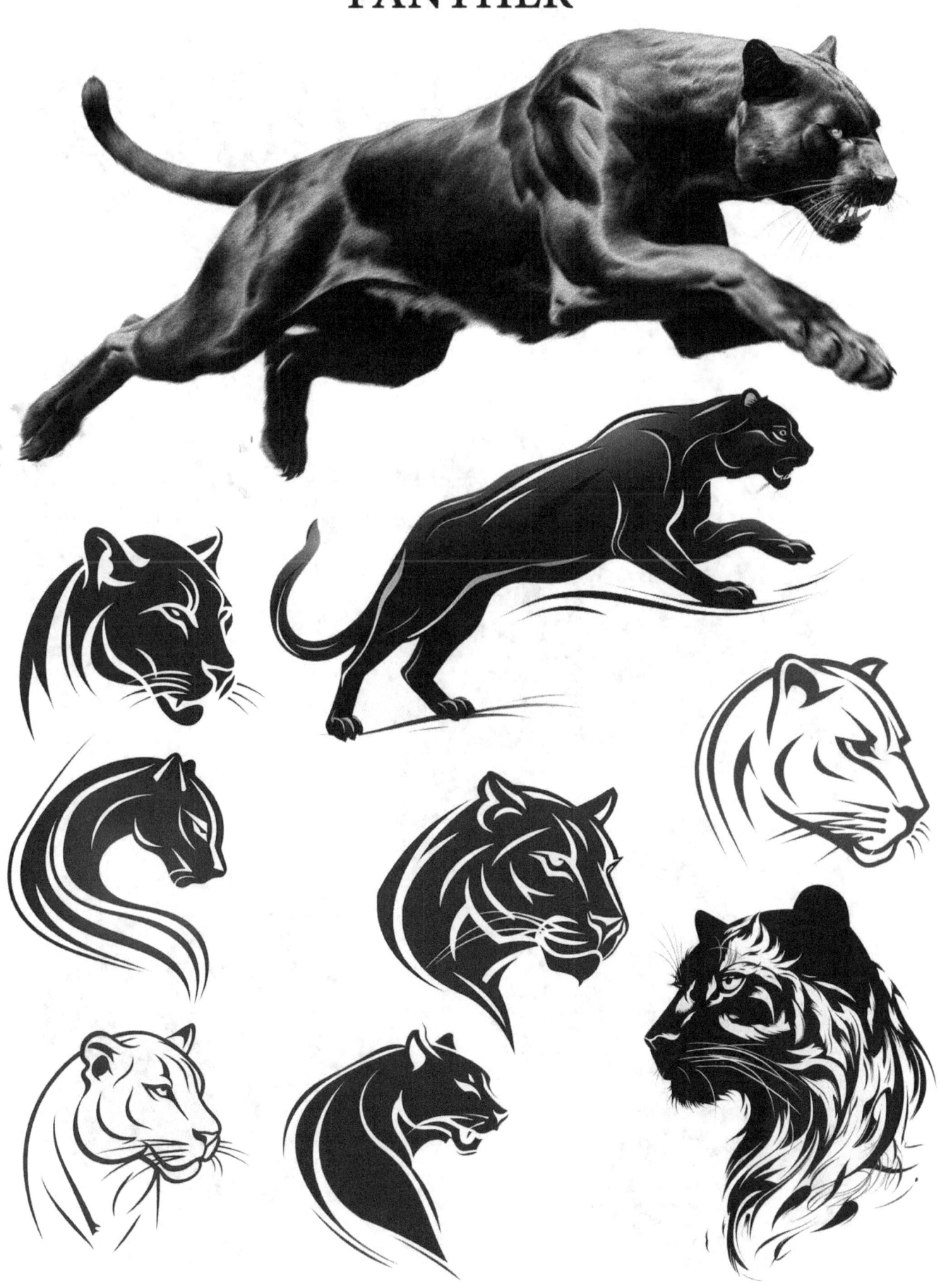

PANTHER

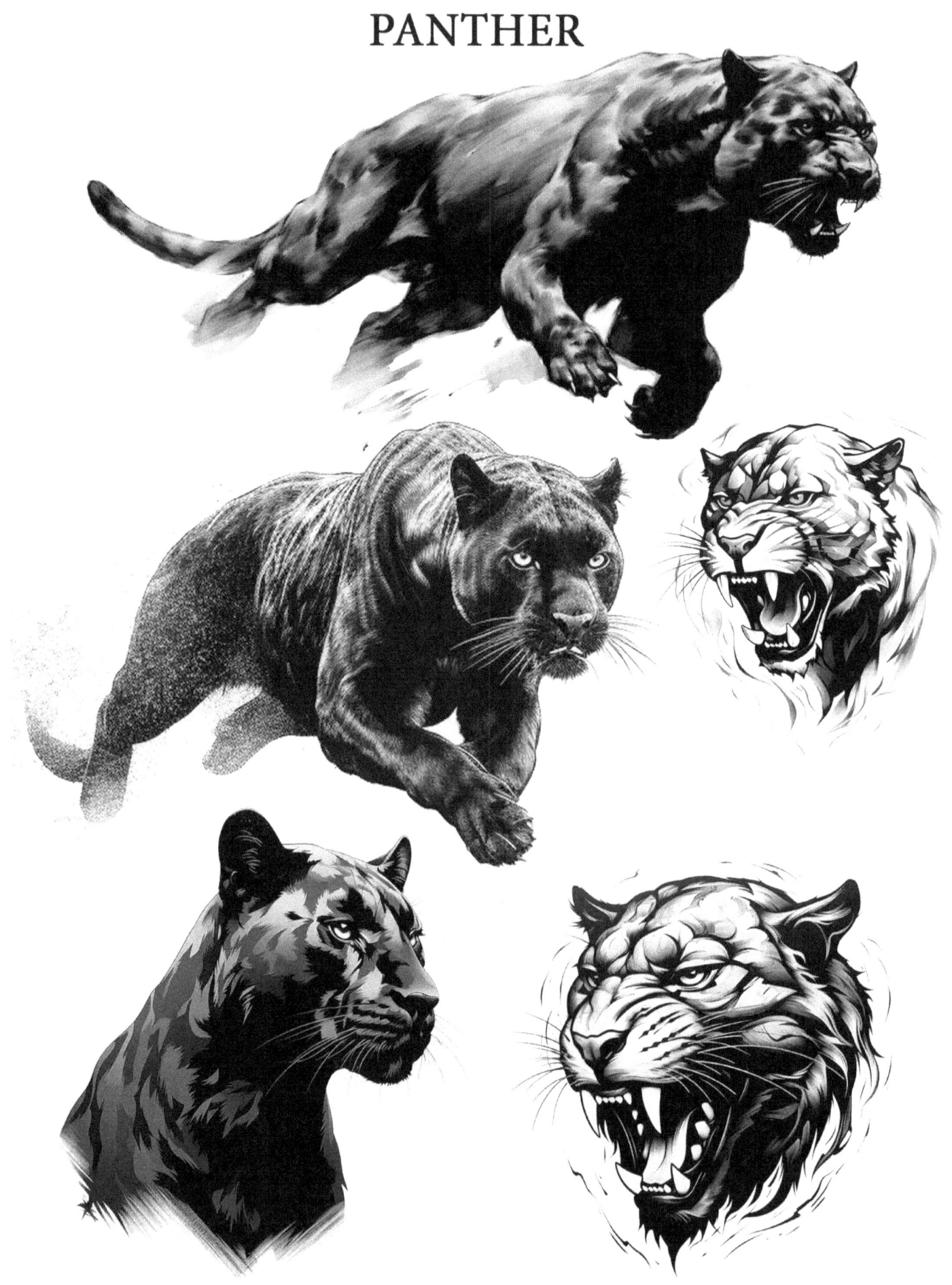

PARROT

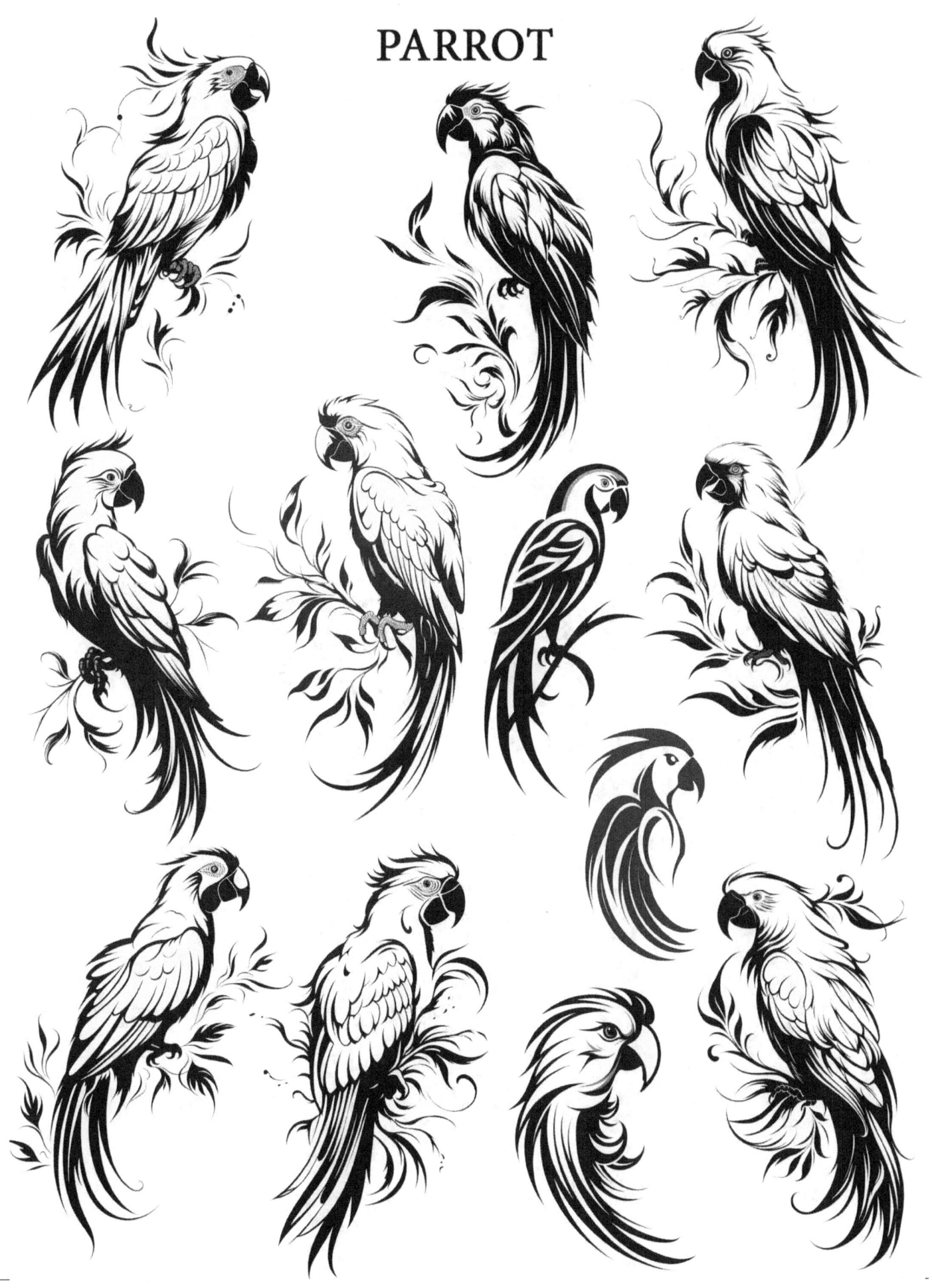

To download scan the below QR code use WINRAR to open and
Use the below password

TheGreatTattooDesignsBook1124

The Great Tattoo designs Book.
v3 Google drive

The Great Tattoo designs Book
V3 download

You can contact us at our Facebook page

Follow us on facebook   Subscribe me at YouTube   My Books on Amazon
SCAN ME

Or visit our Link tree for all goodies

AlexartsOriginals linktree

Tiktok AlexartsOriginals

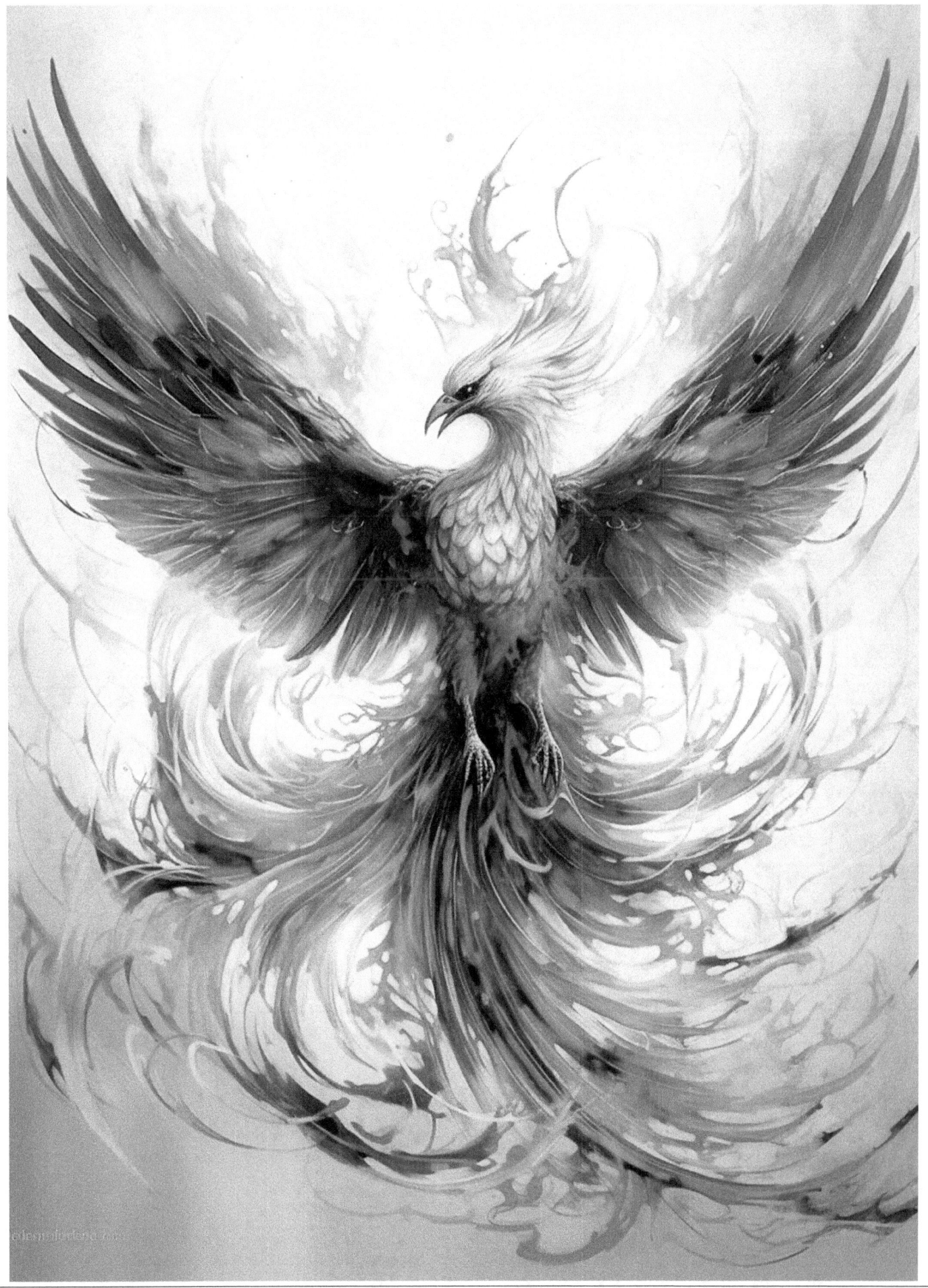

PHOENIX

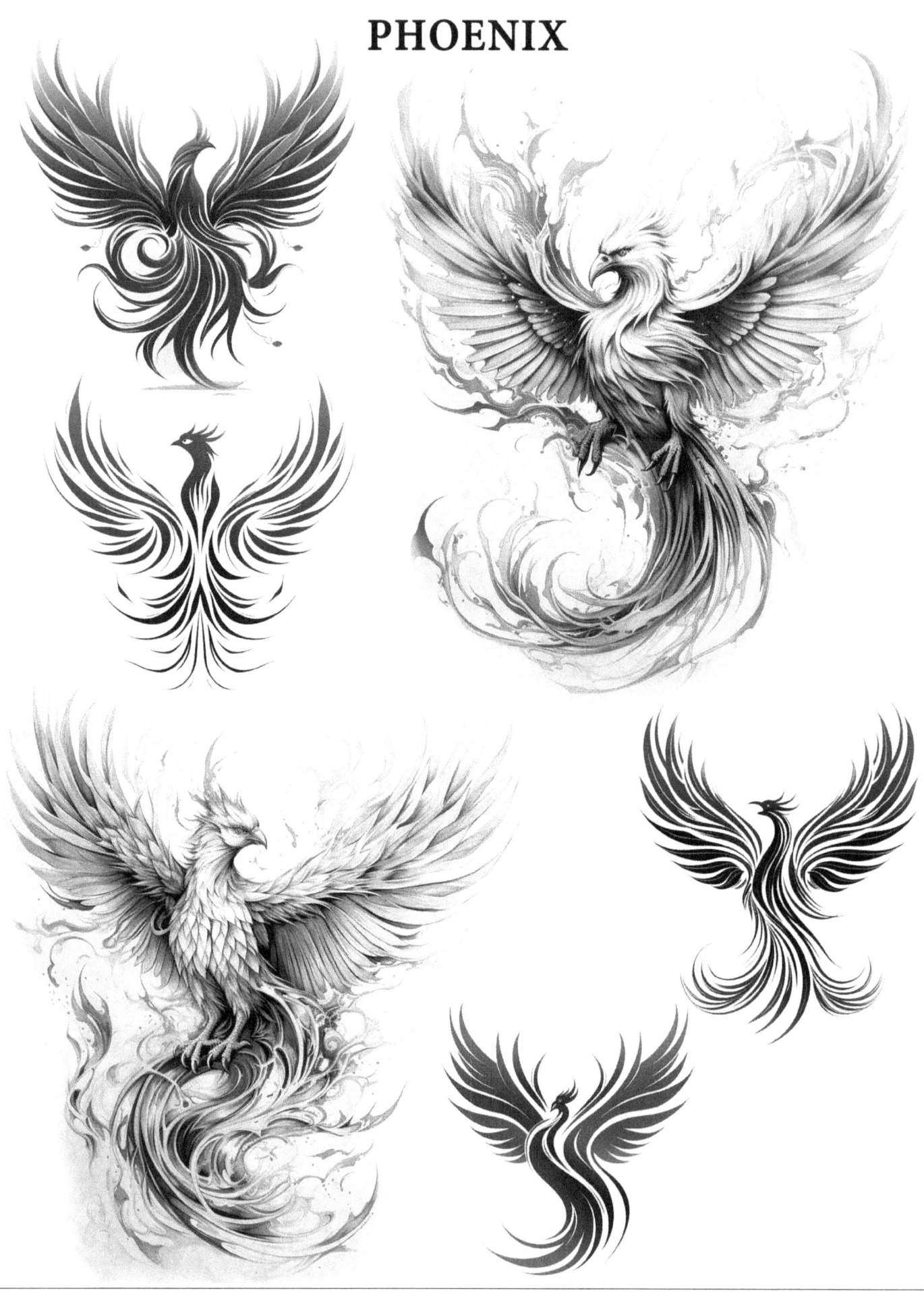

PHOENIX

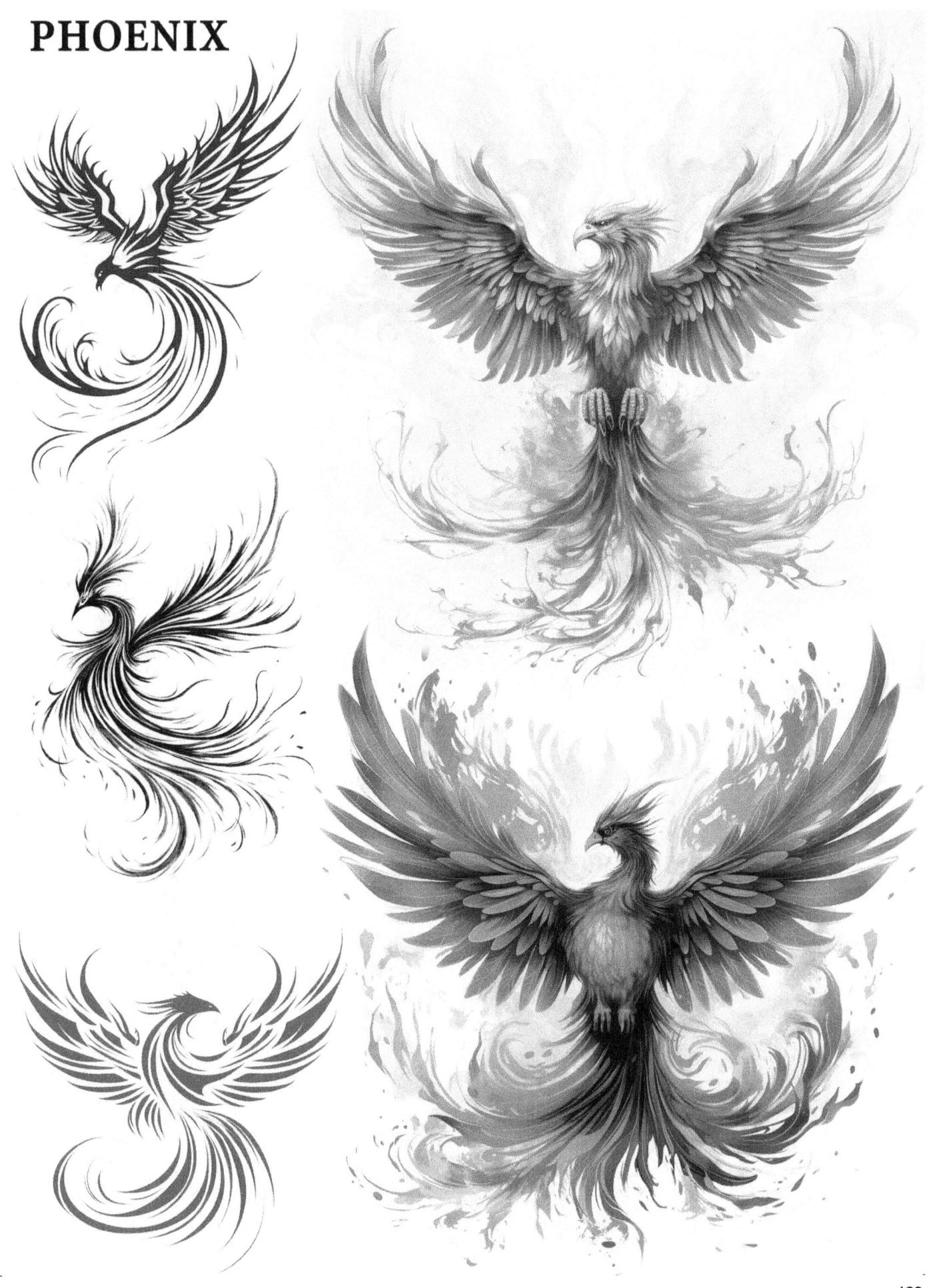

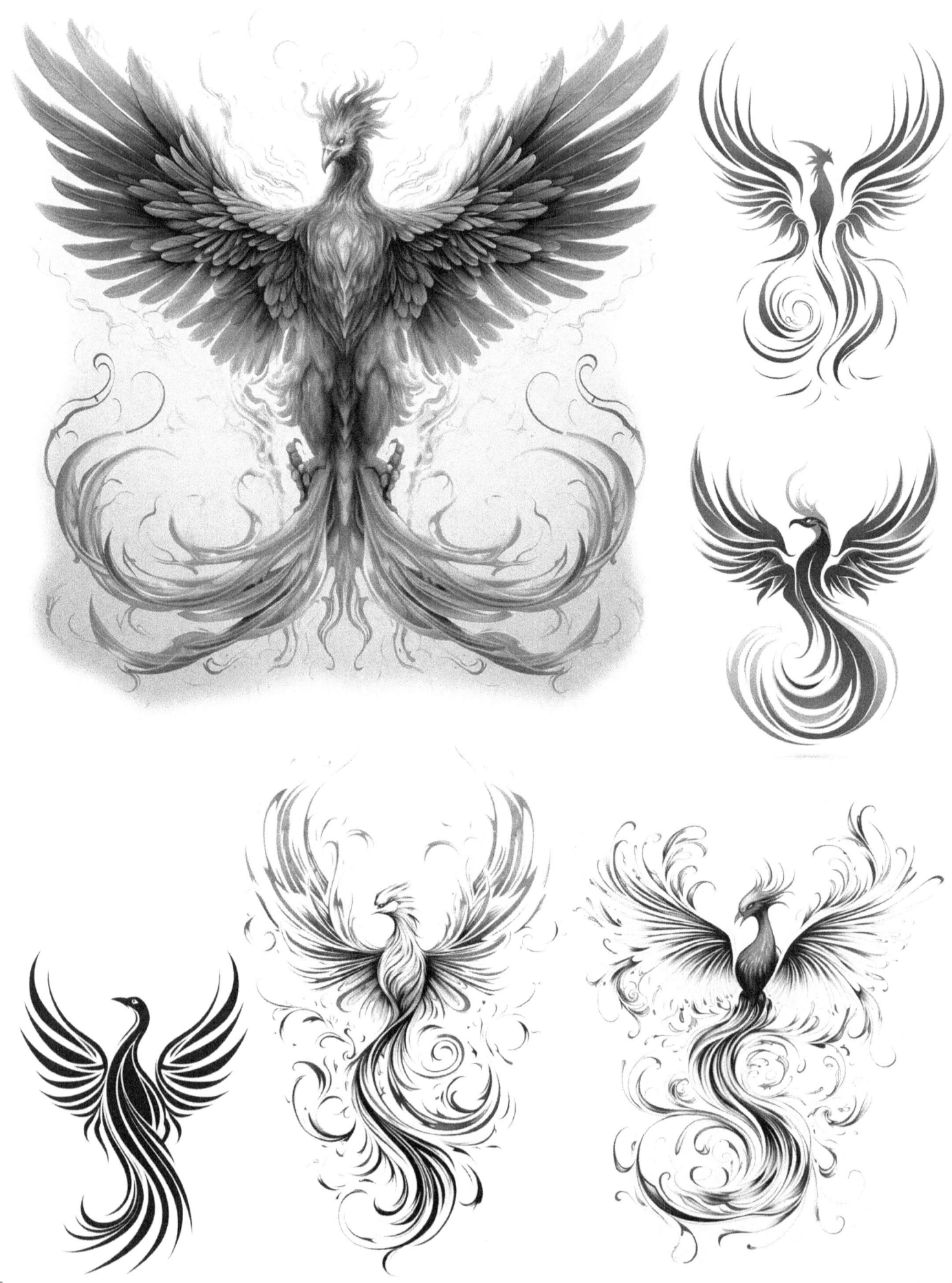

ROOSTER

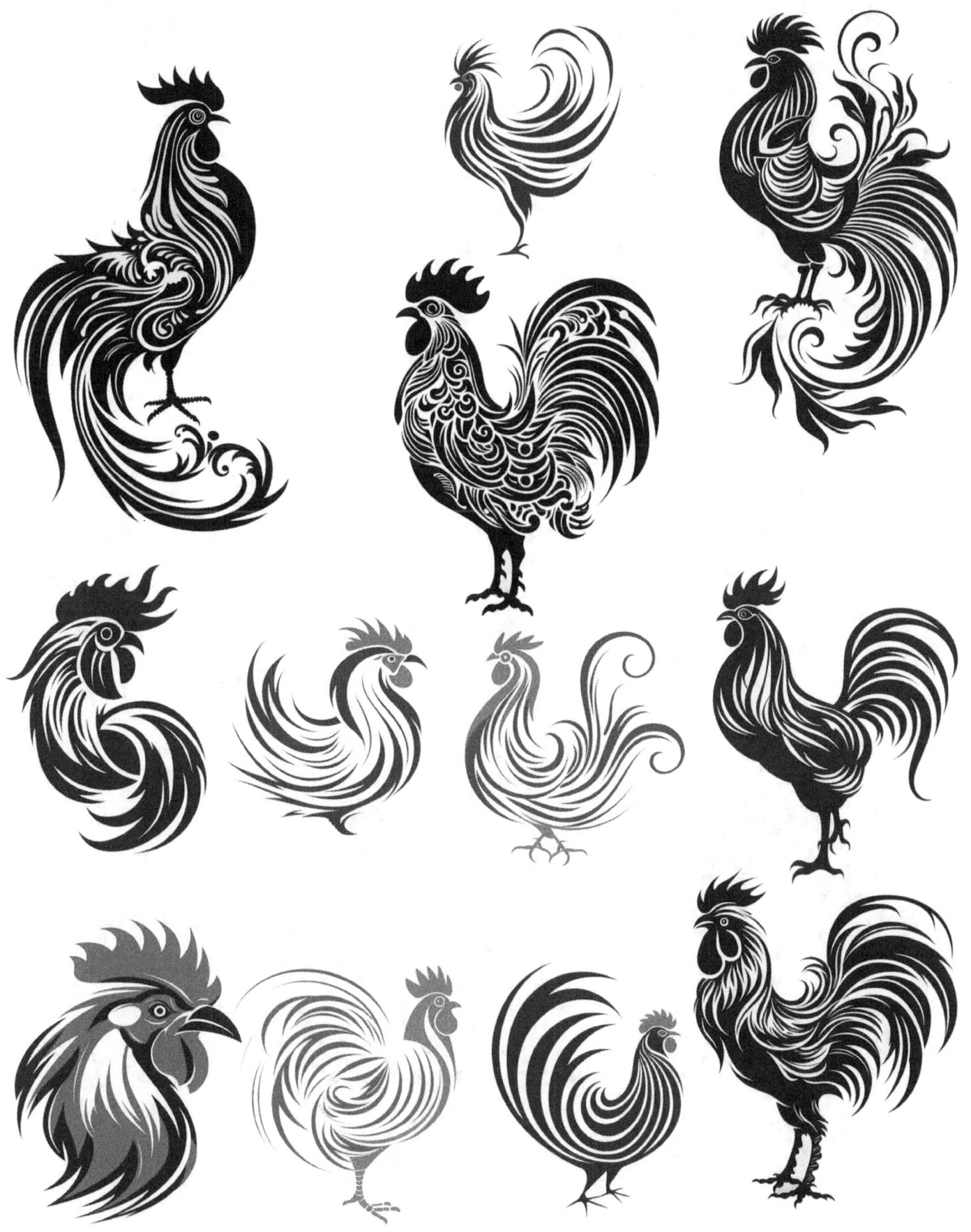

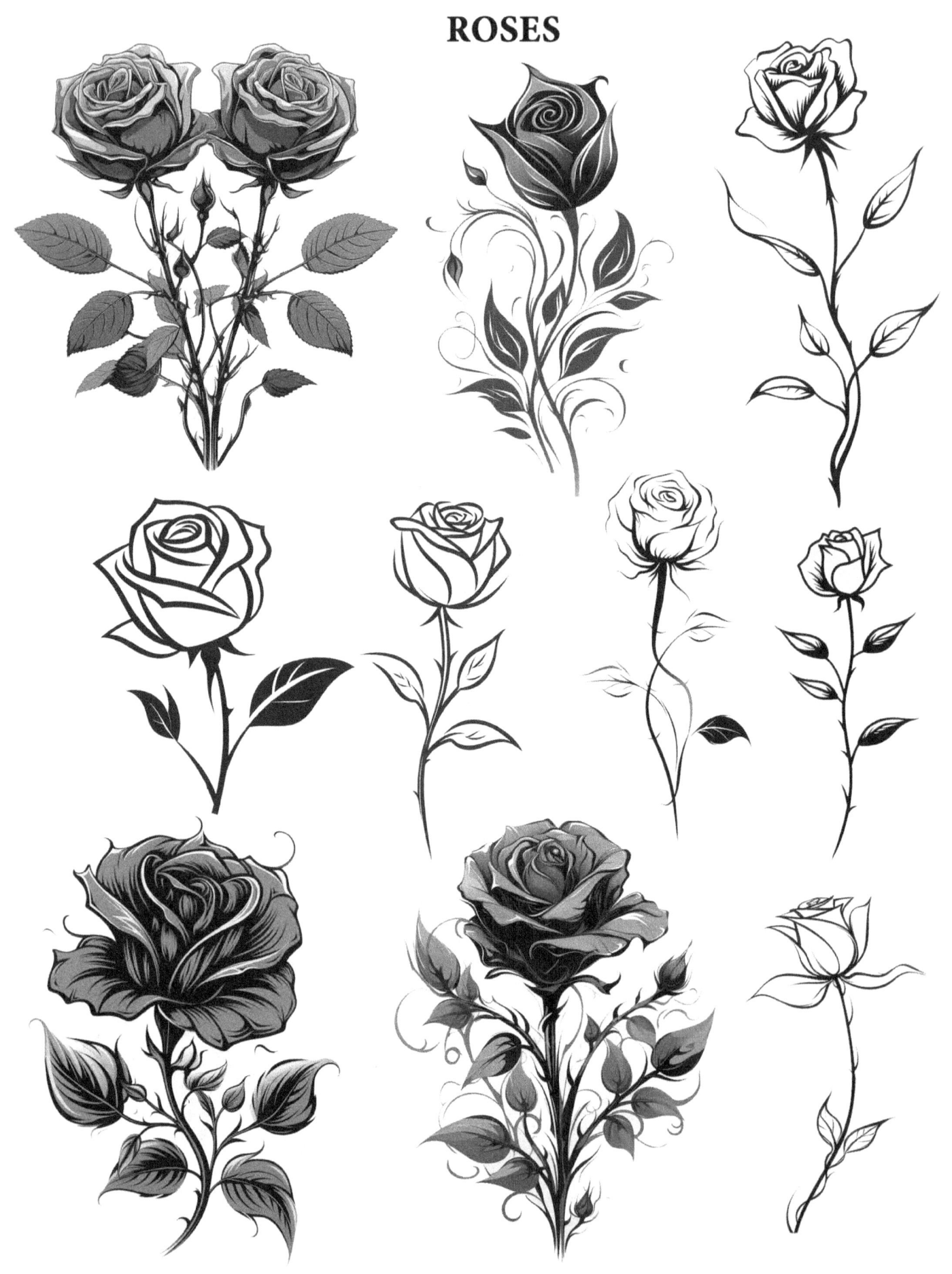

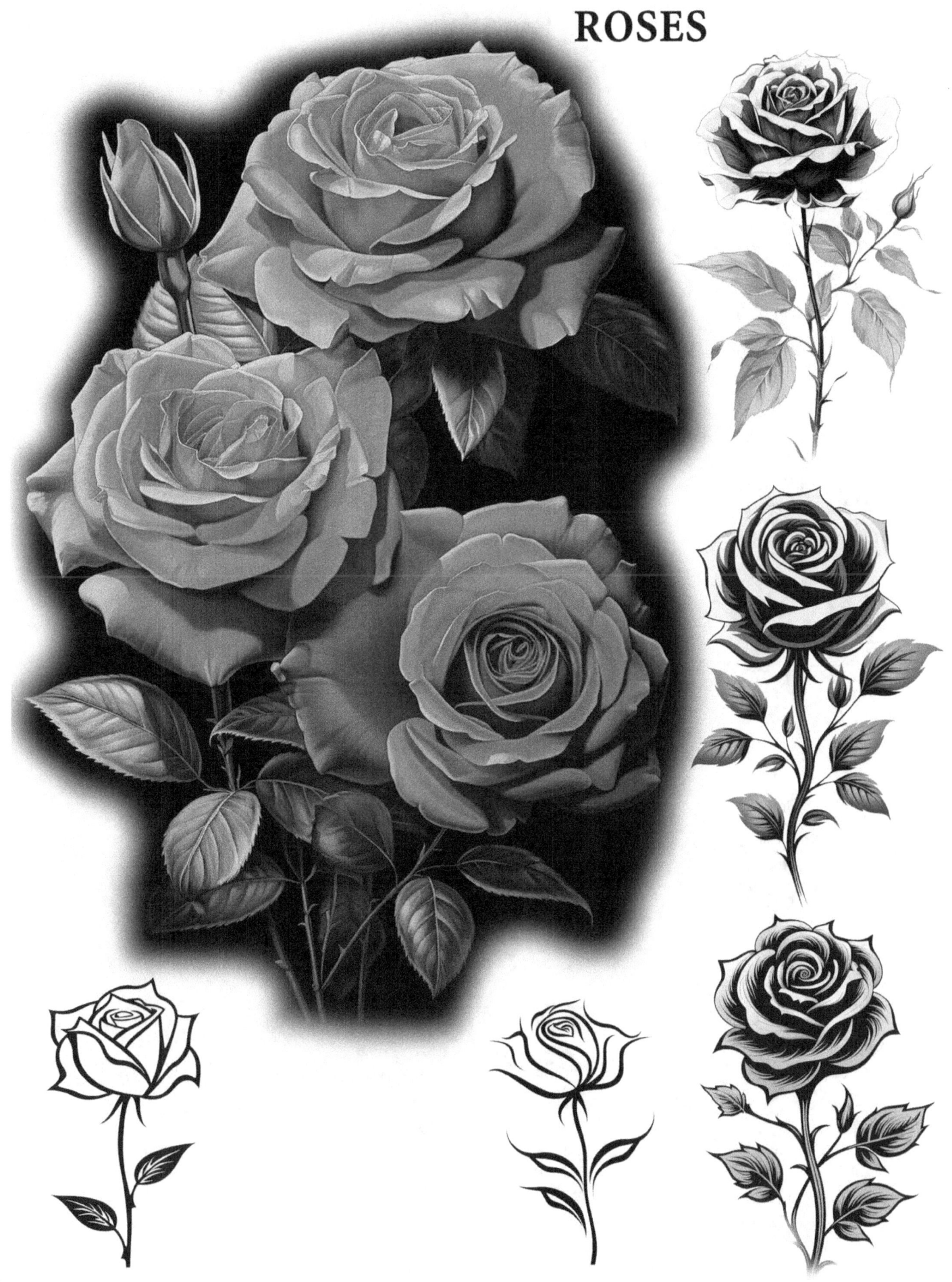

ROSES

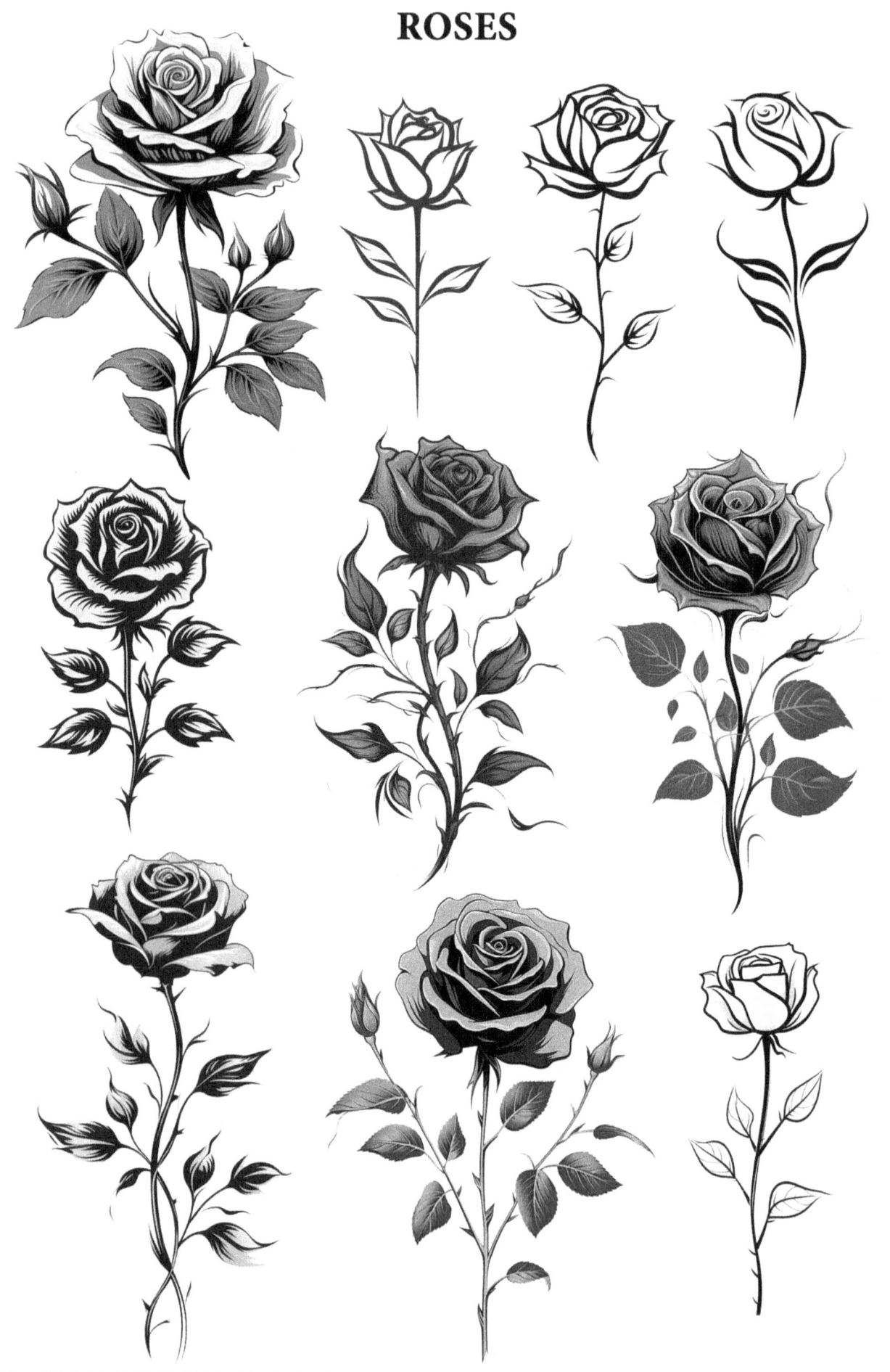

ROSES

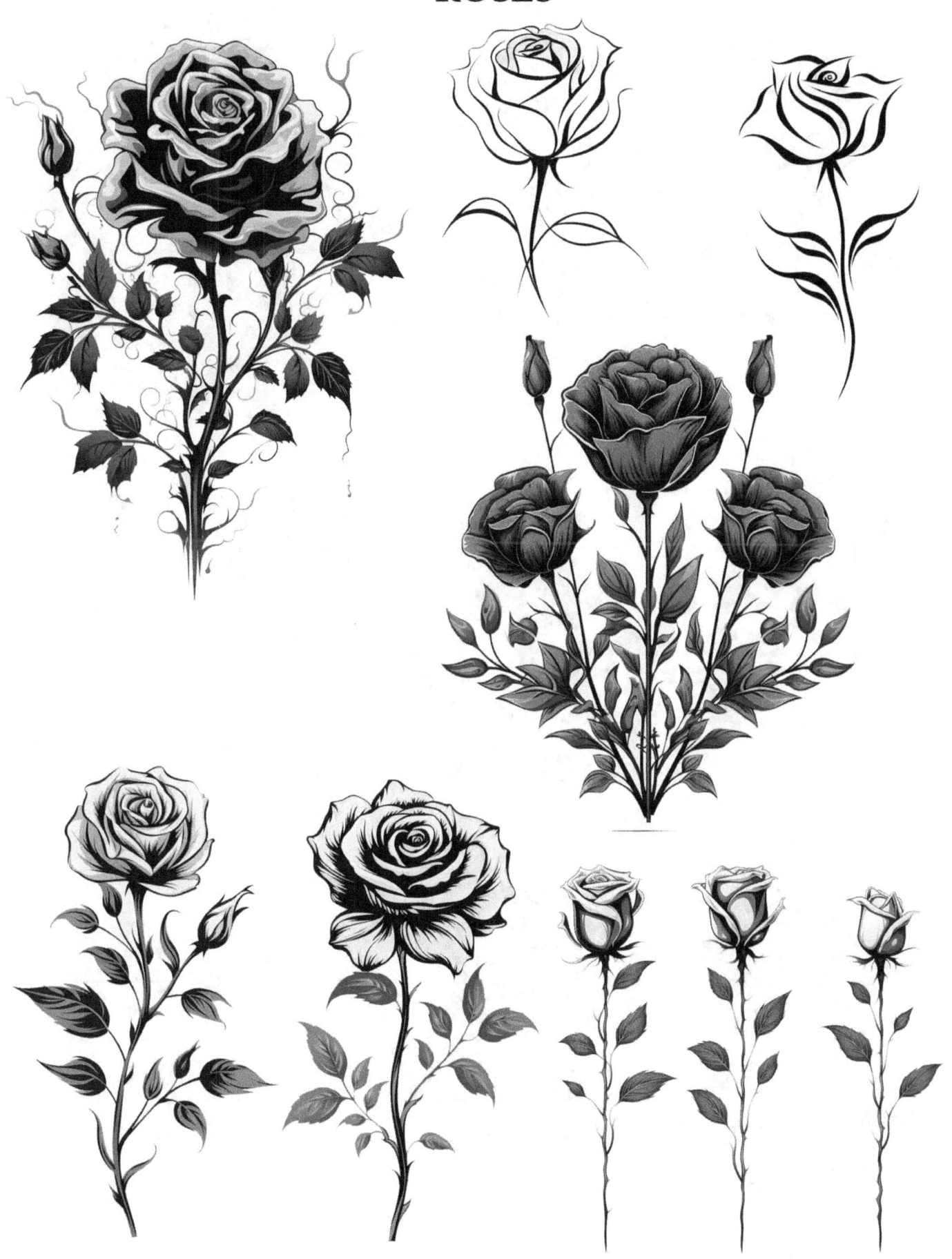

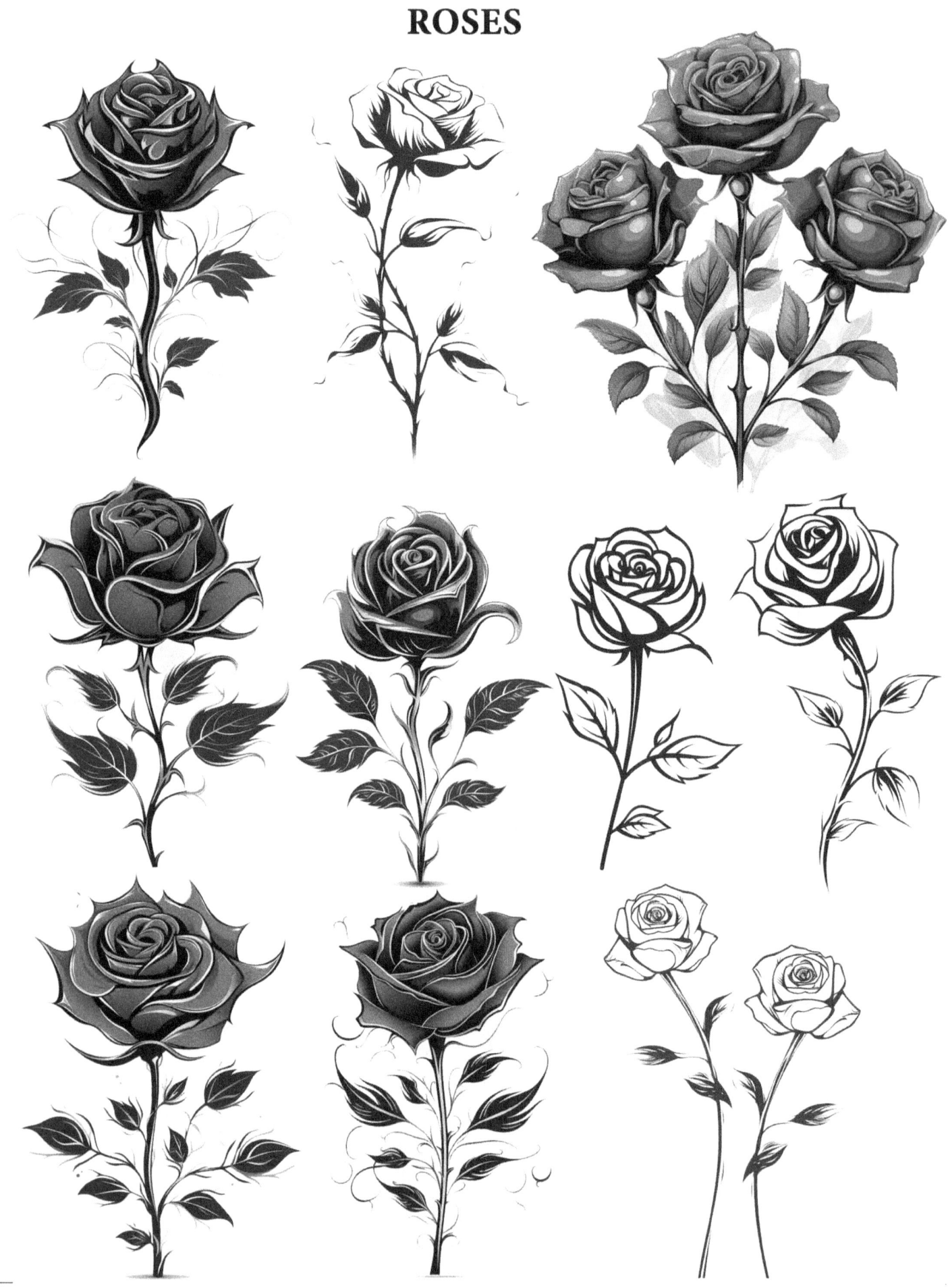

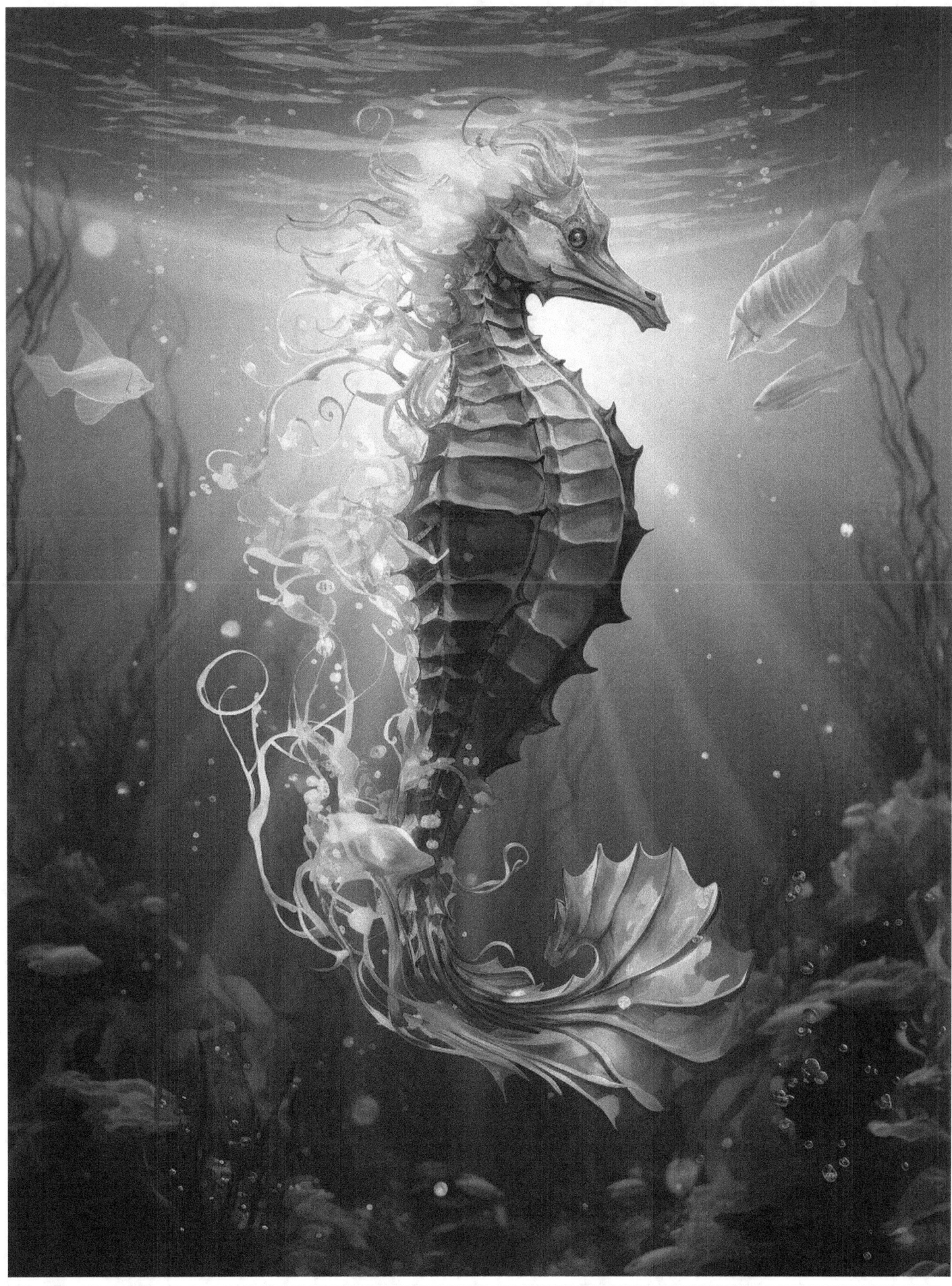

SEA HORSE

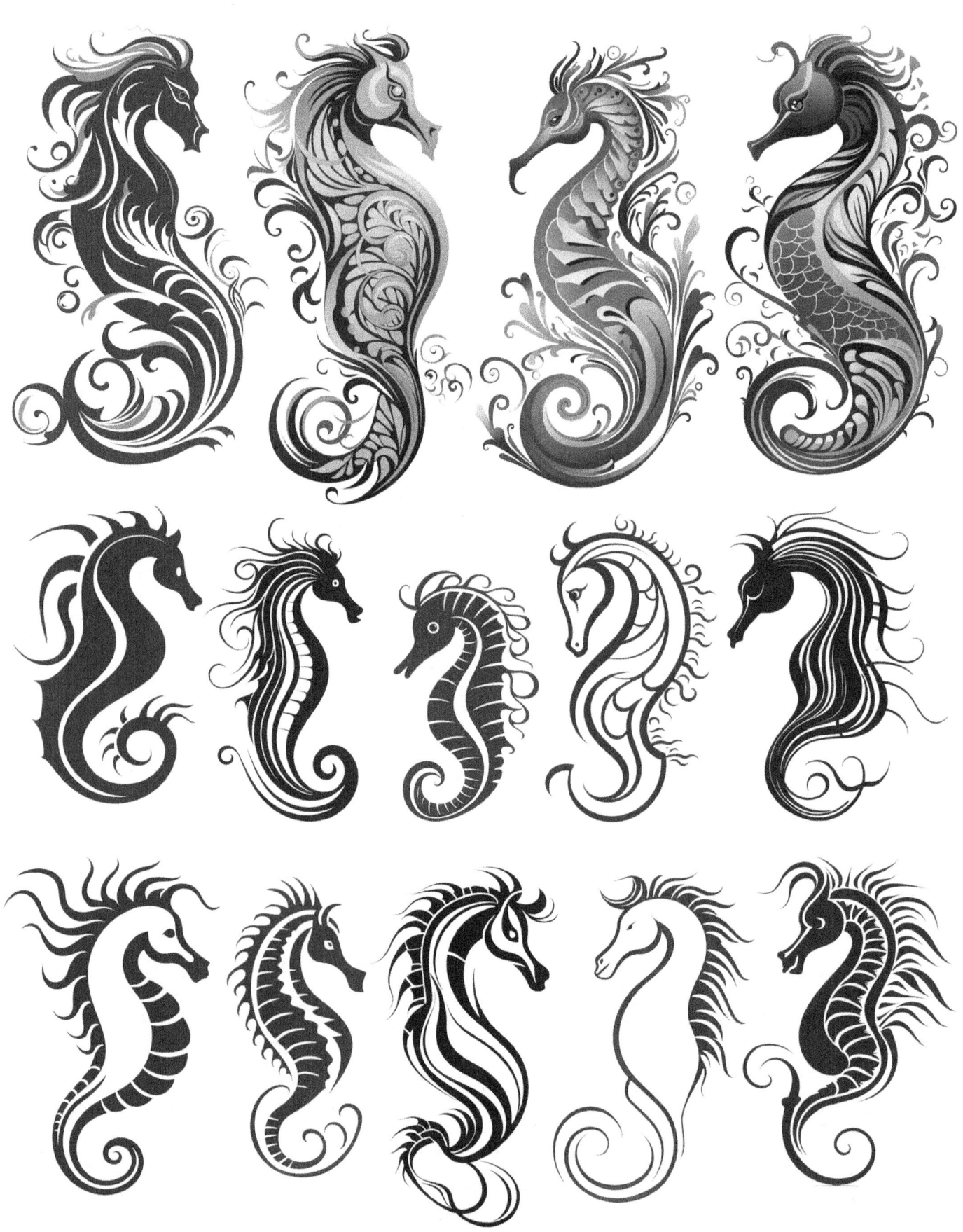

SEA HORSE

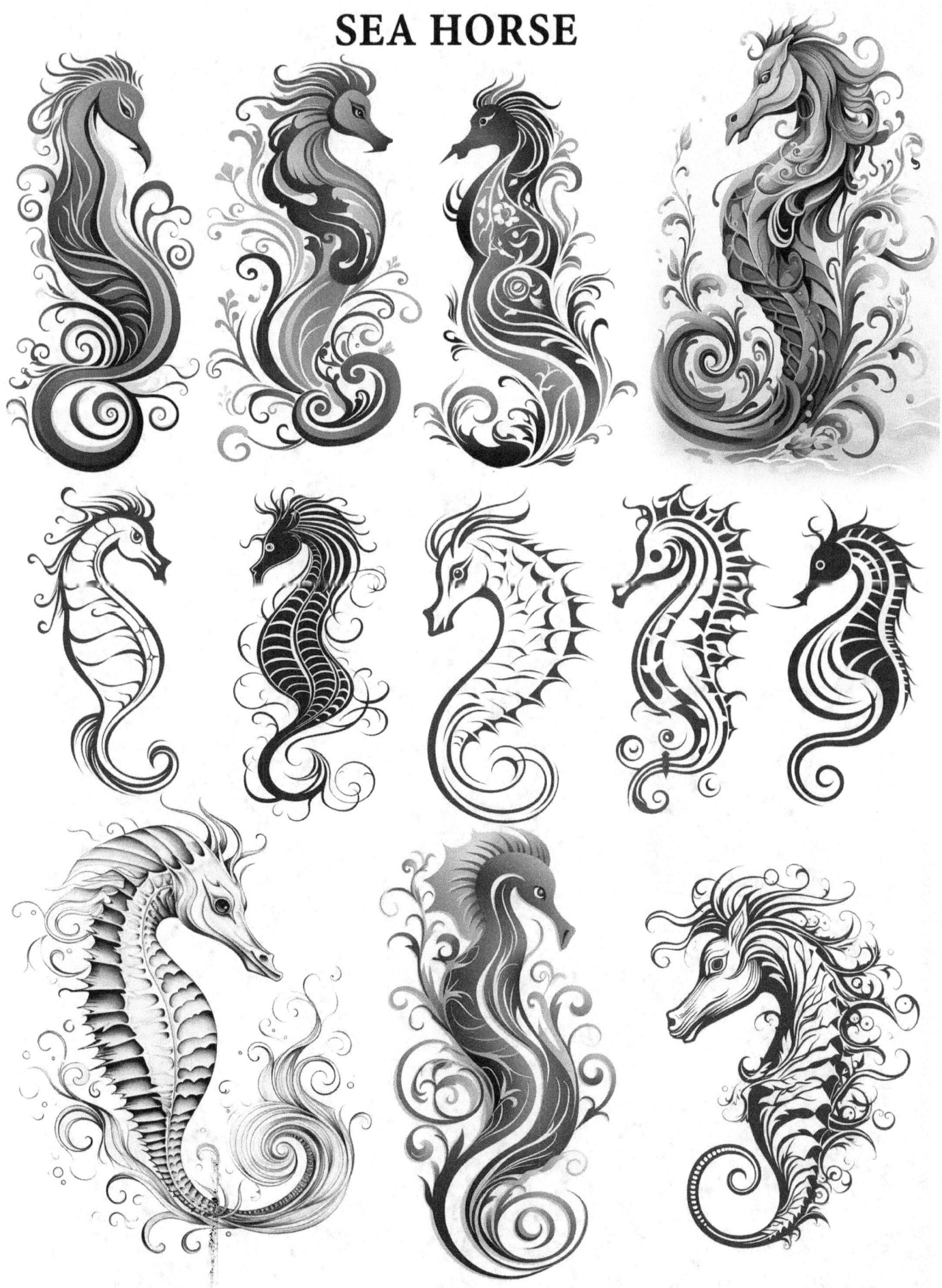

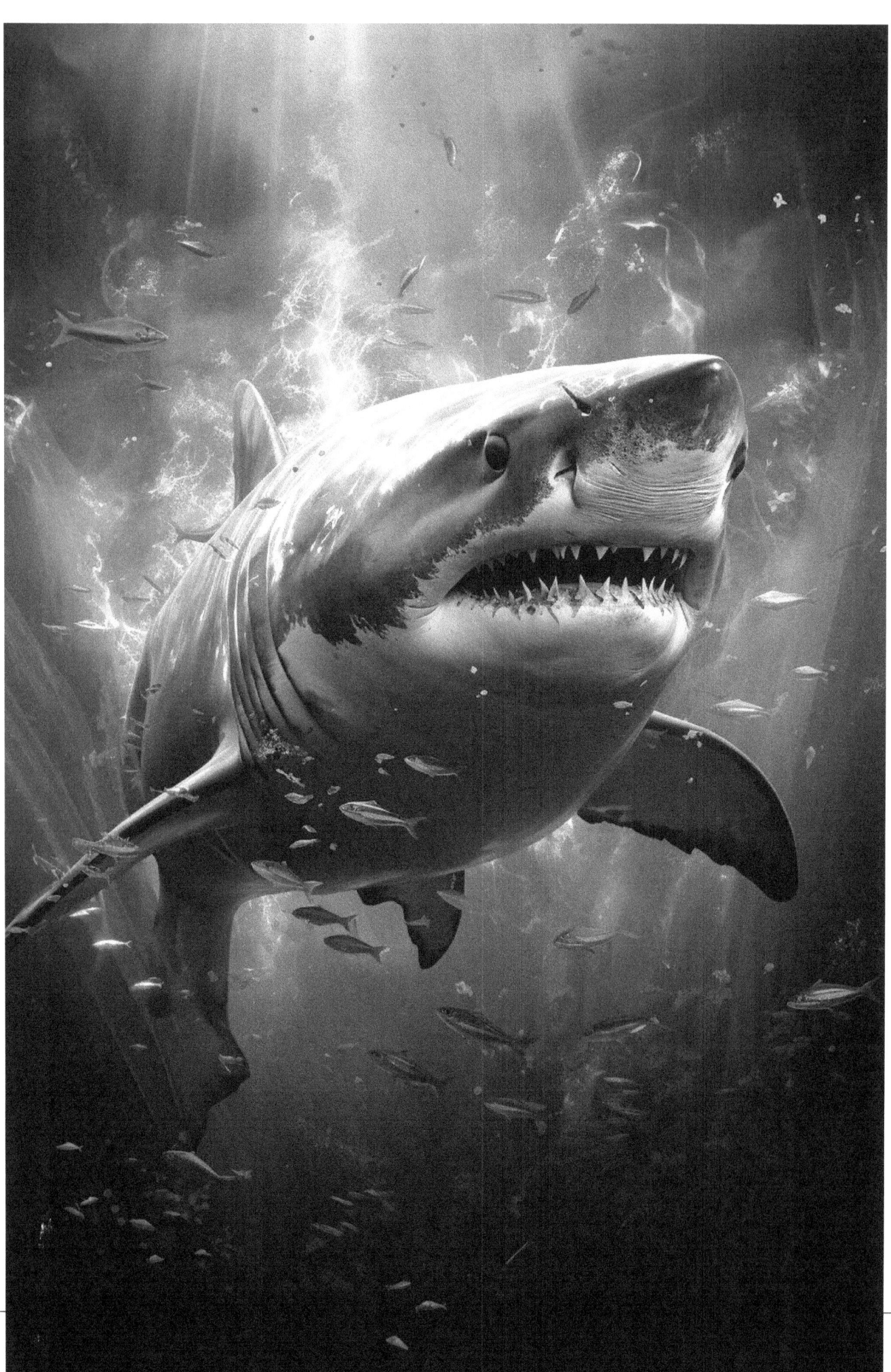

SHARK

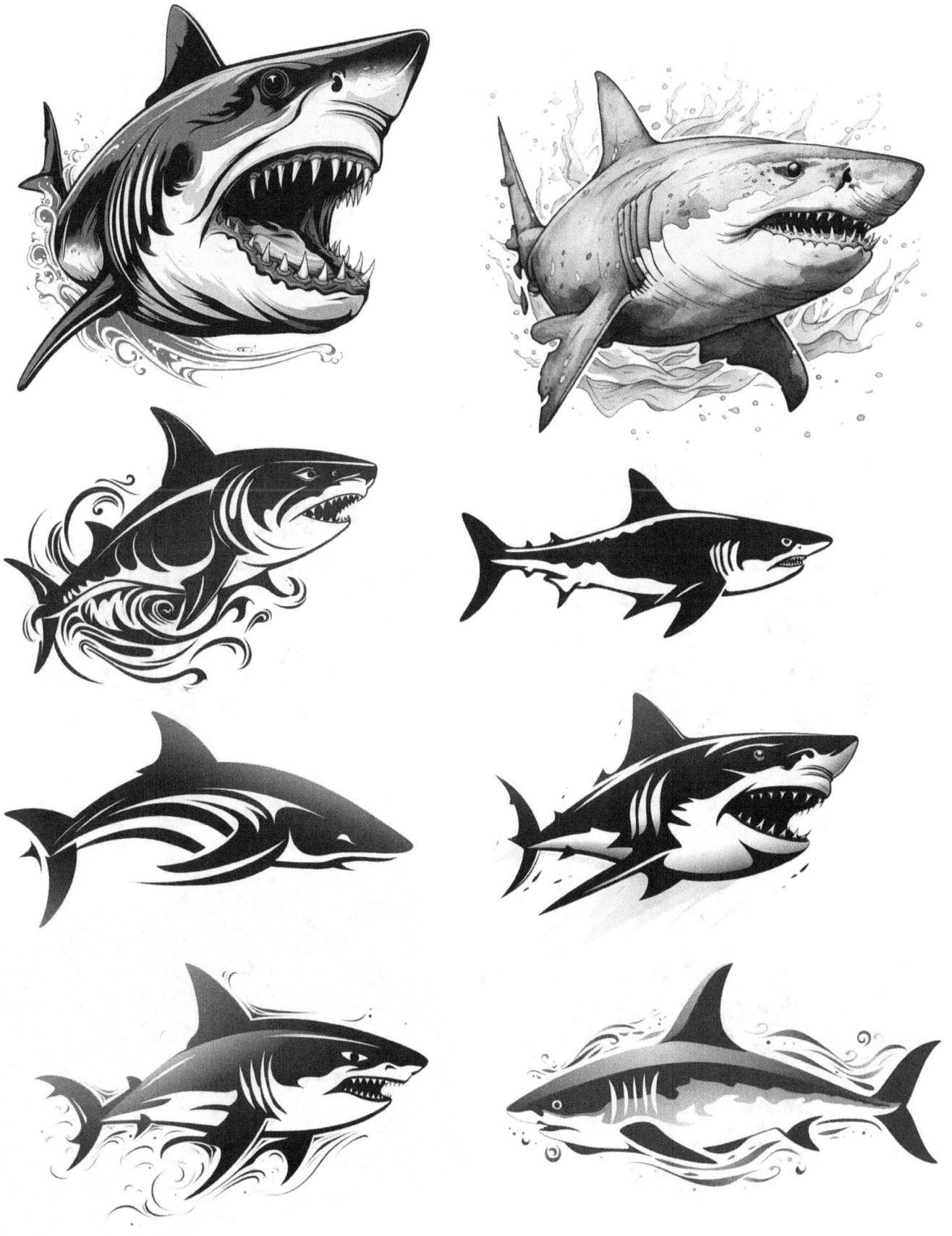

SHARK

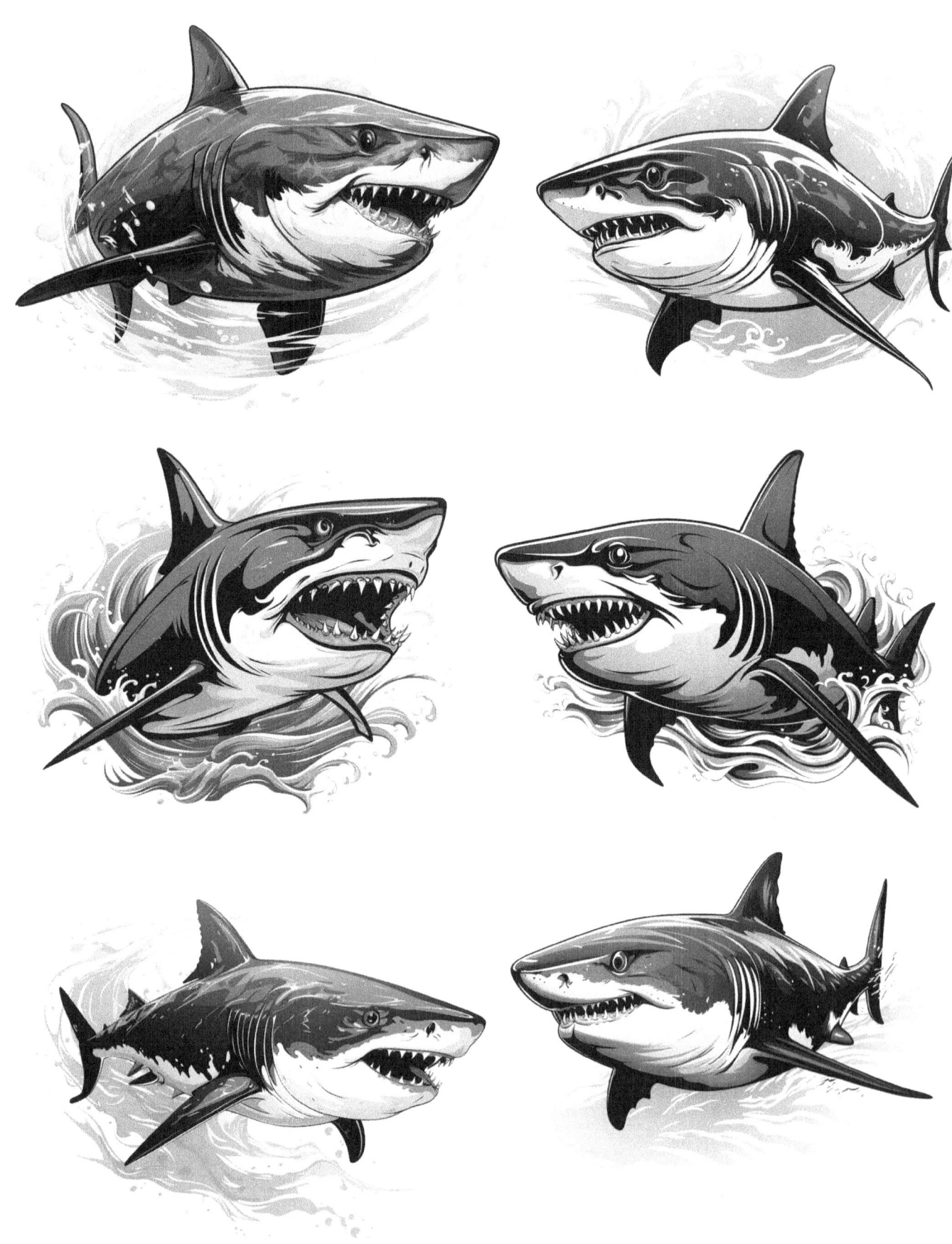

STARFISH

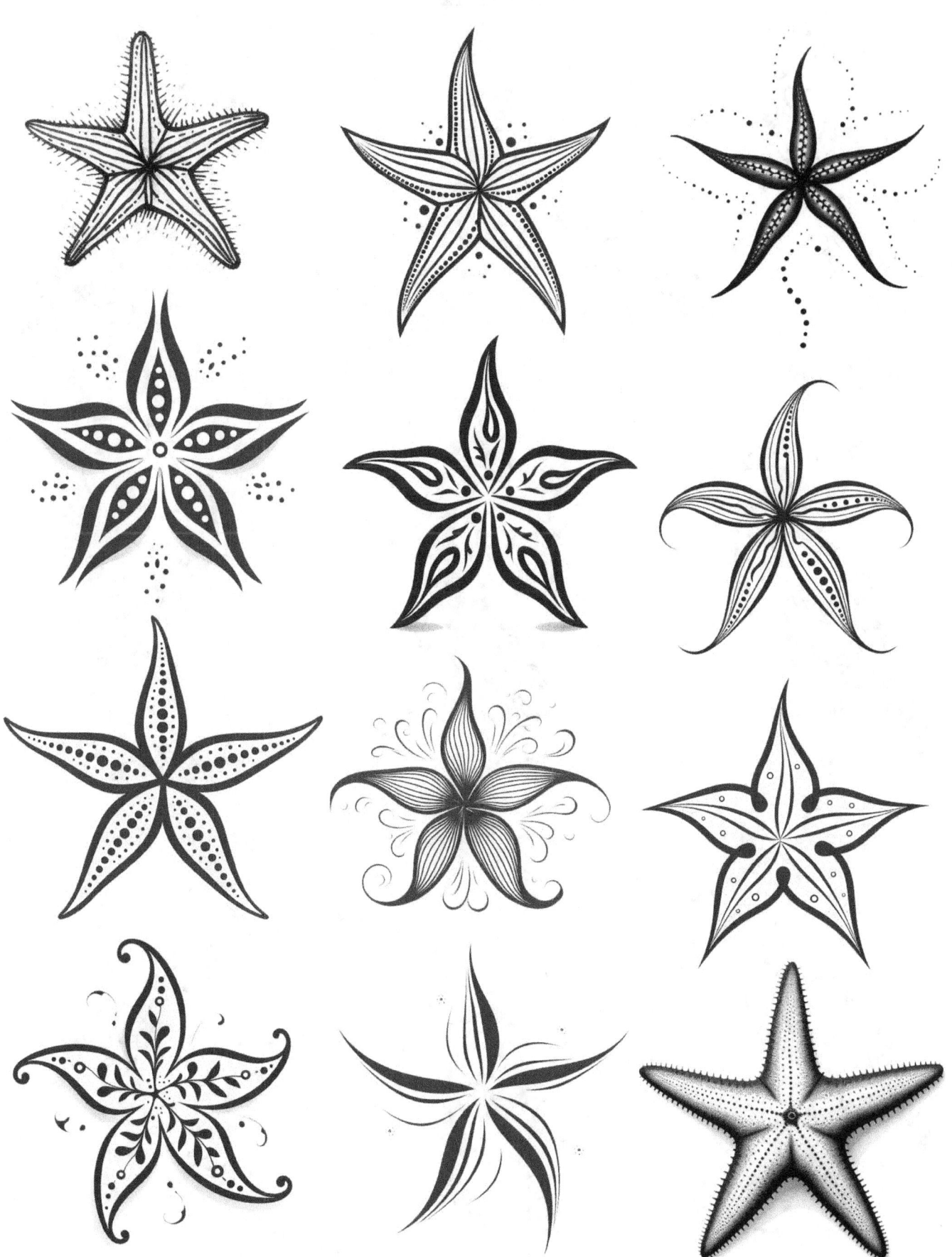

STORK

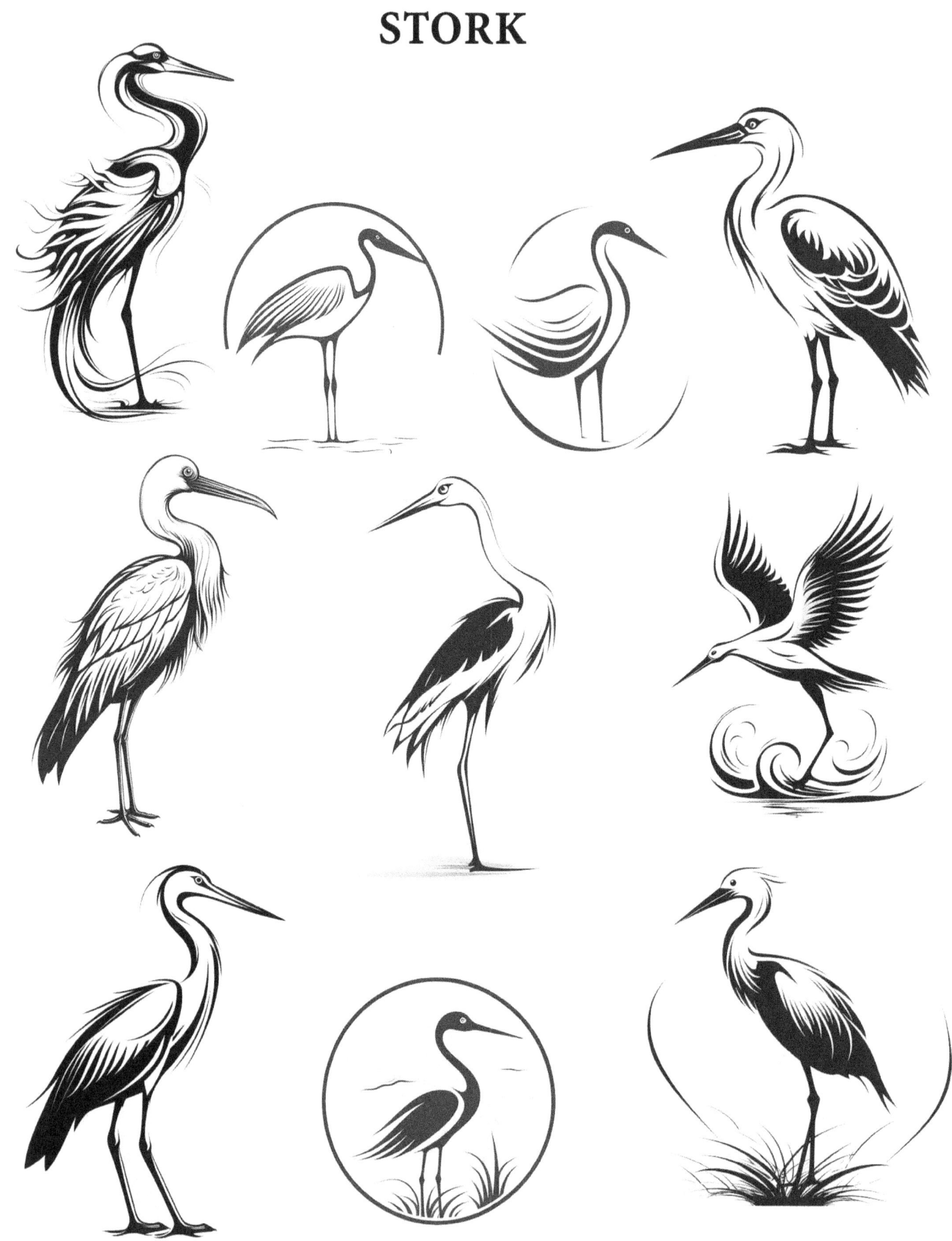

SUN - MOON

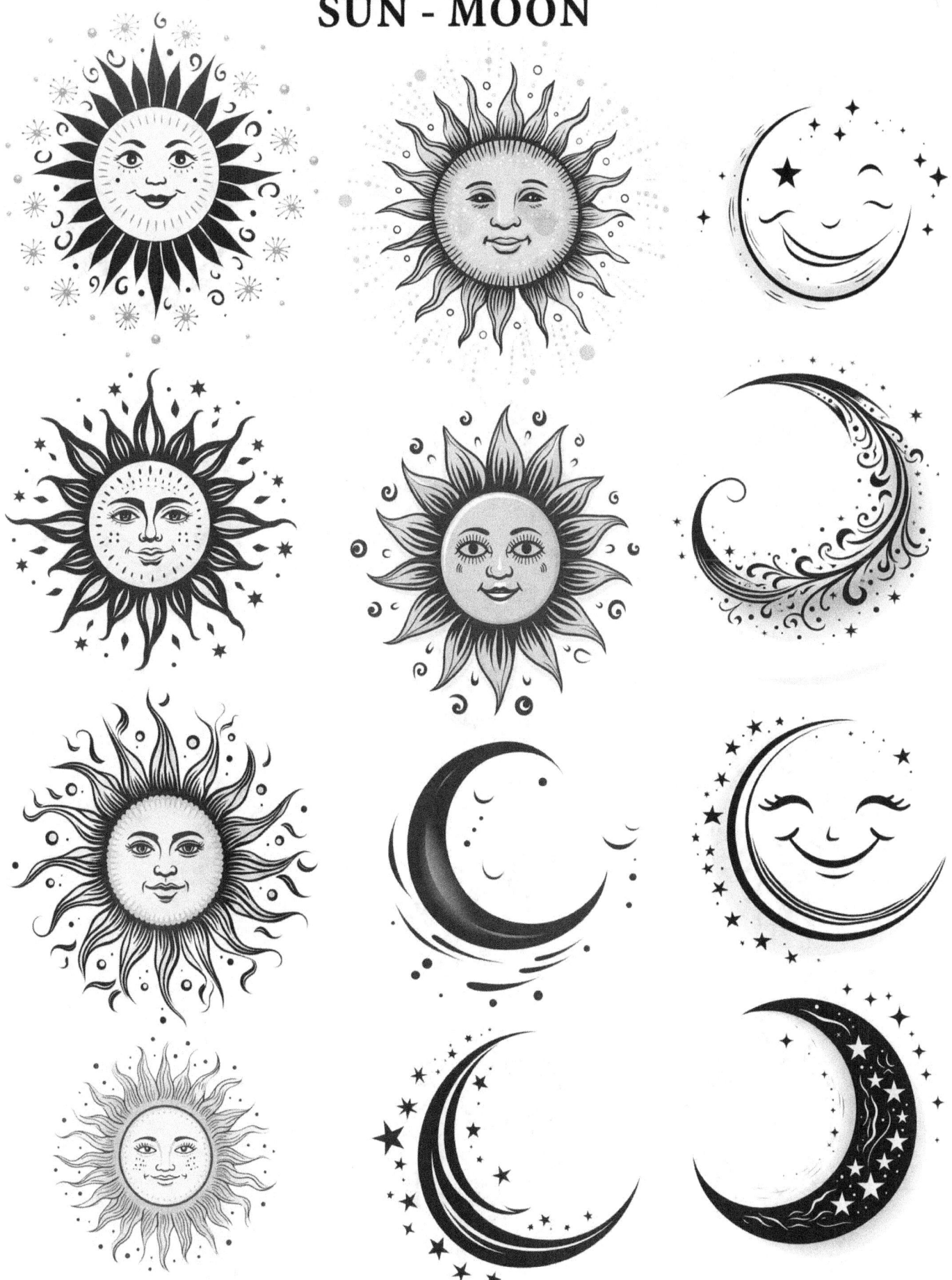

SUN - MOON

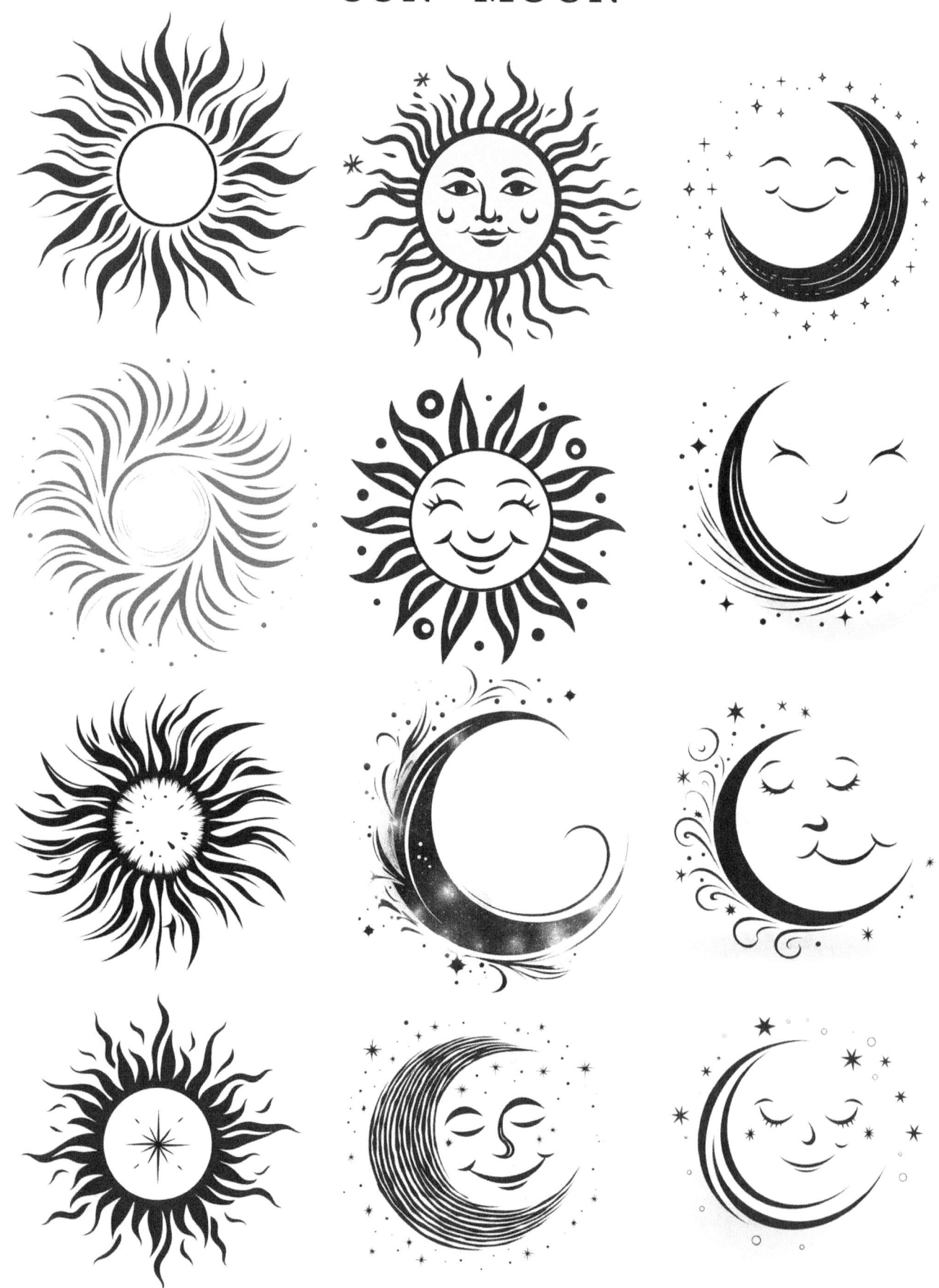

SUNFLOWER

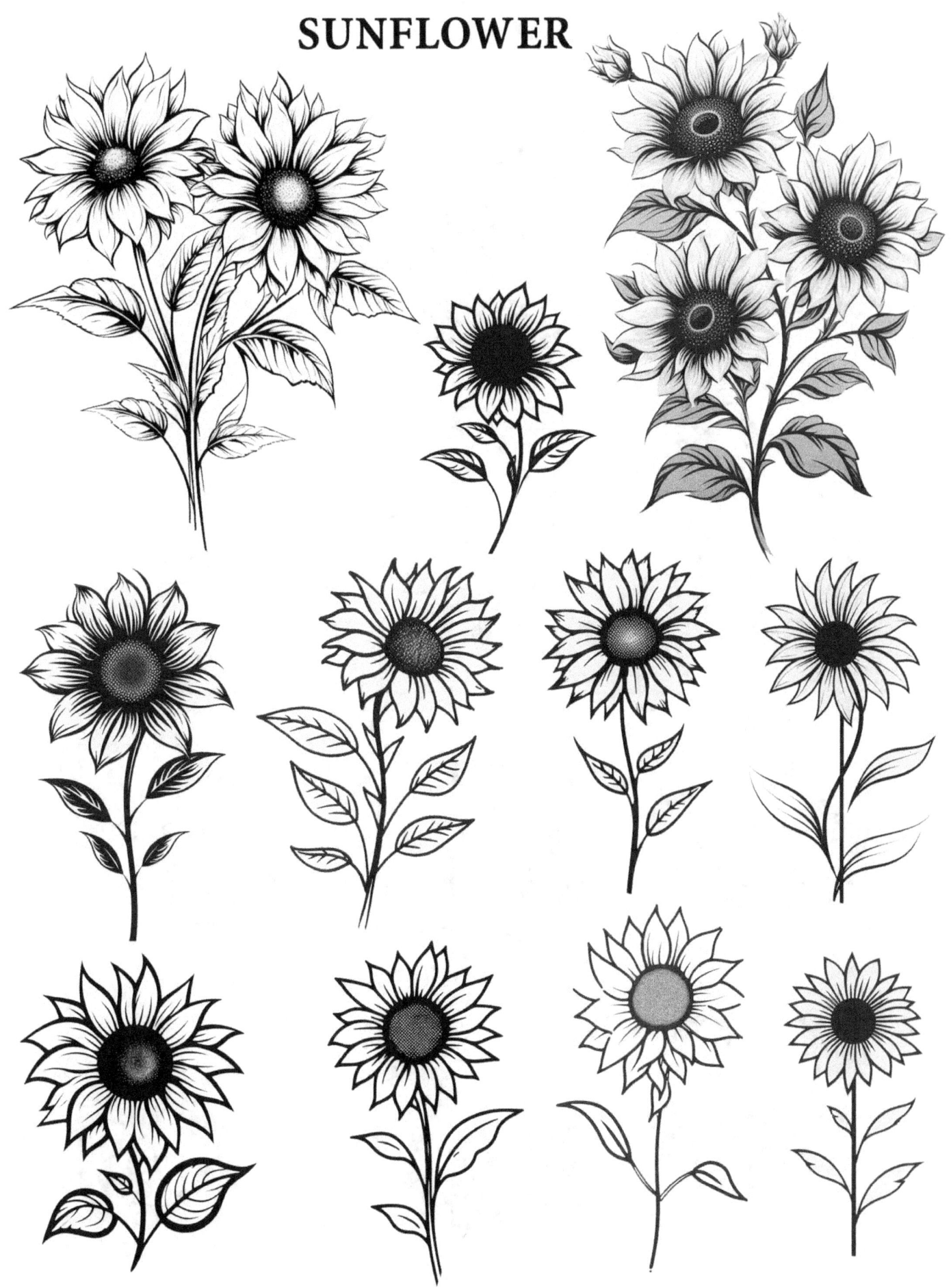

SWAN

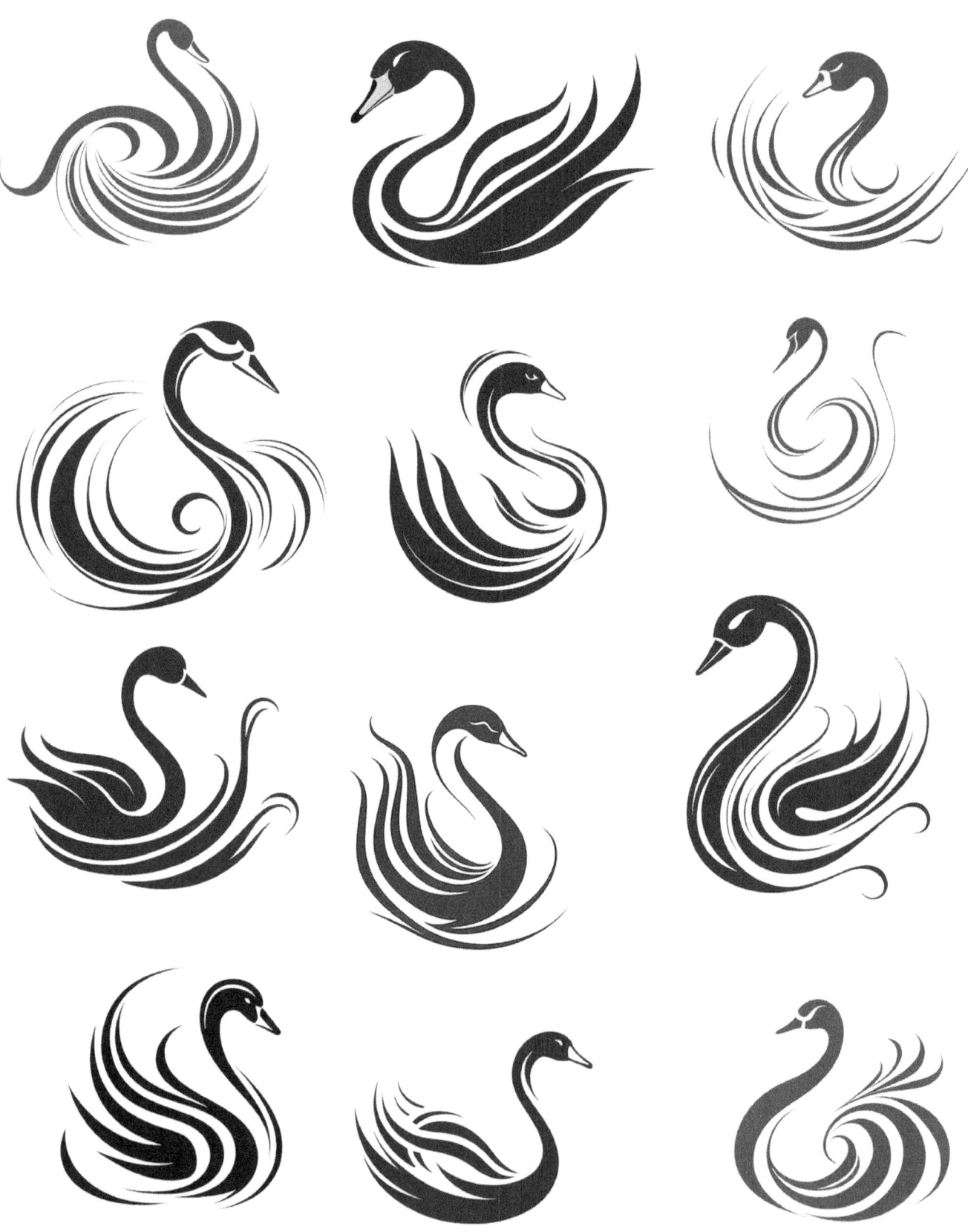

TIGER

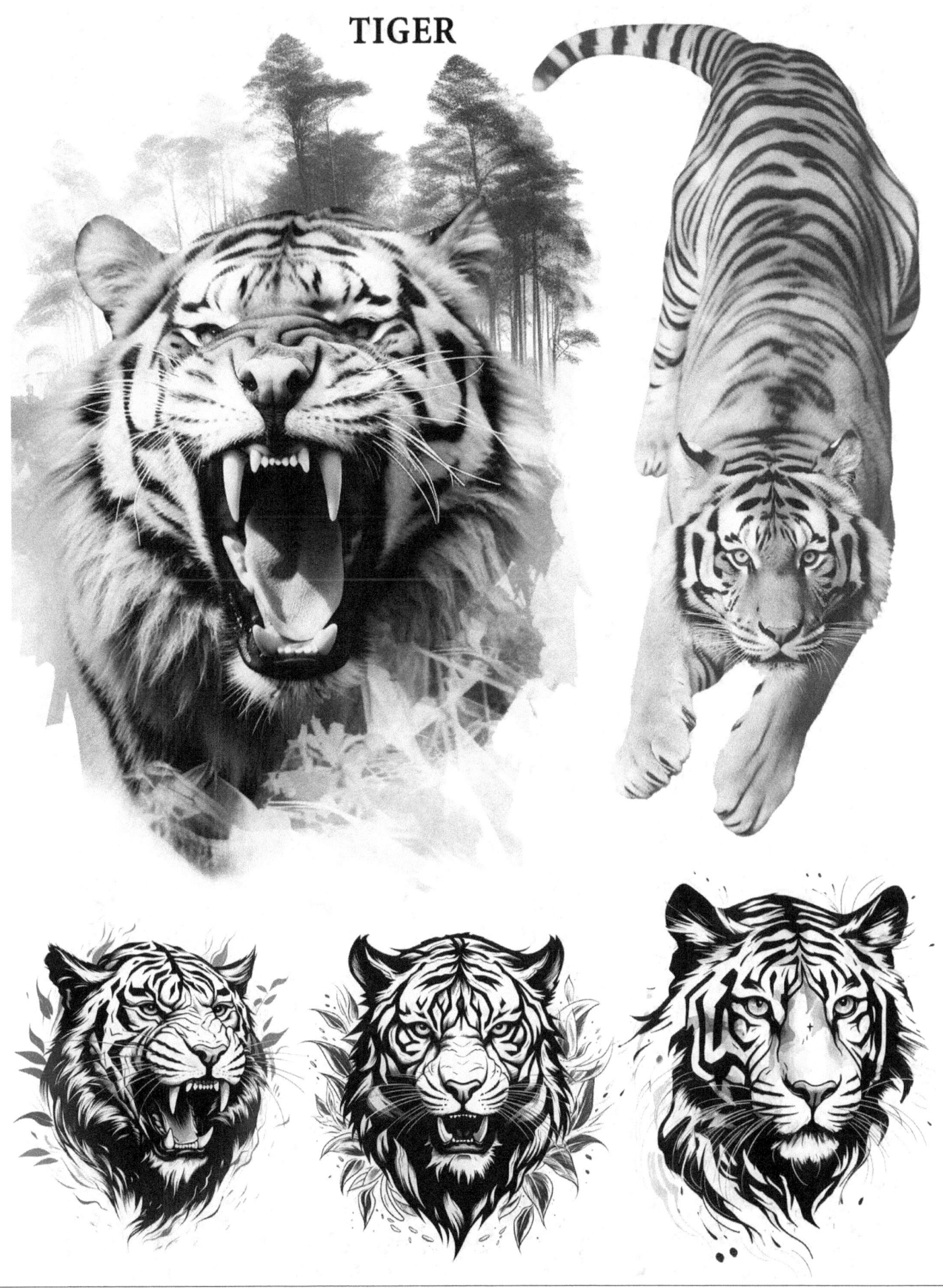

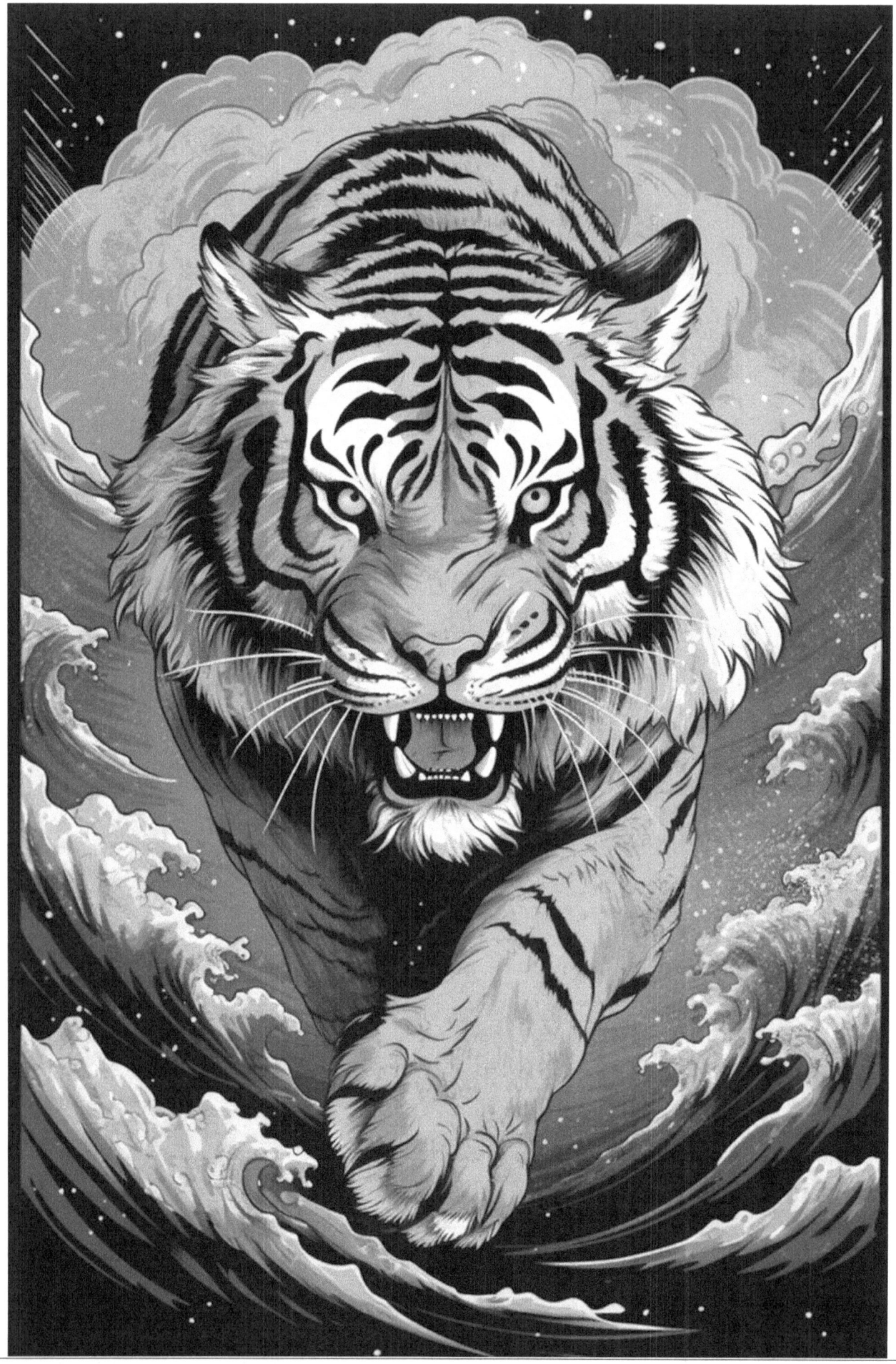

TIGER

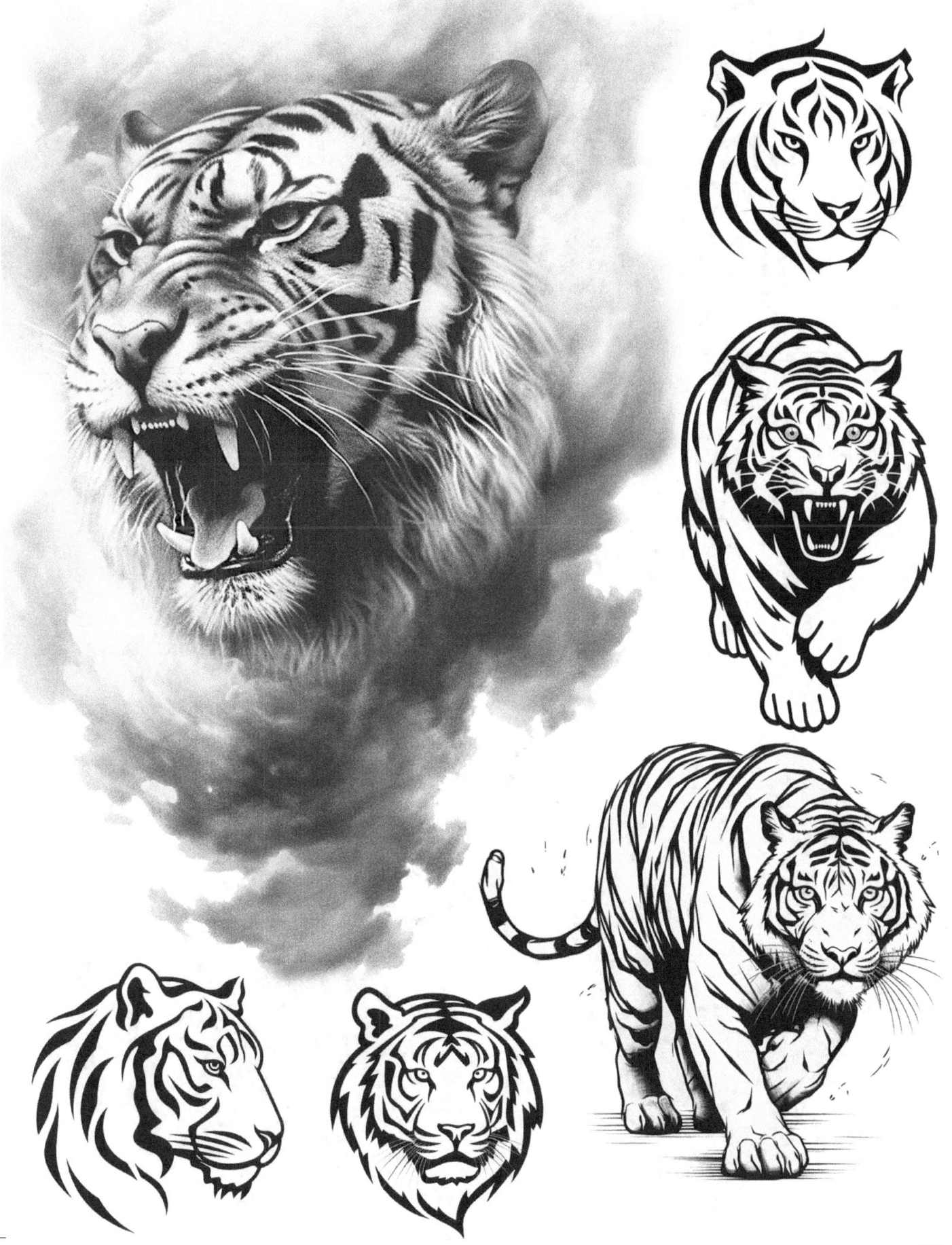

TIGER

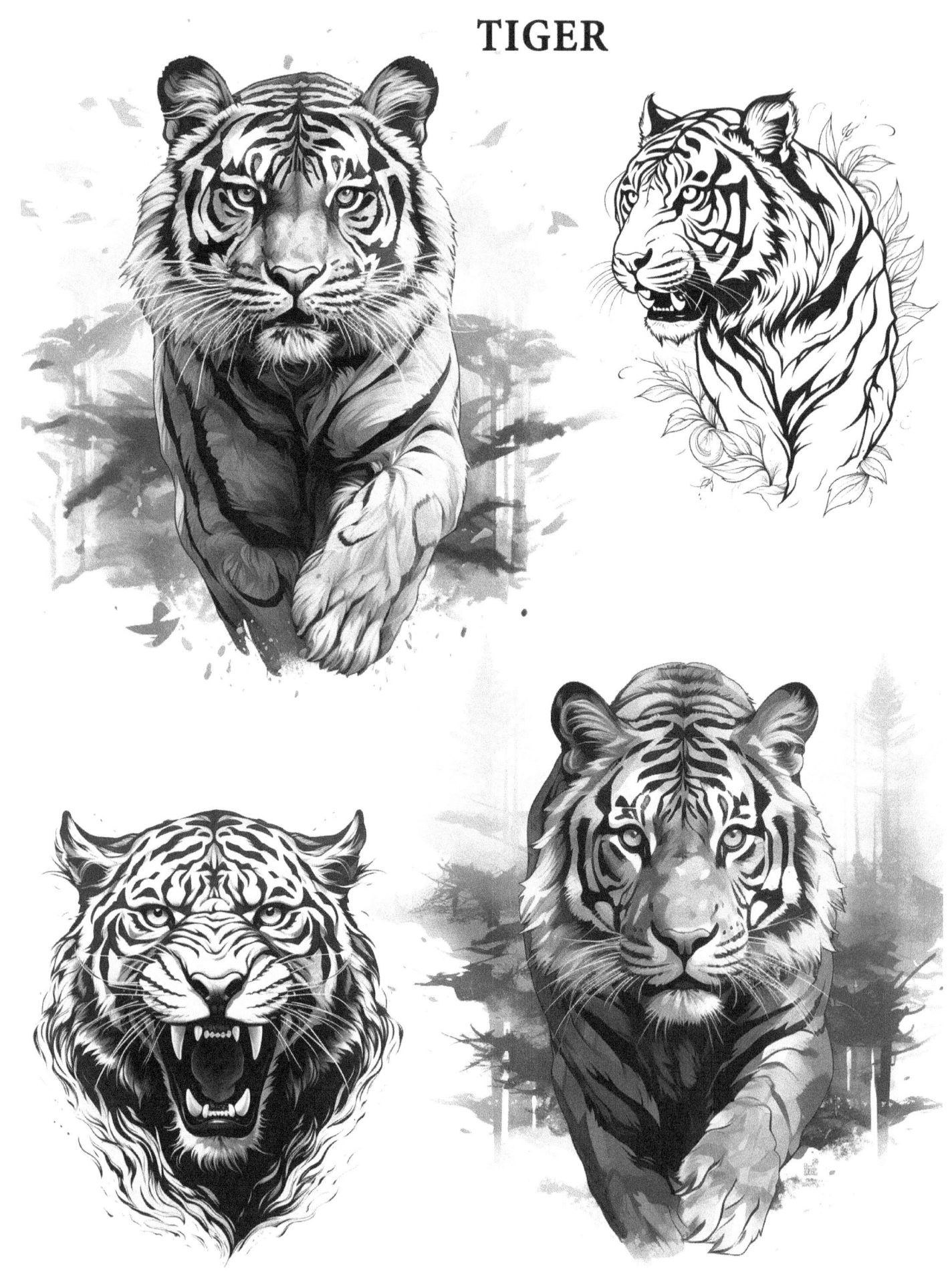

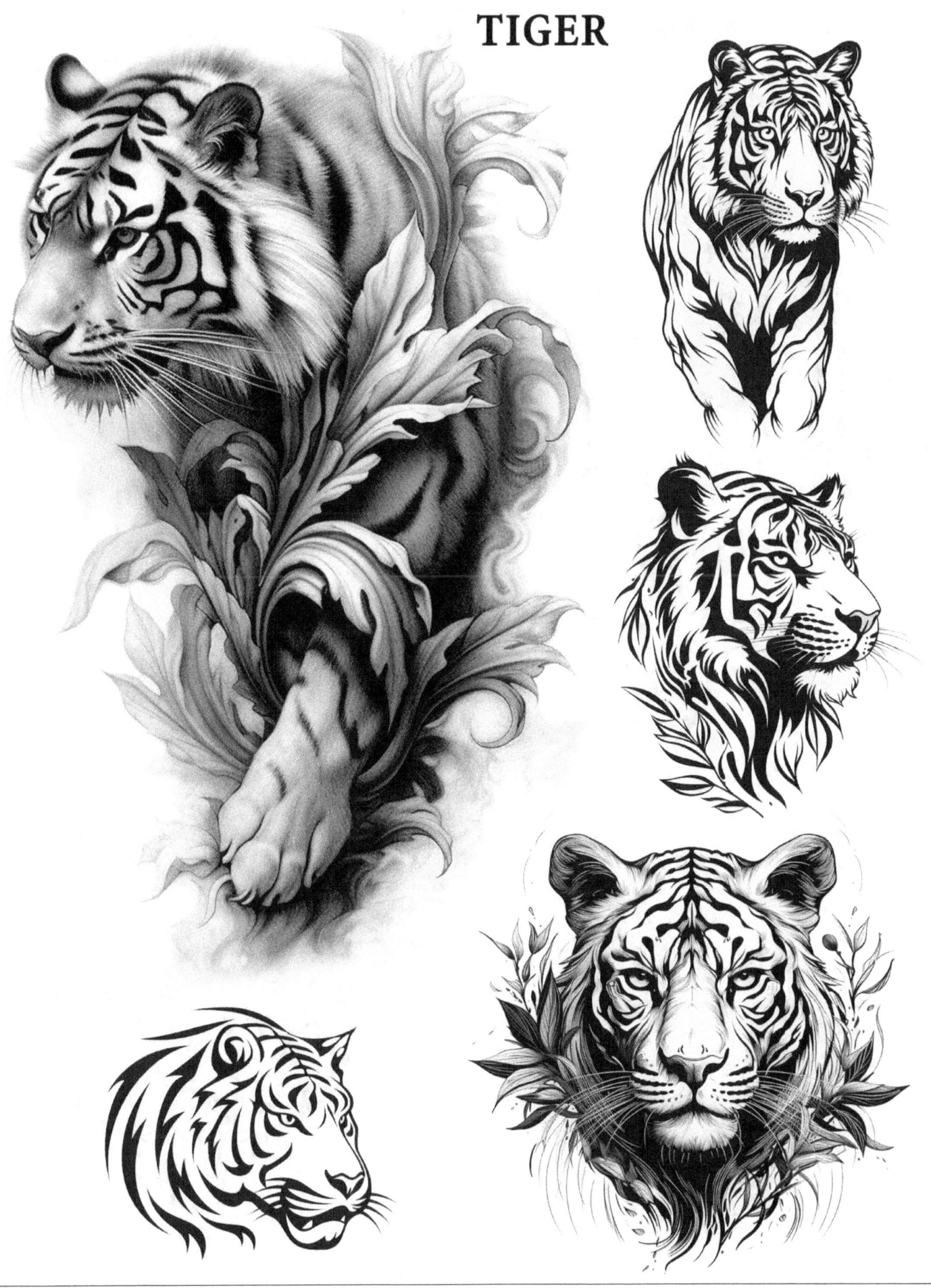

TIGER

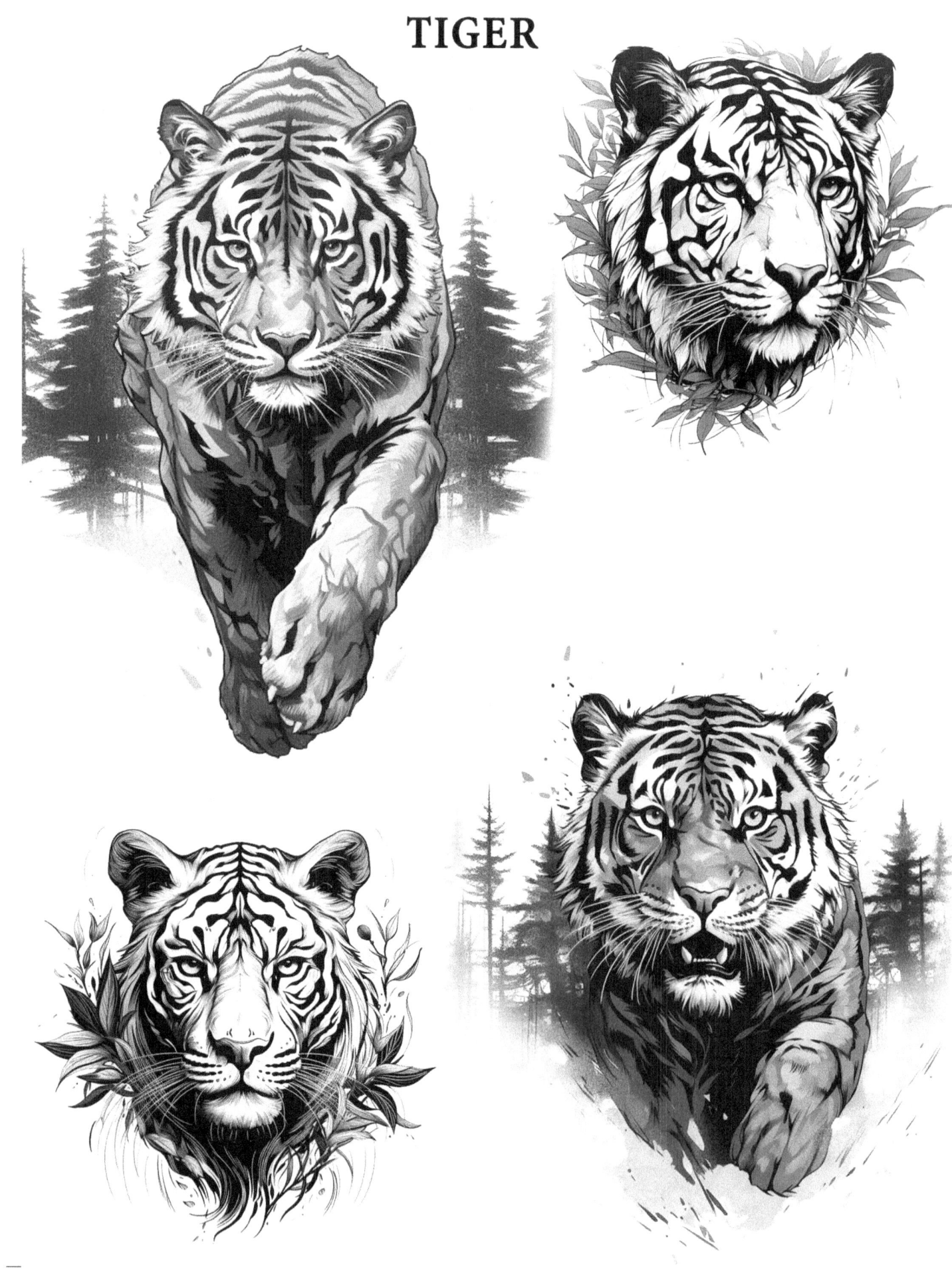

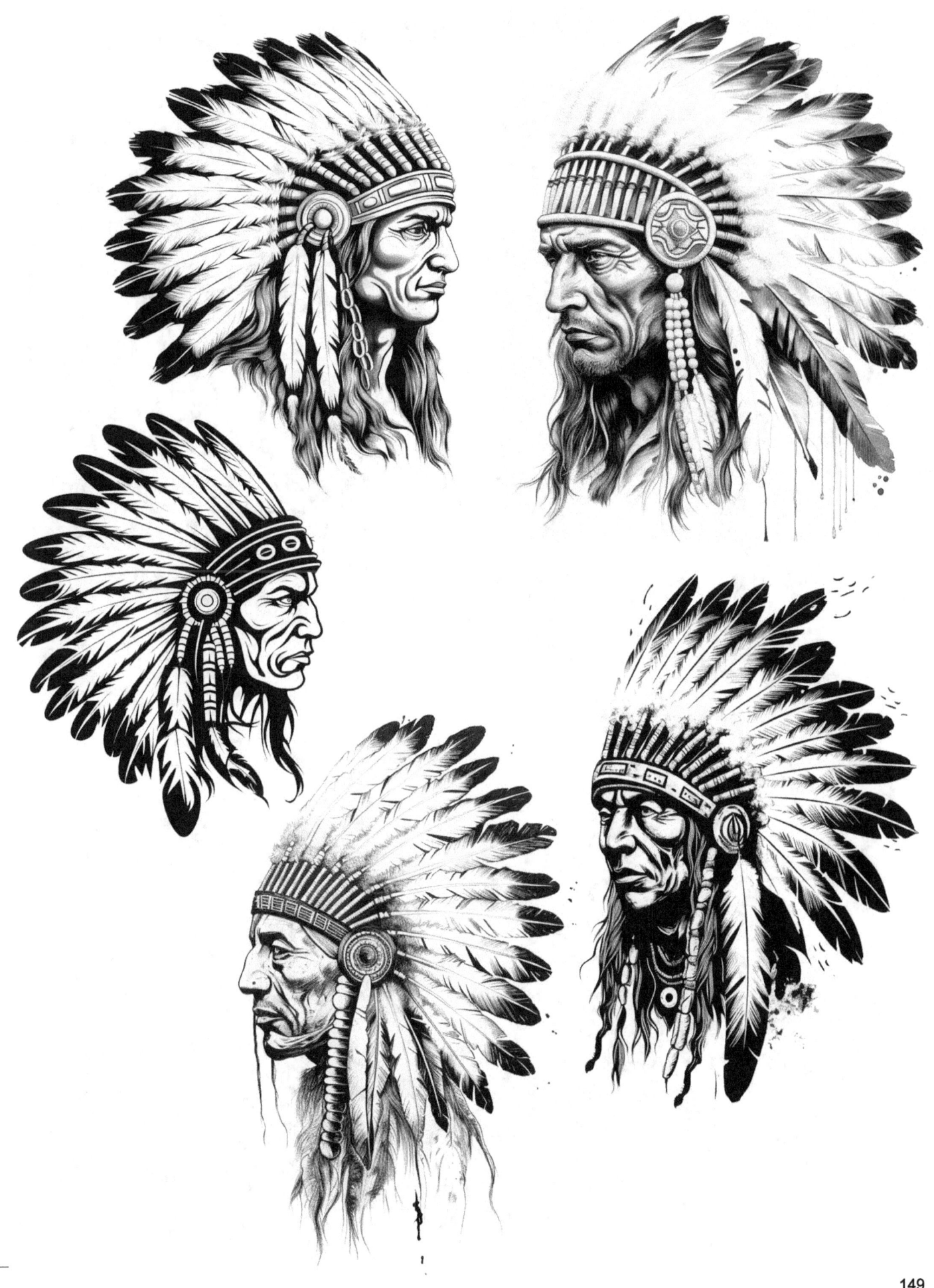

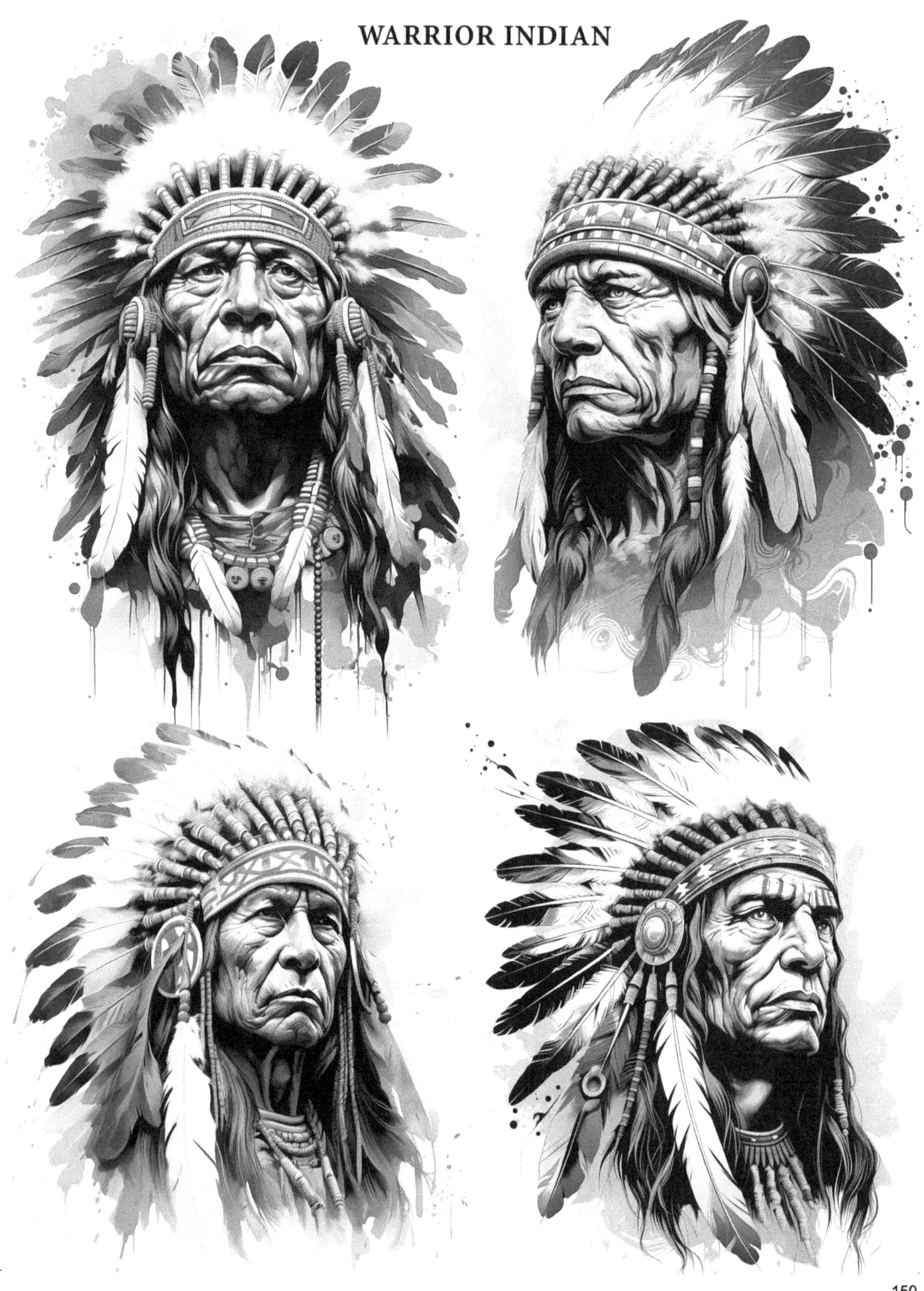

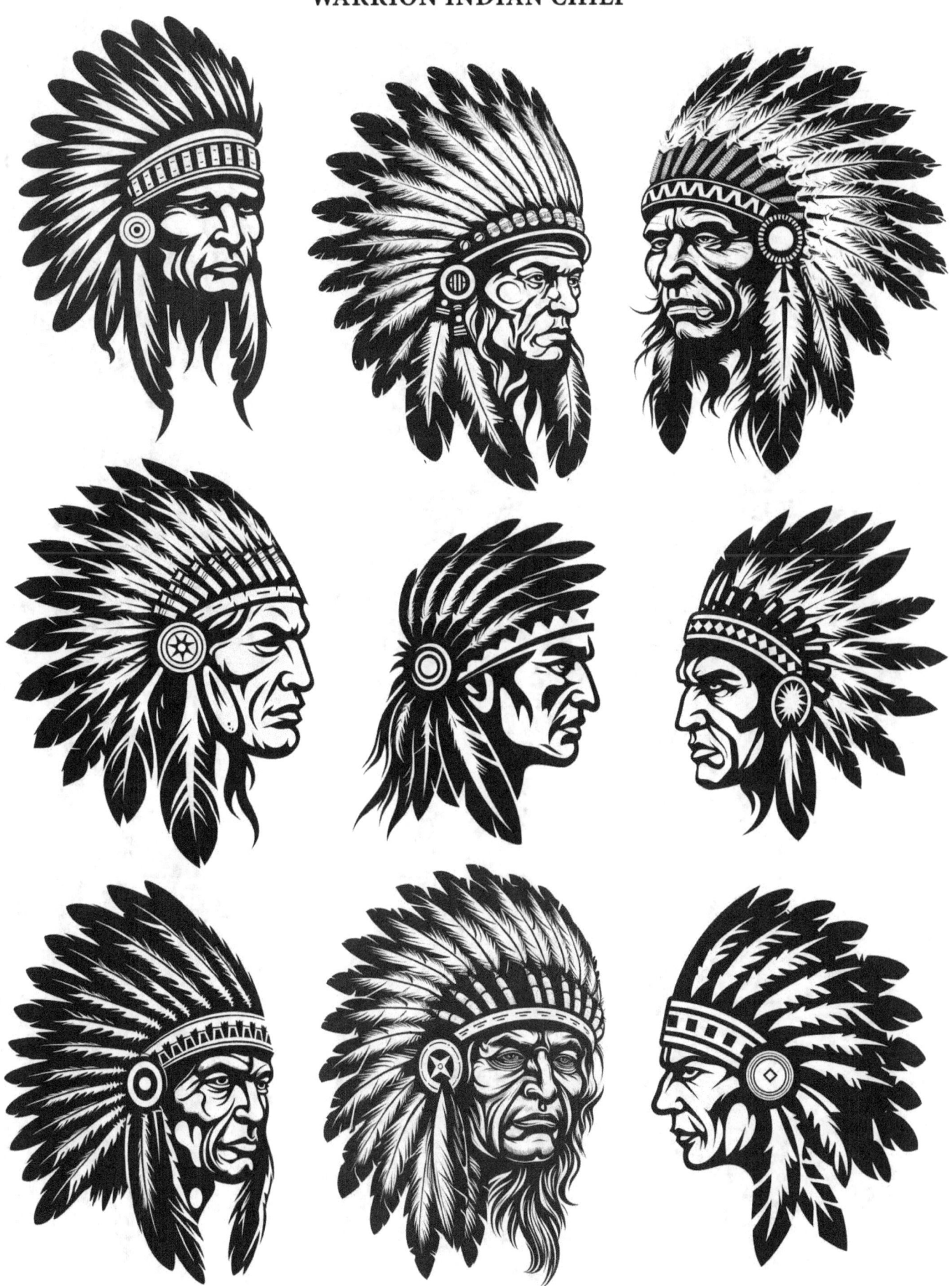

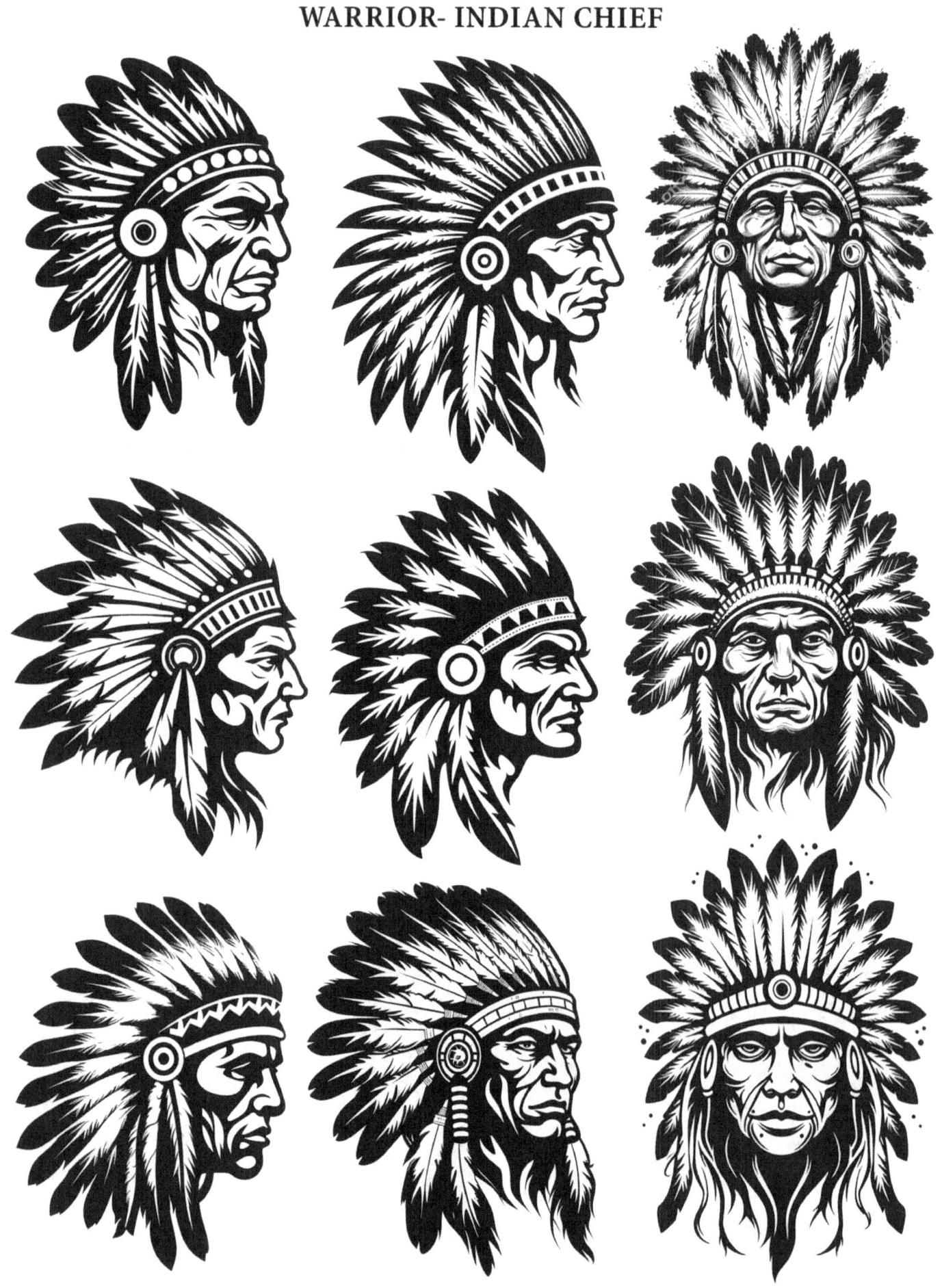

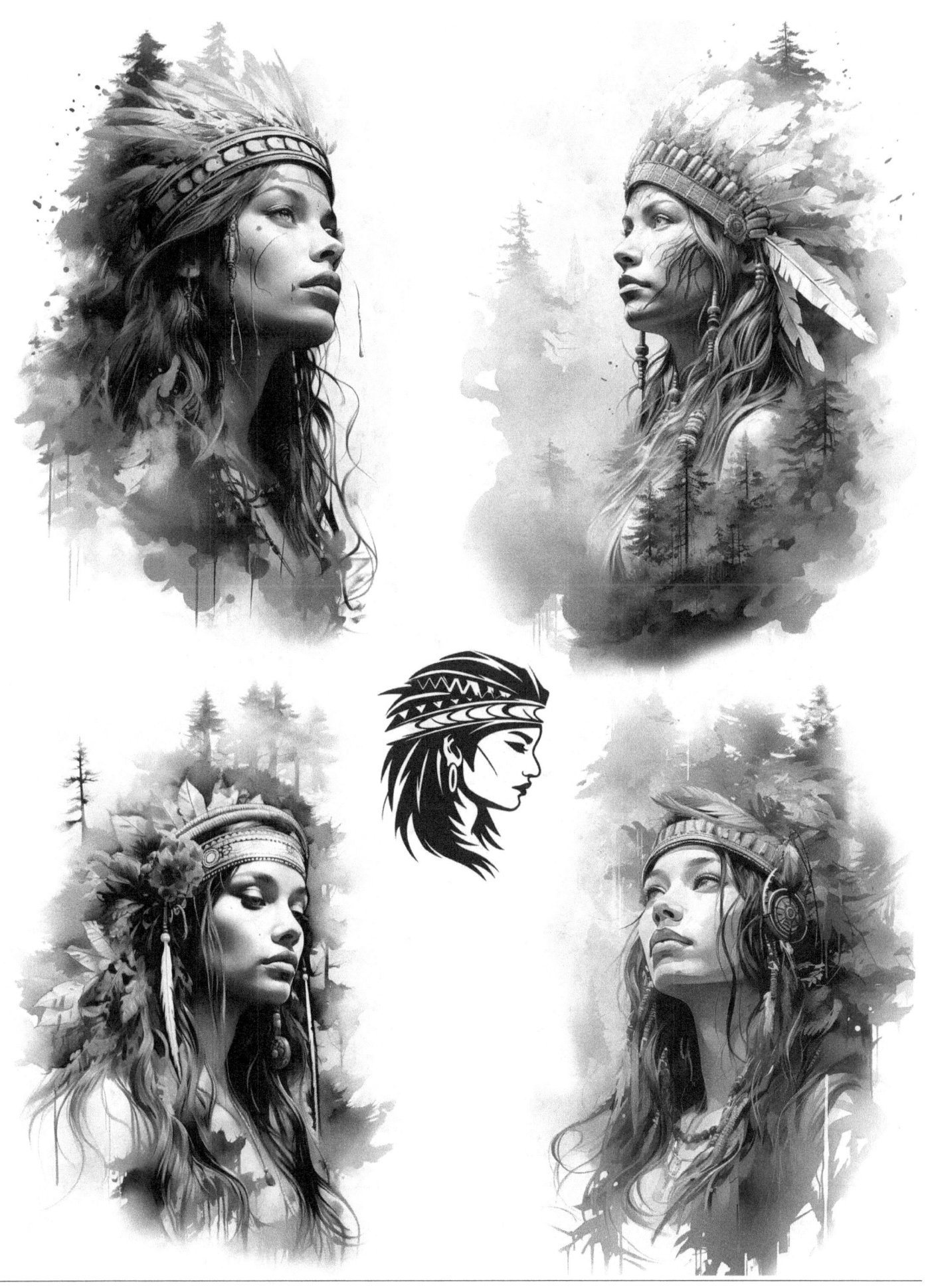

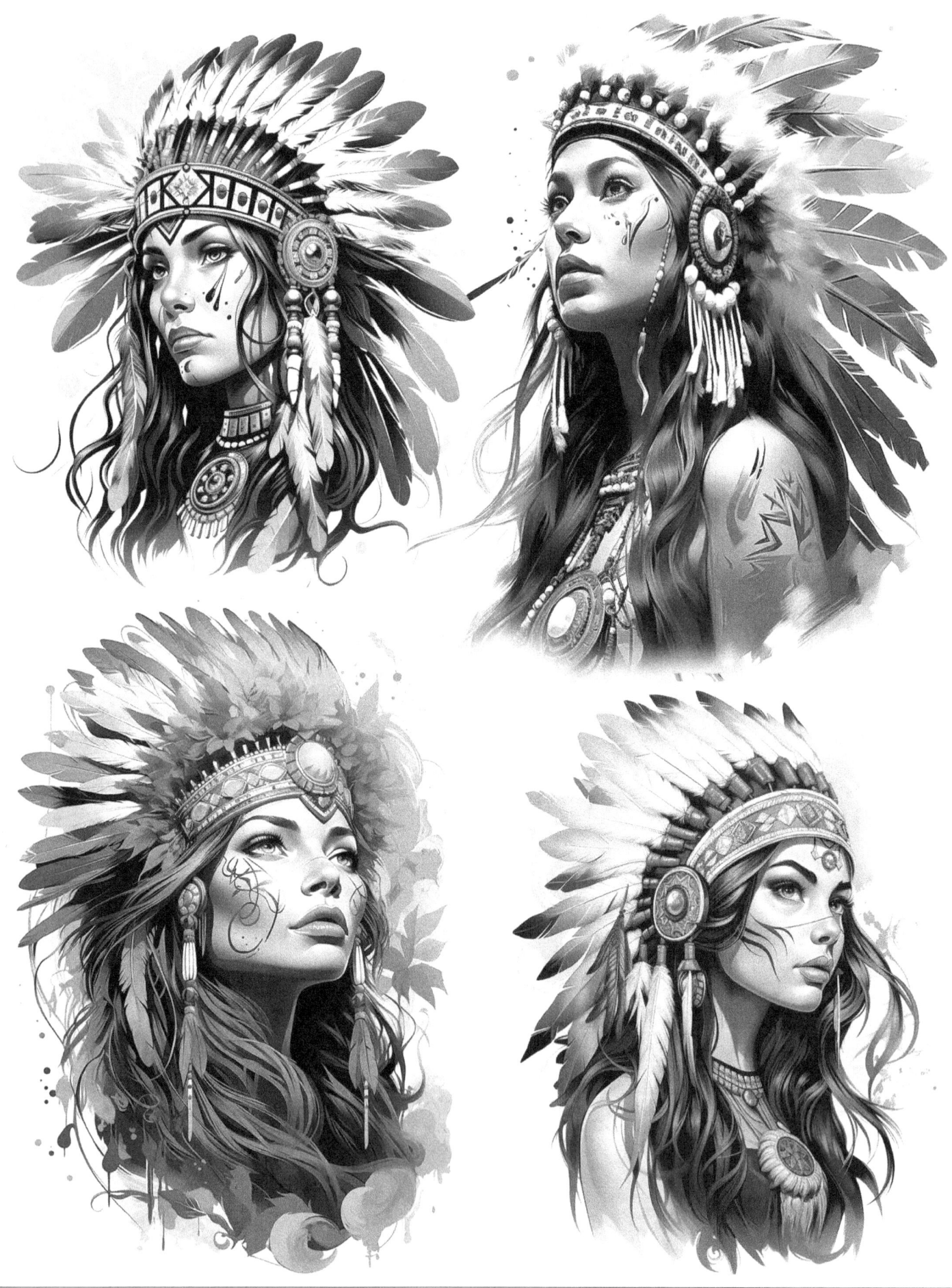

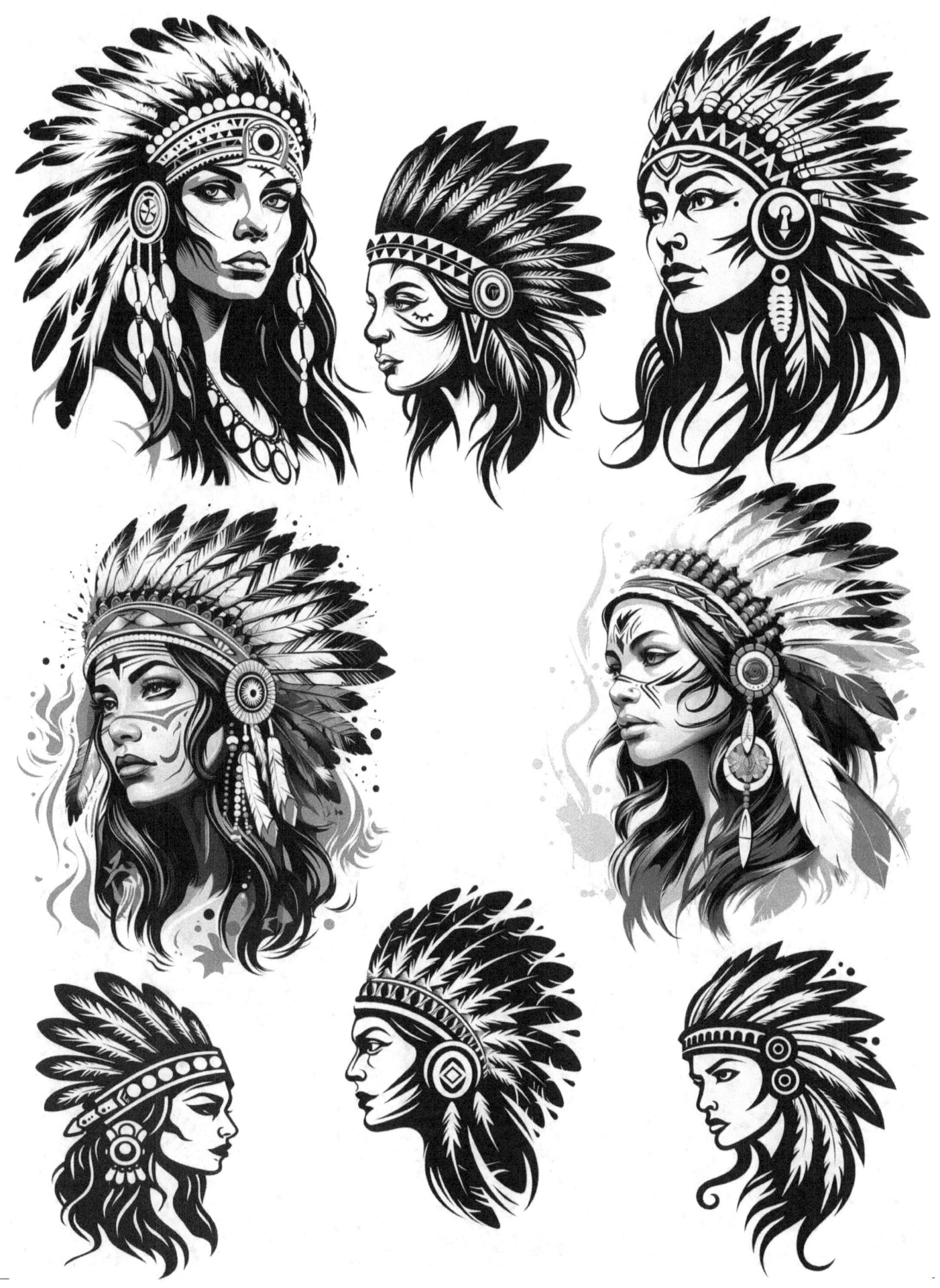

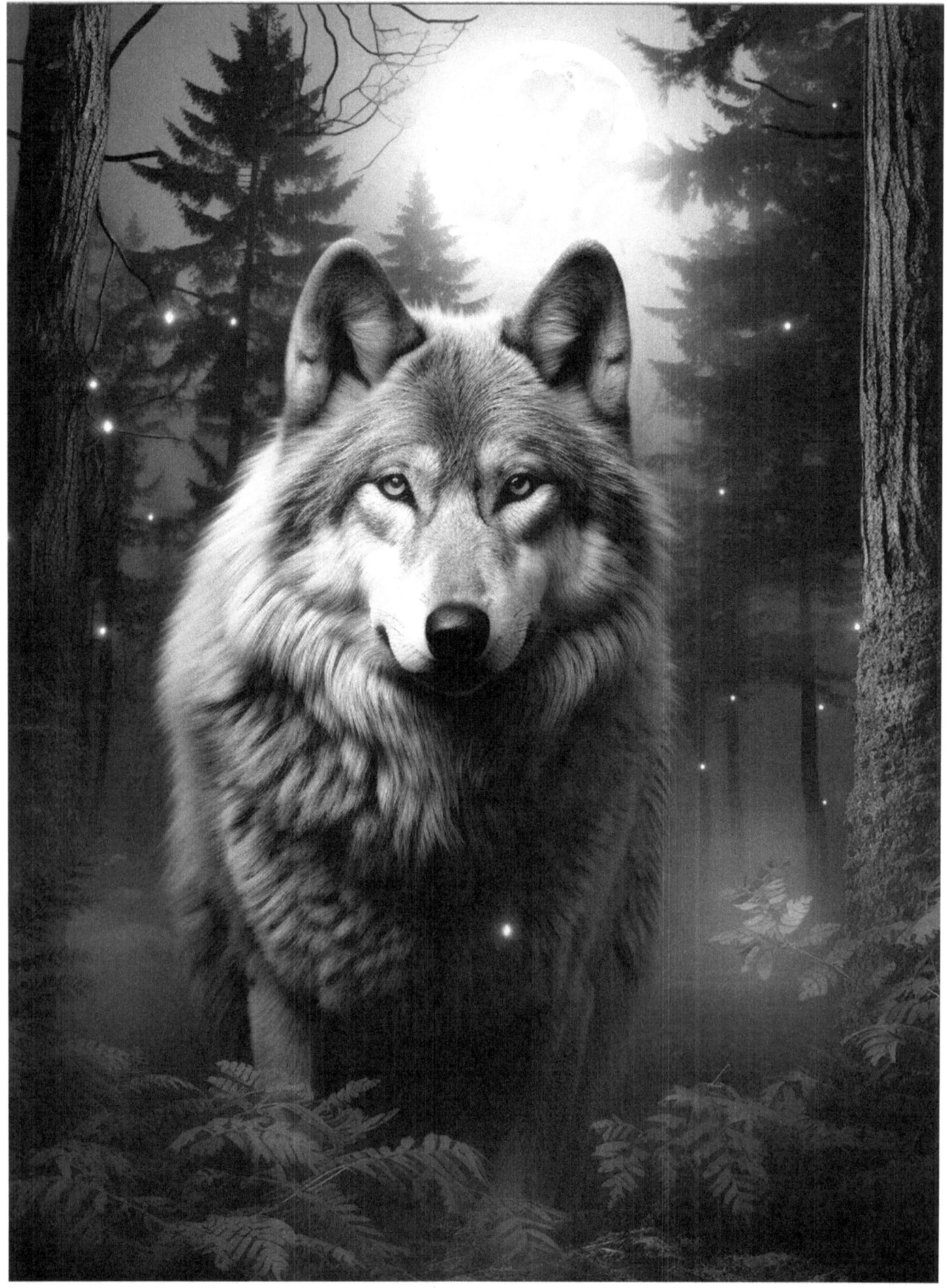

WOLF

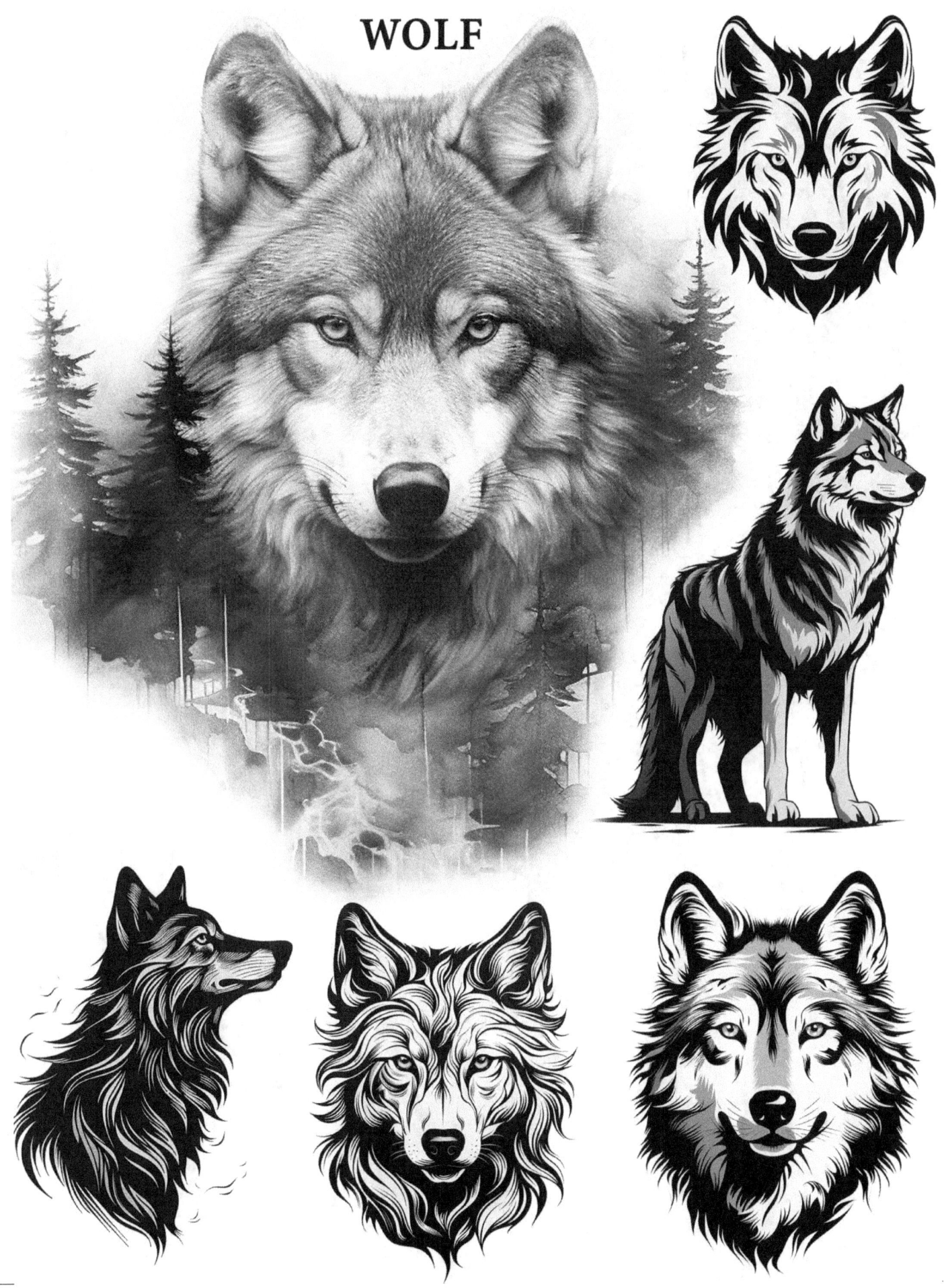

WOLF

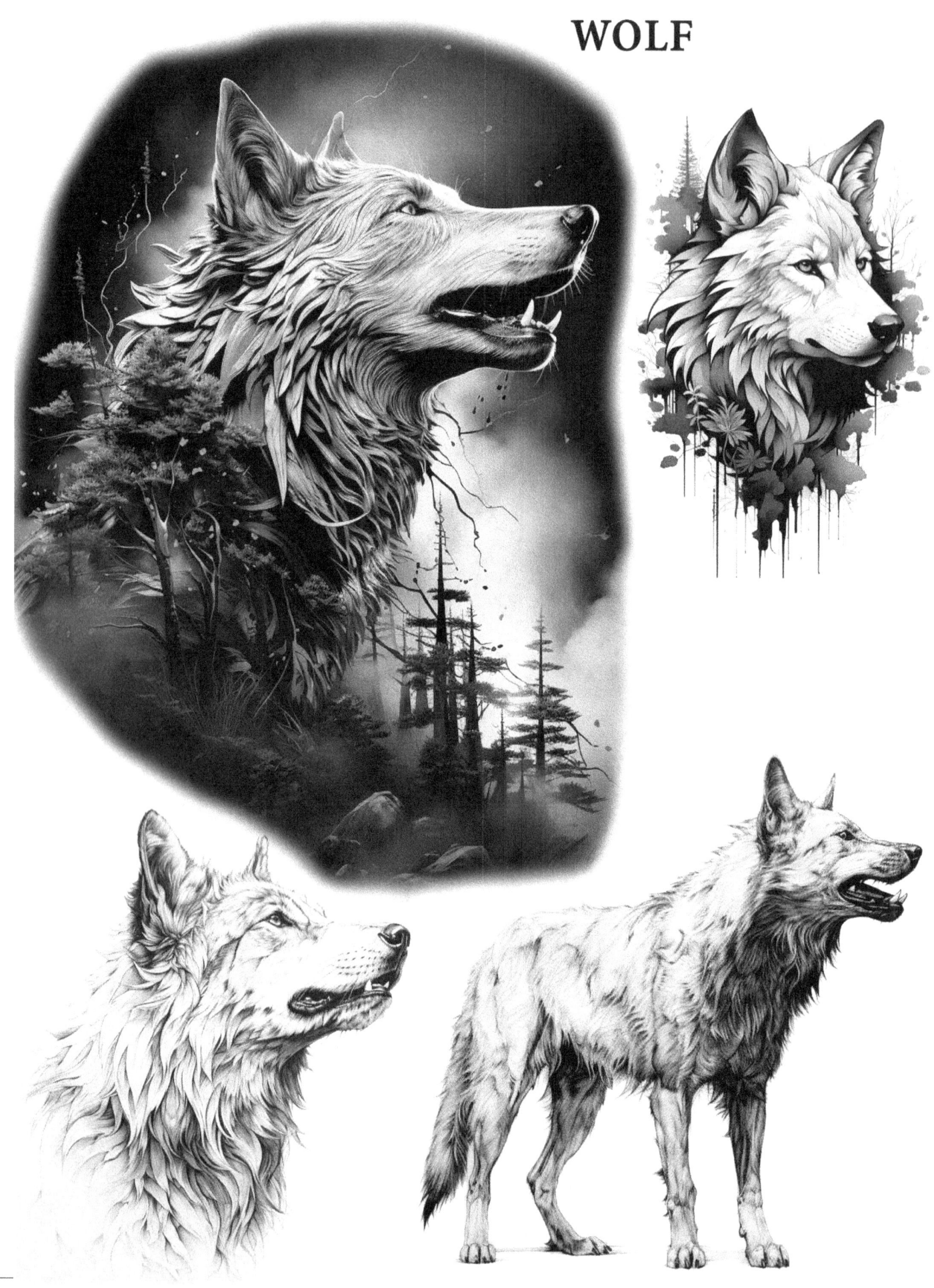

WOLF

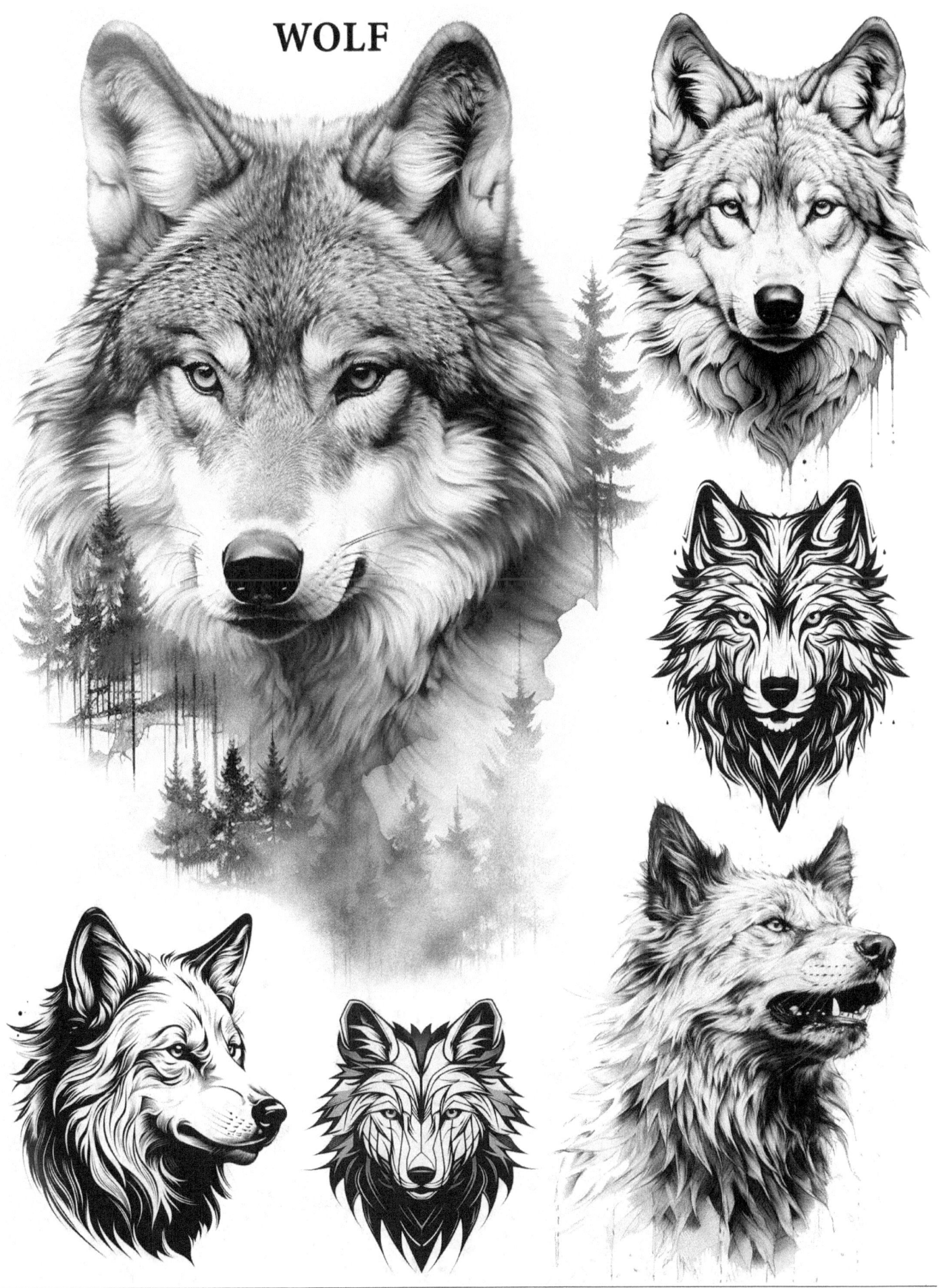

WOLF

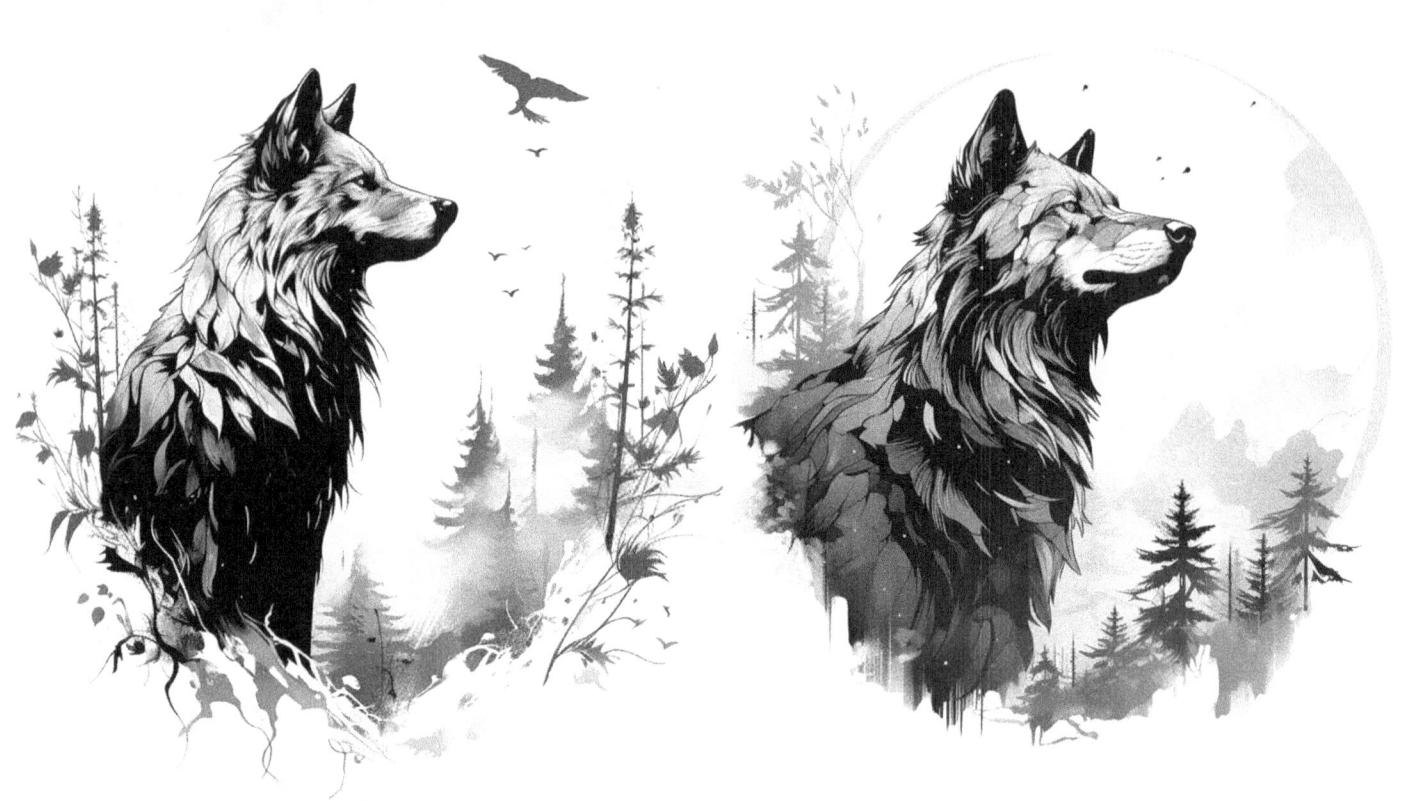

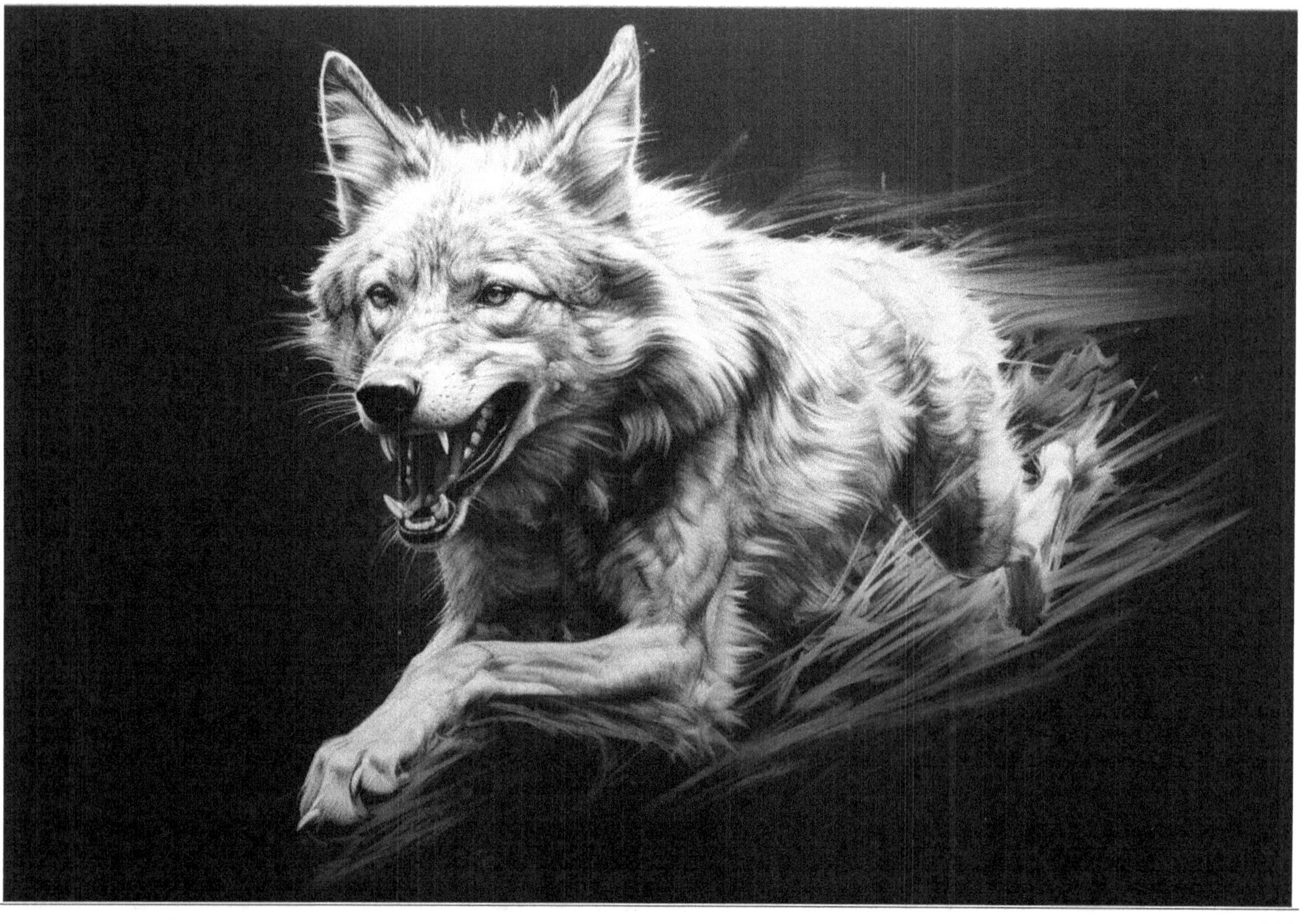

Below are the Revision pages. These extra pages are added in 2025, with new styles and designs. Available also as a download from the below QR code, or can be found through our Facebook page, any time and available to all owners of this book (older versions owners are also eligible to free download of th e revisions)   Use same password as the main download of the book to get it opened with WINRAR

REVISION PAGES

Astronaut   10
Butterfly   20
Cats   20
Dolphin   30
Eagle   15
Leopard   19
  Lion   19
Mermaid   10
Owl   5
 Panther   26
Parrot   15
Phoenix 9
All Seeing Eye 18
 Samurai 5
Spartan 8
Tigers   13
 Viking 6
 Total = 248

ASTRONAUT

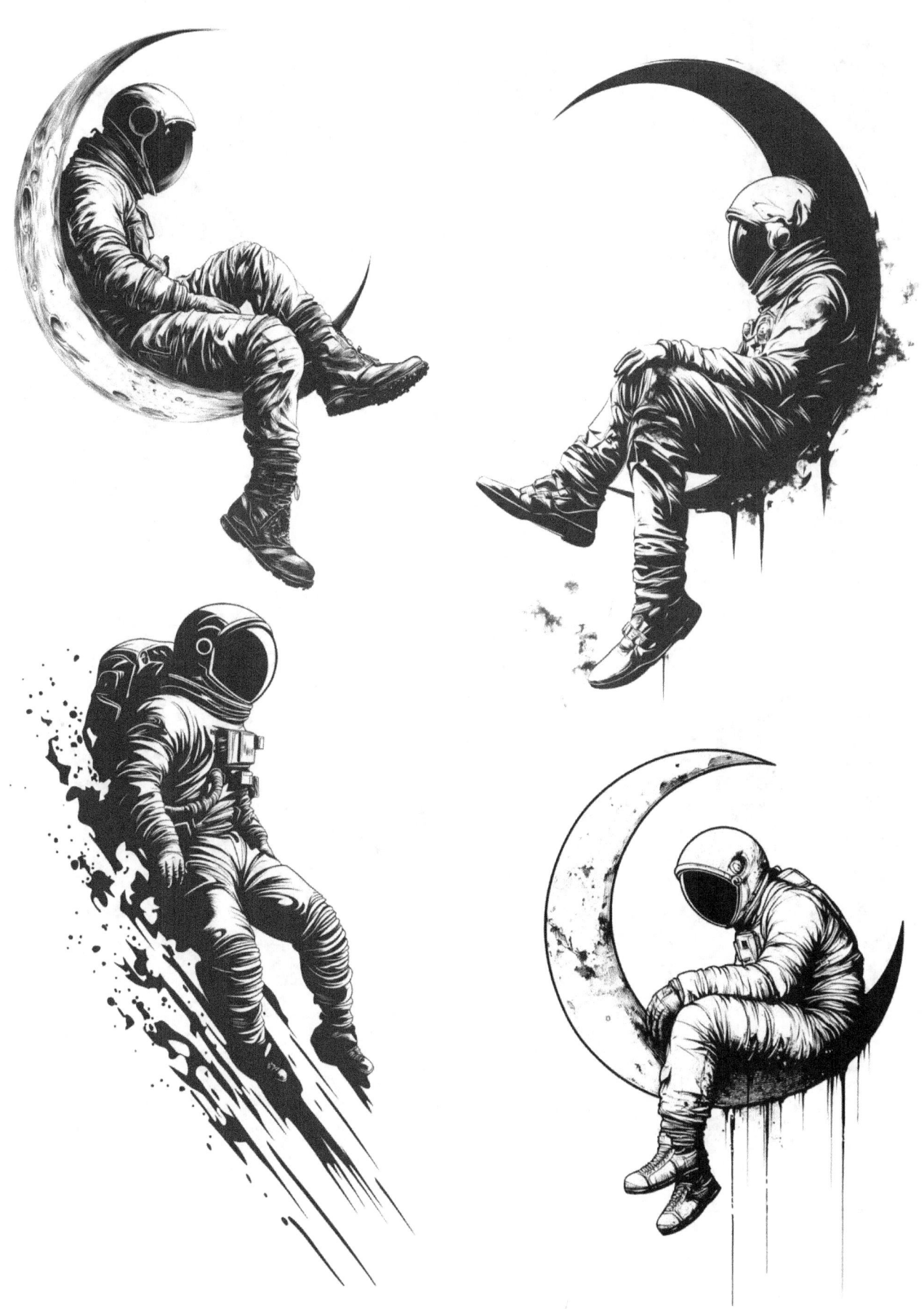

ASTRONAUT

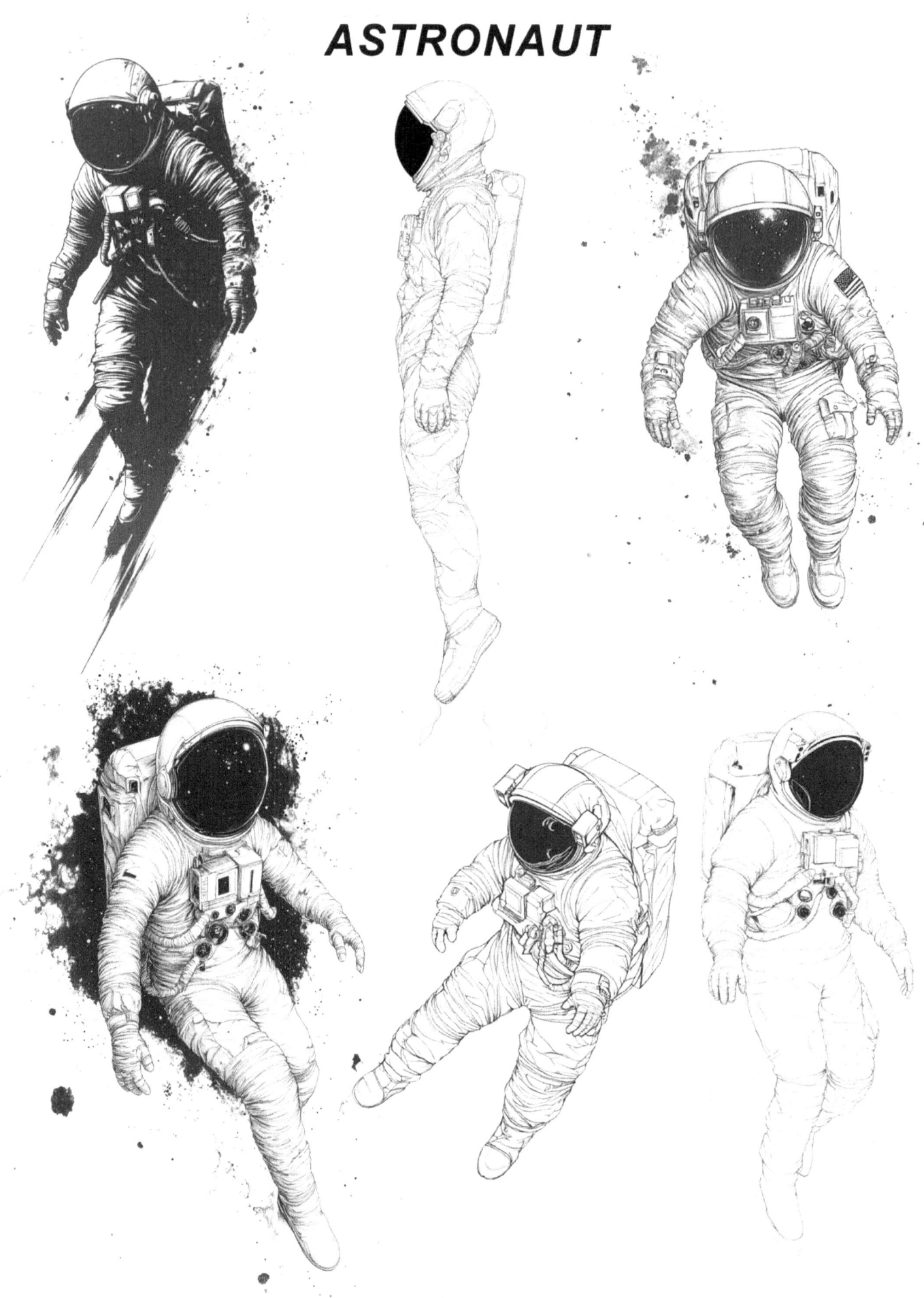

BUTTERFLY

CATS

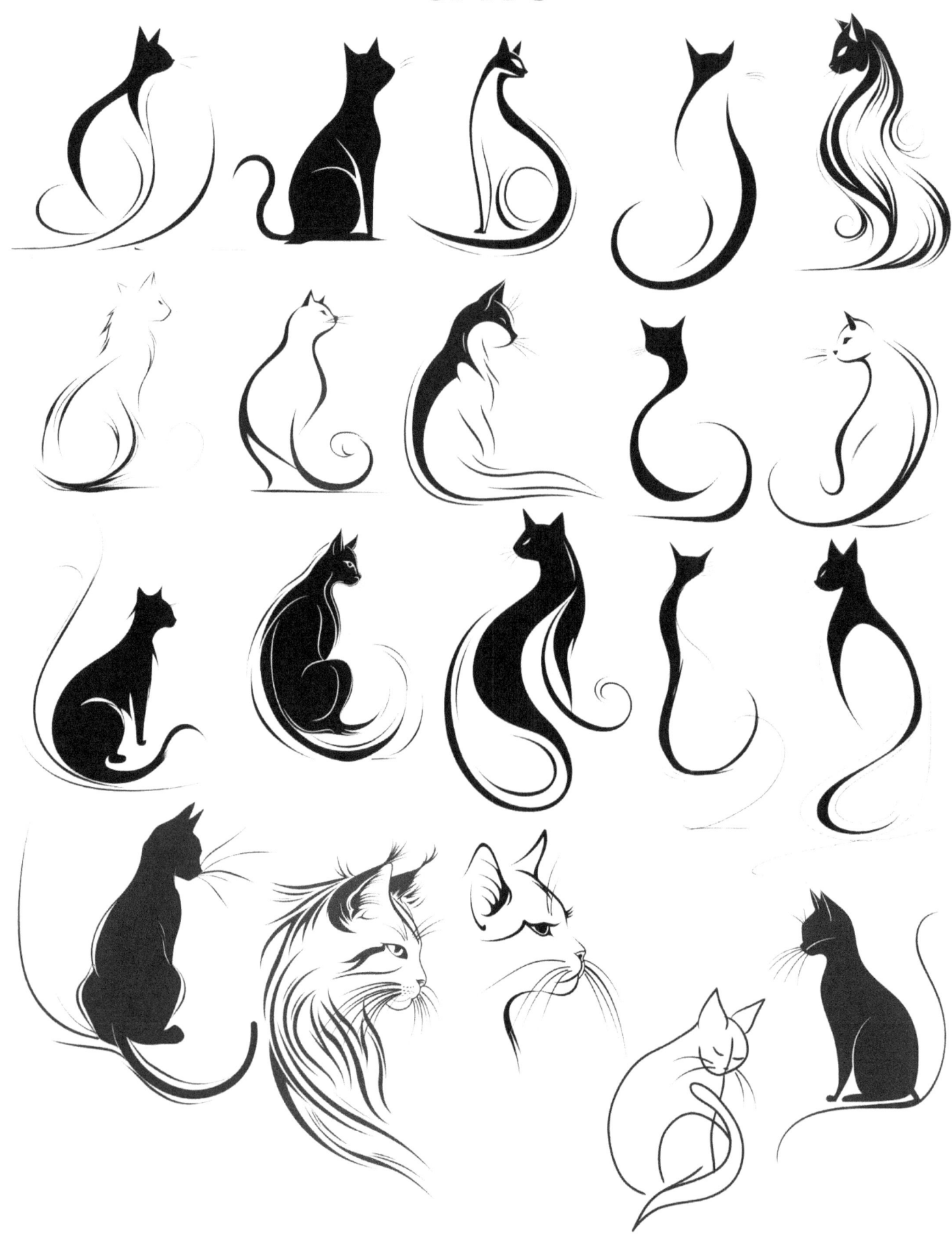

DOLPHIN

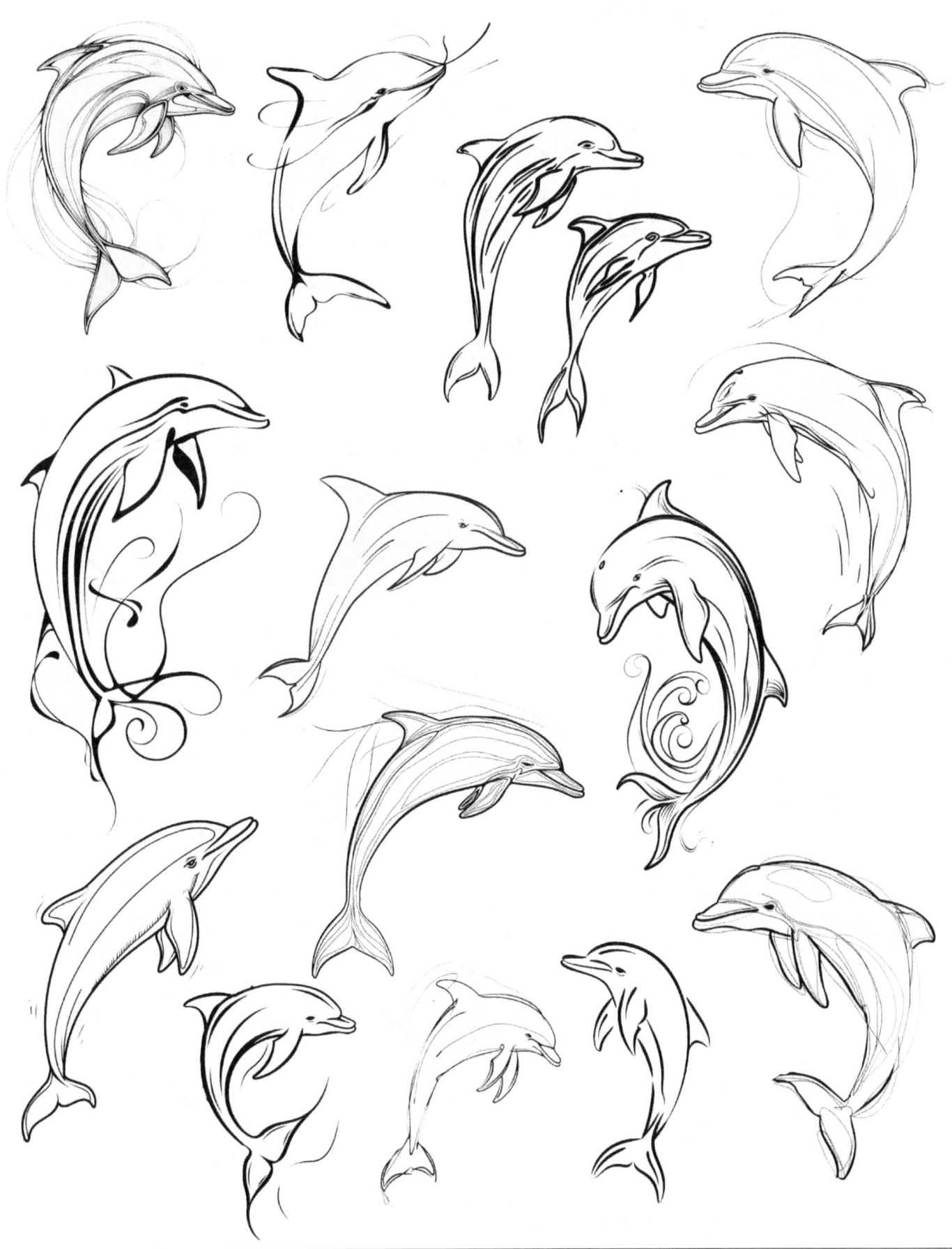

DOLPHINS

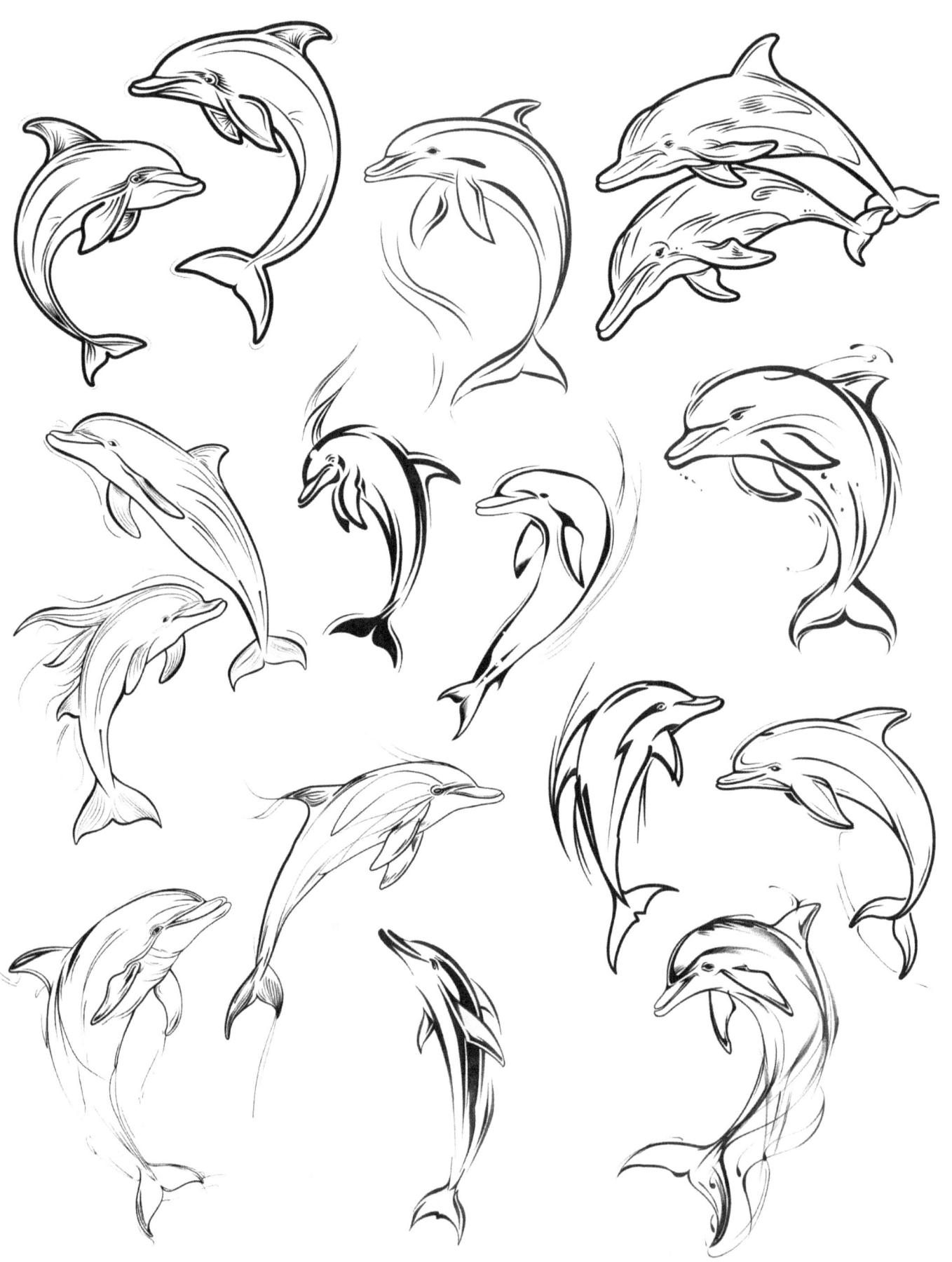

EAGLE

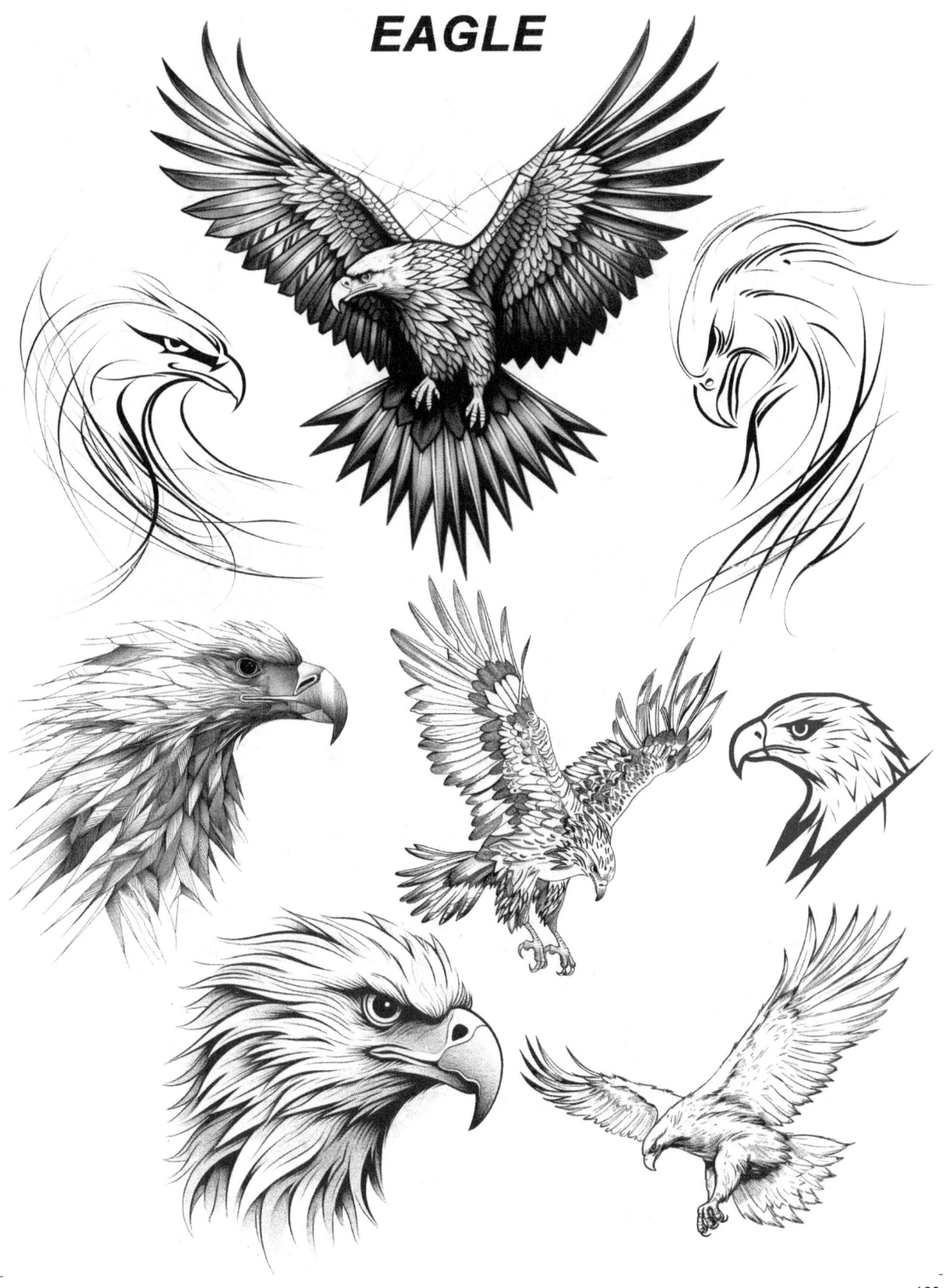

EAGLE

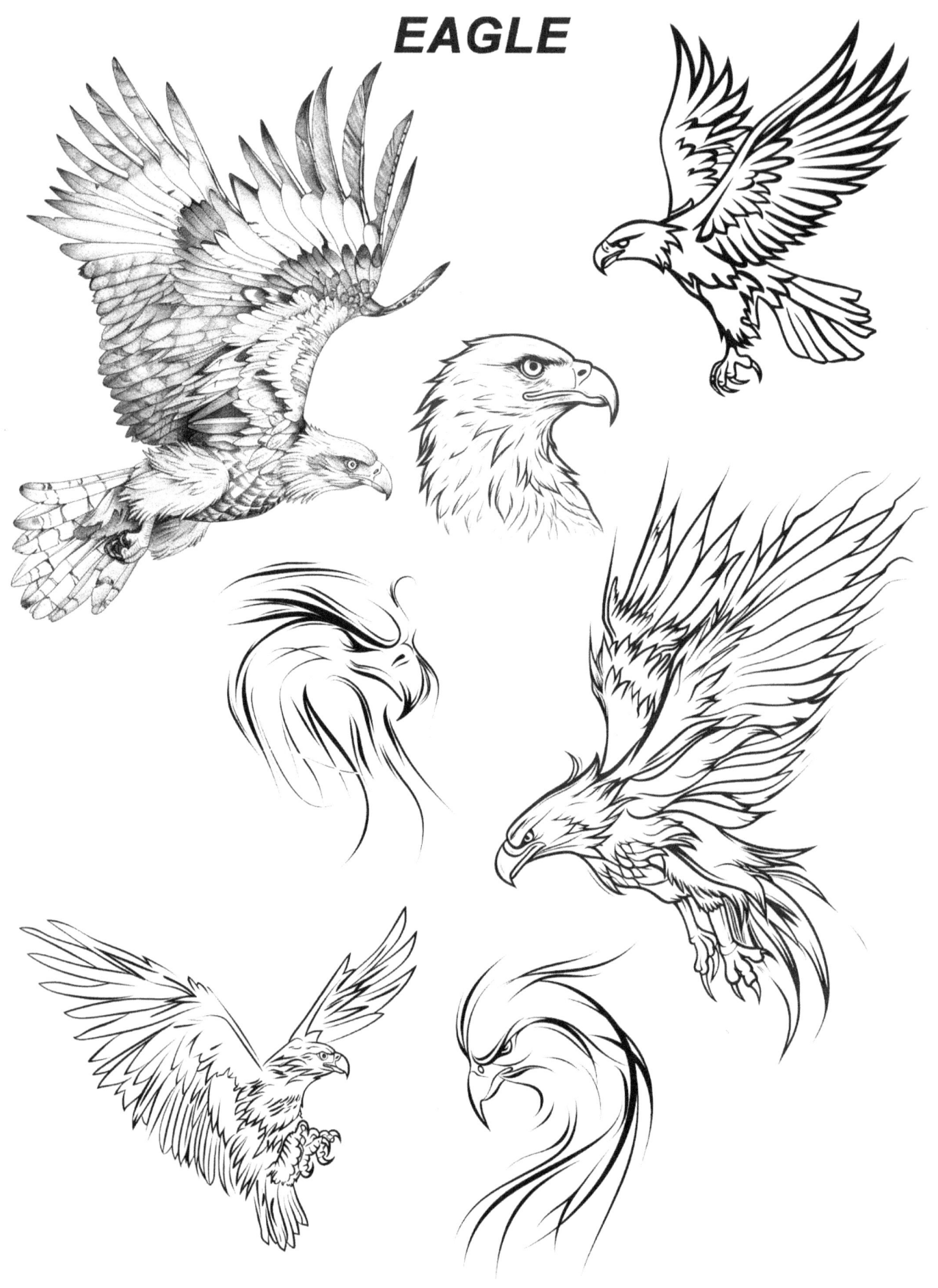

LEOPARD

LEOPARD

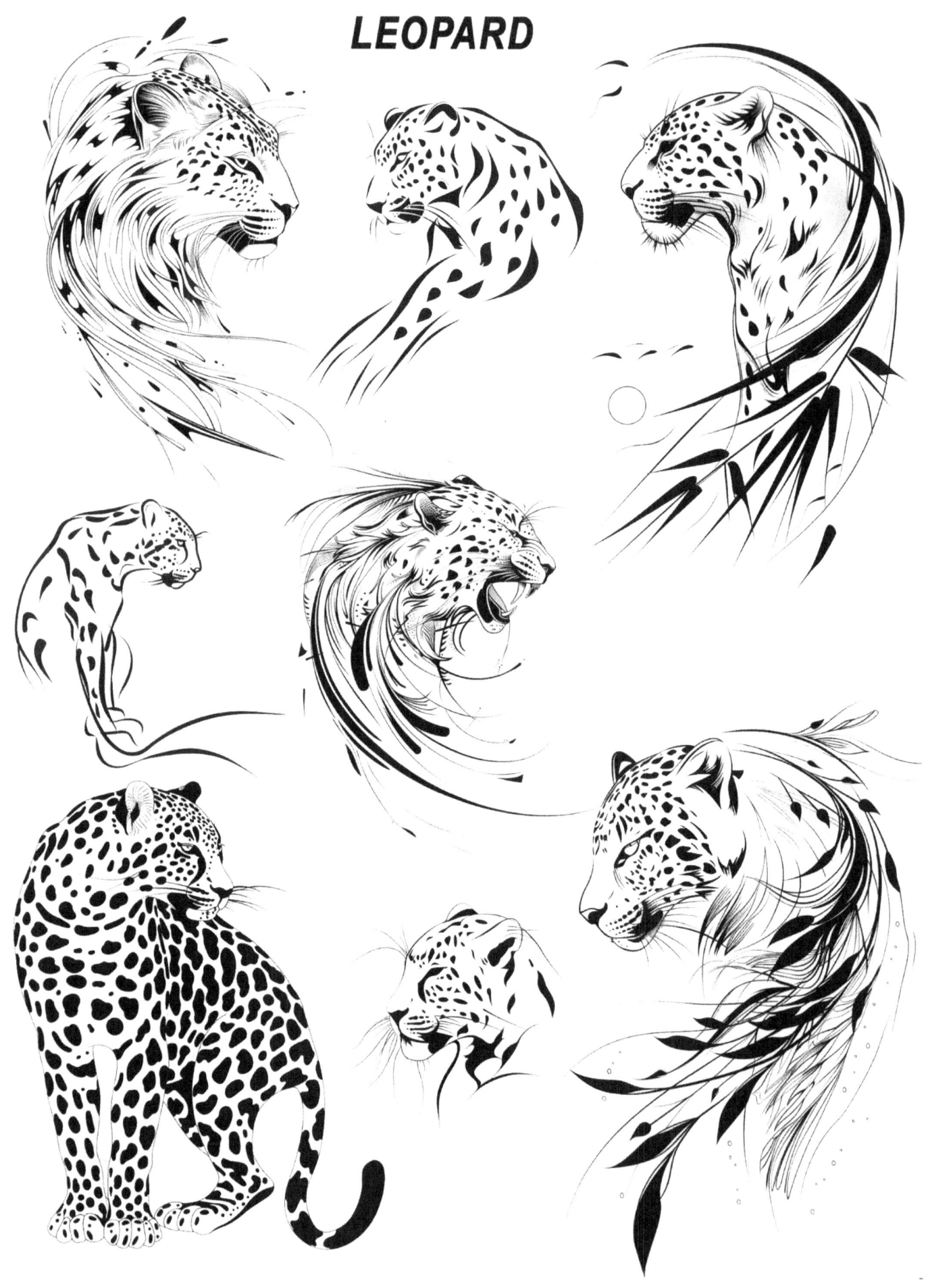

LION

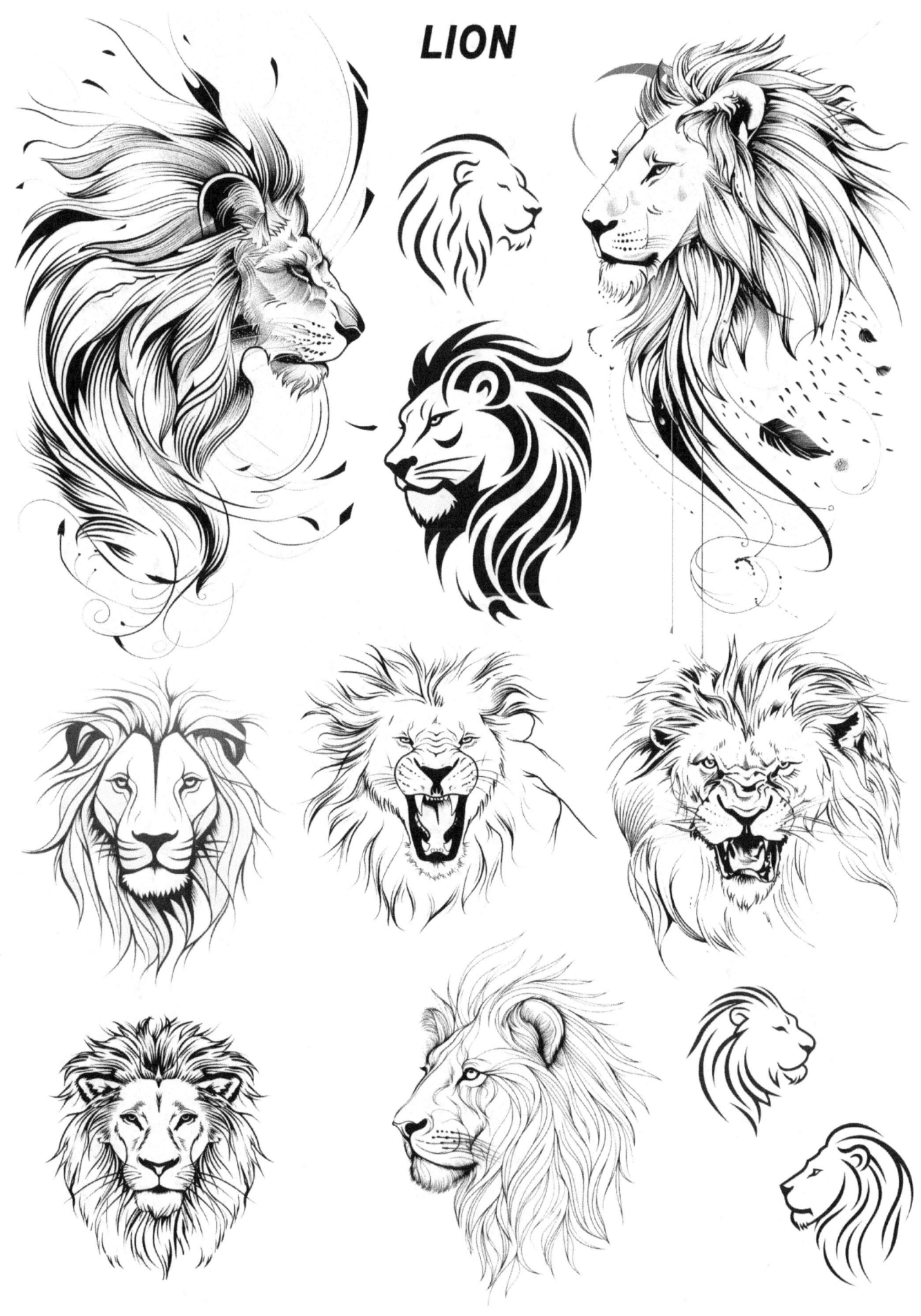

LION

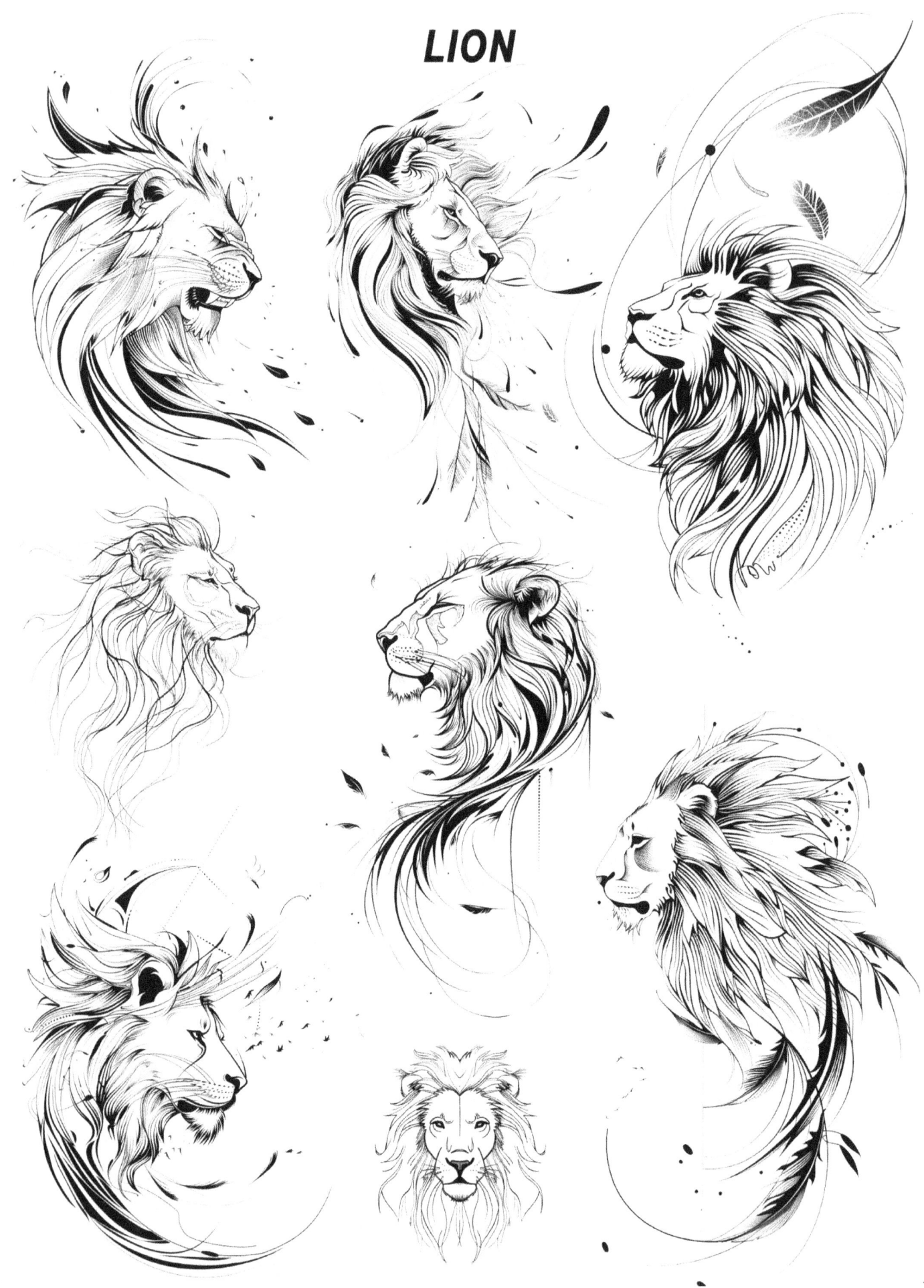

MERMAIDS

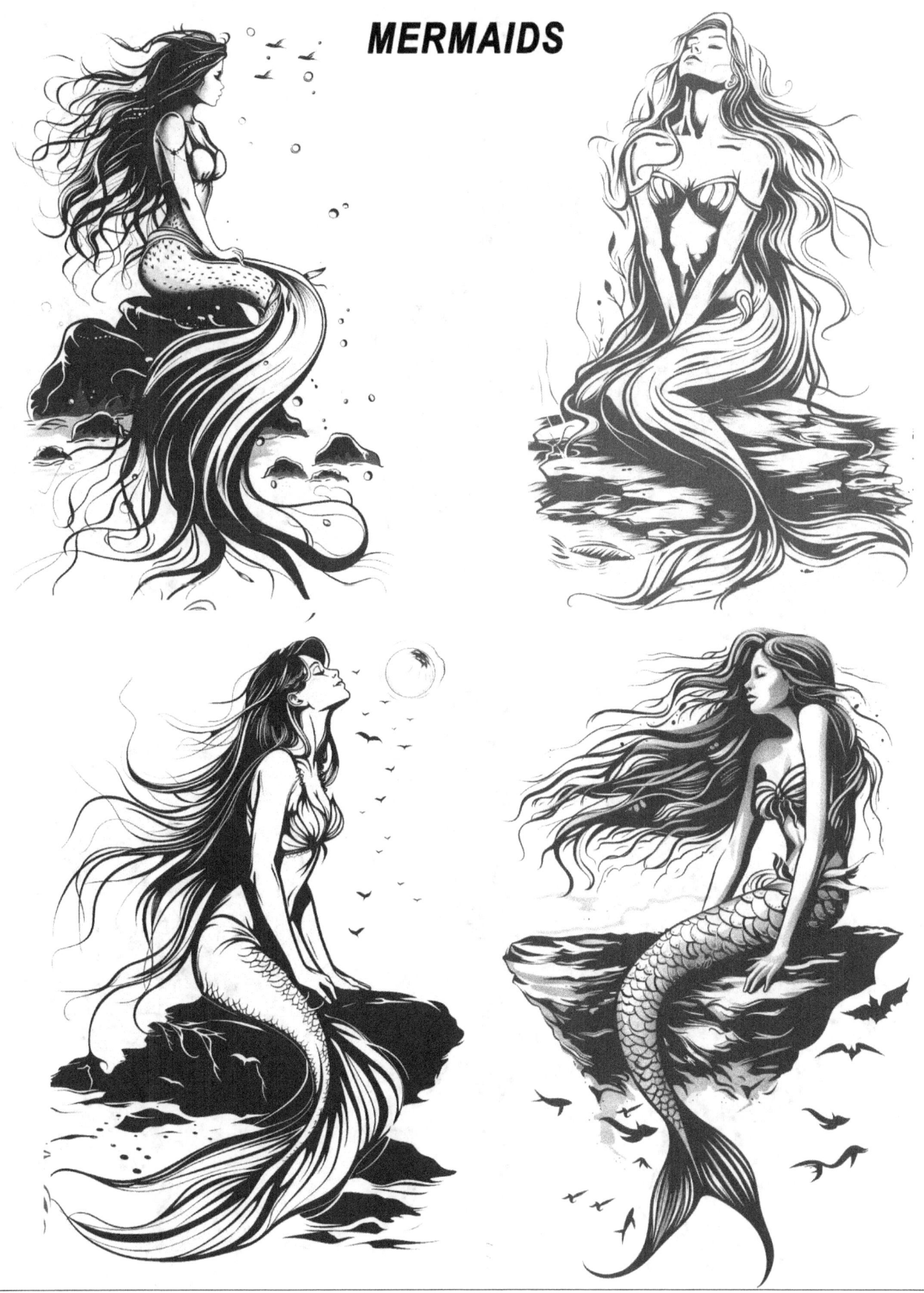

MERMAIDS

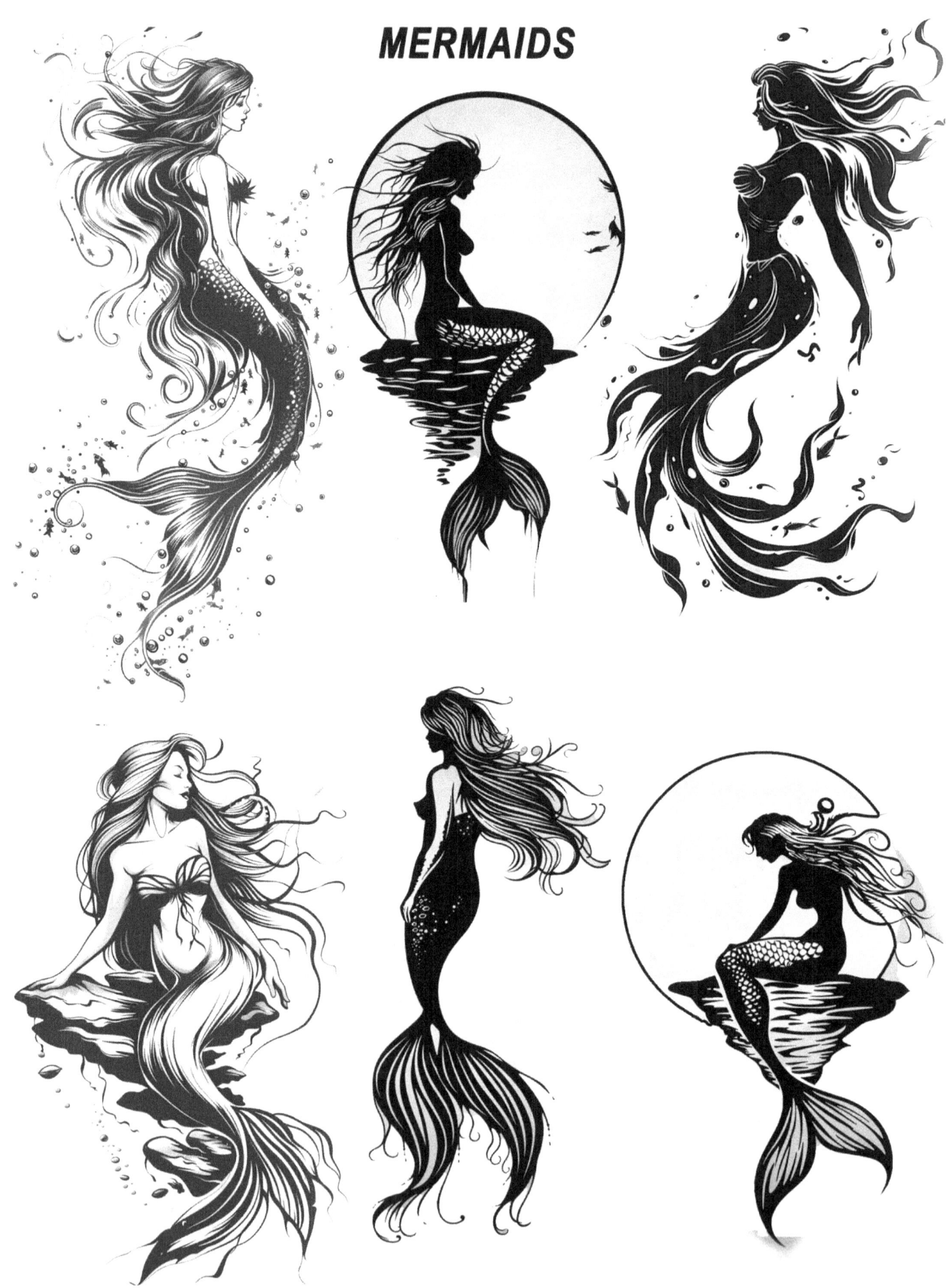

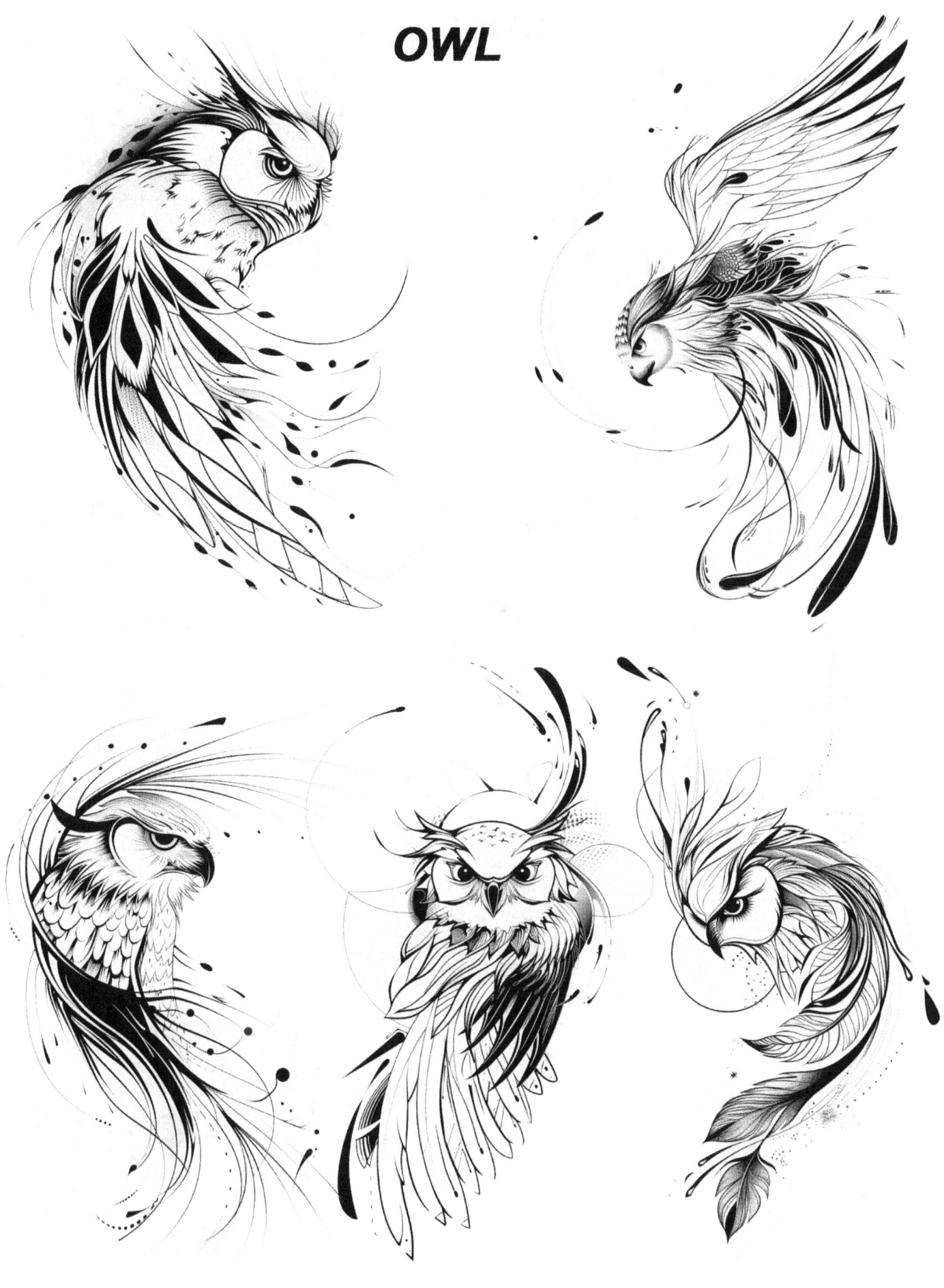

PANTHER

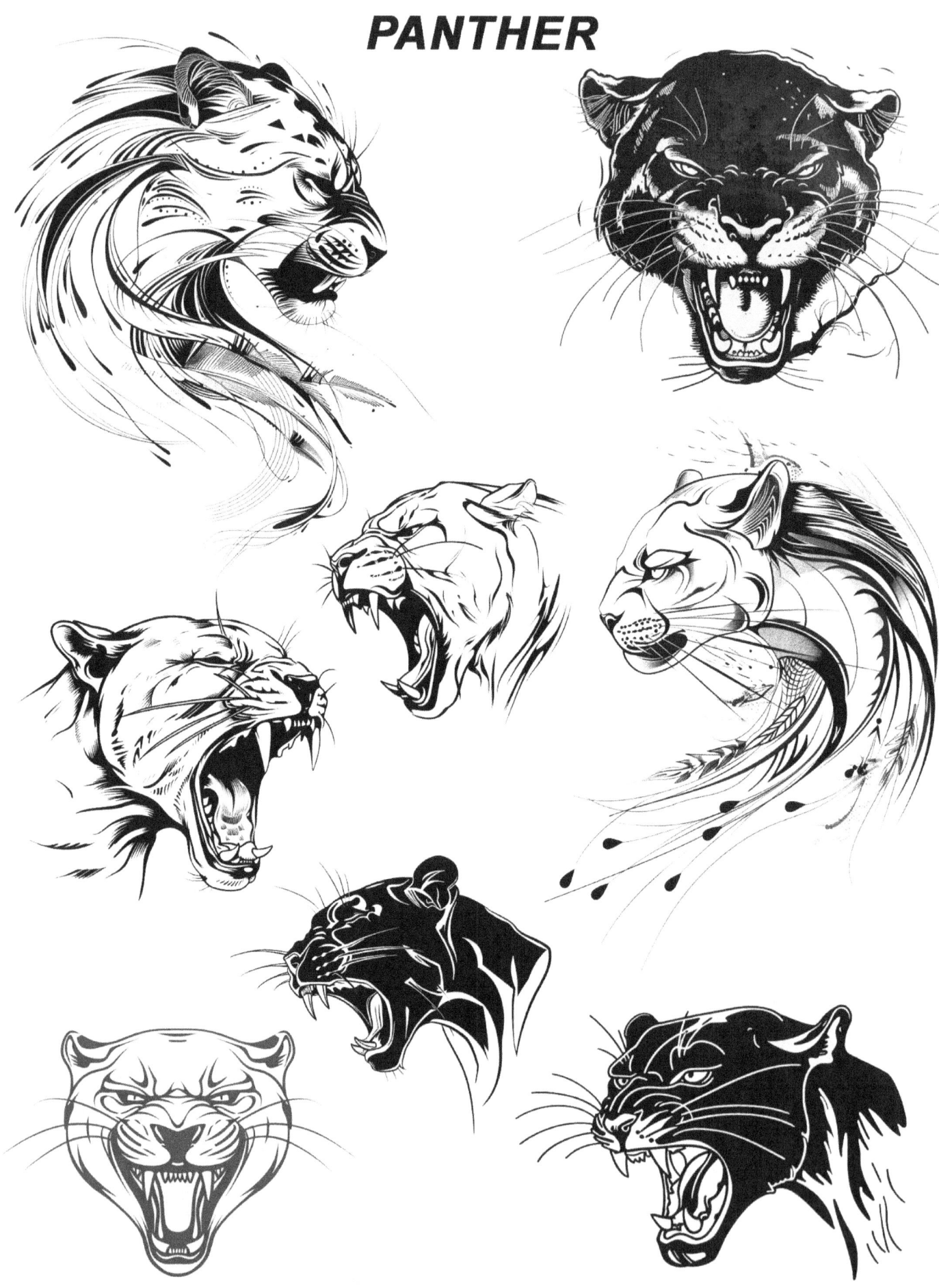

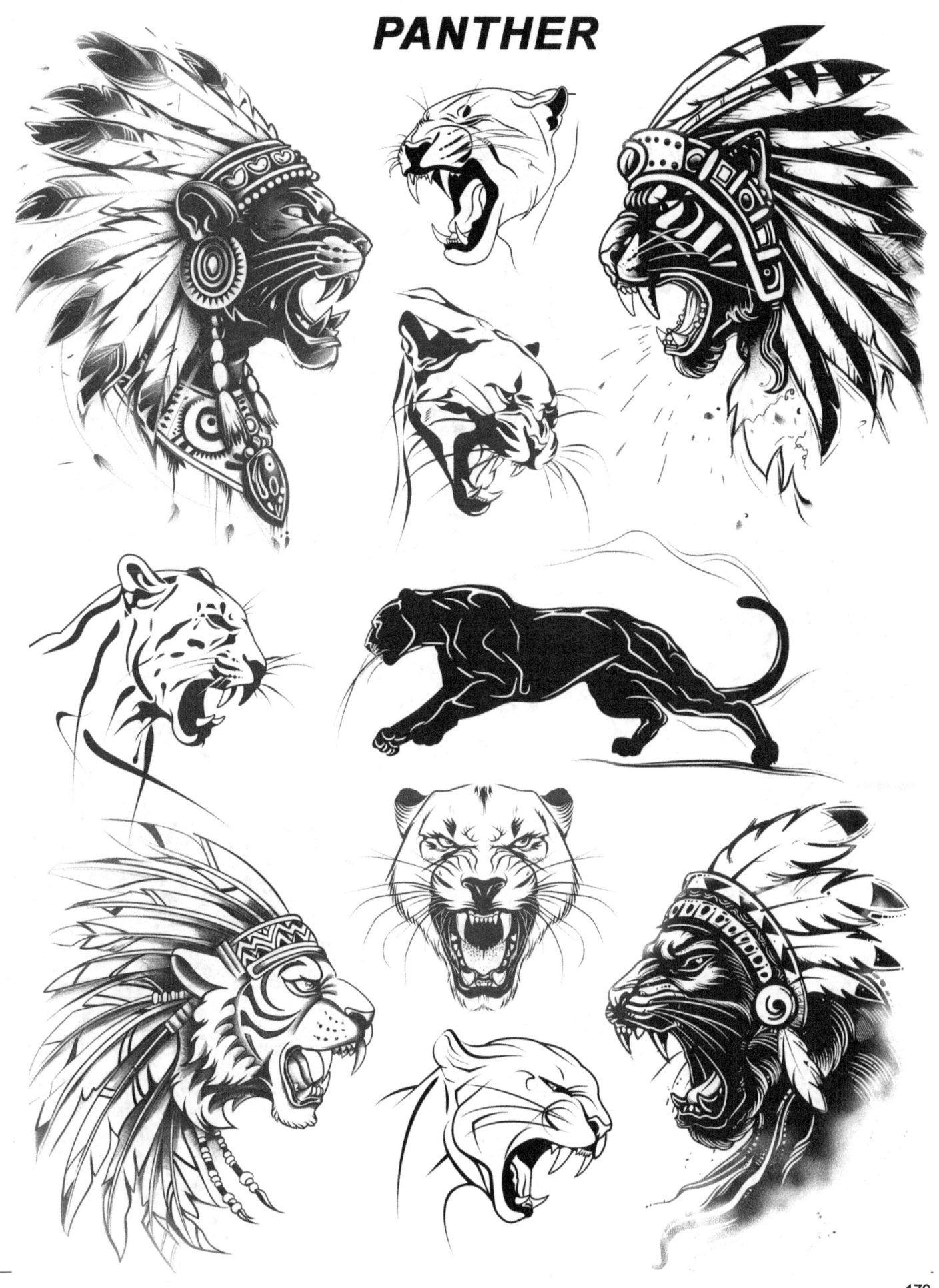

PANTHER

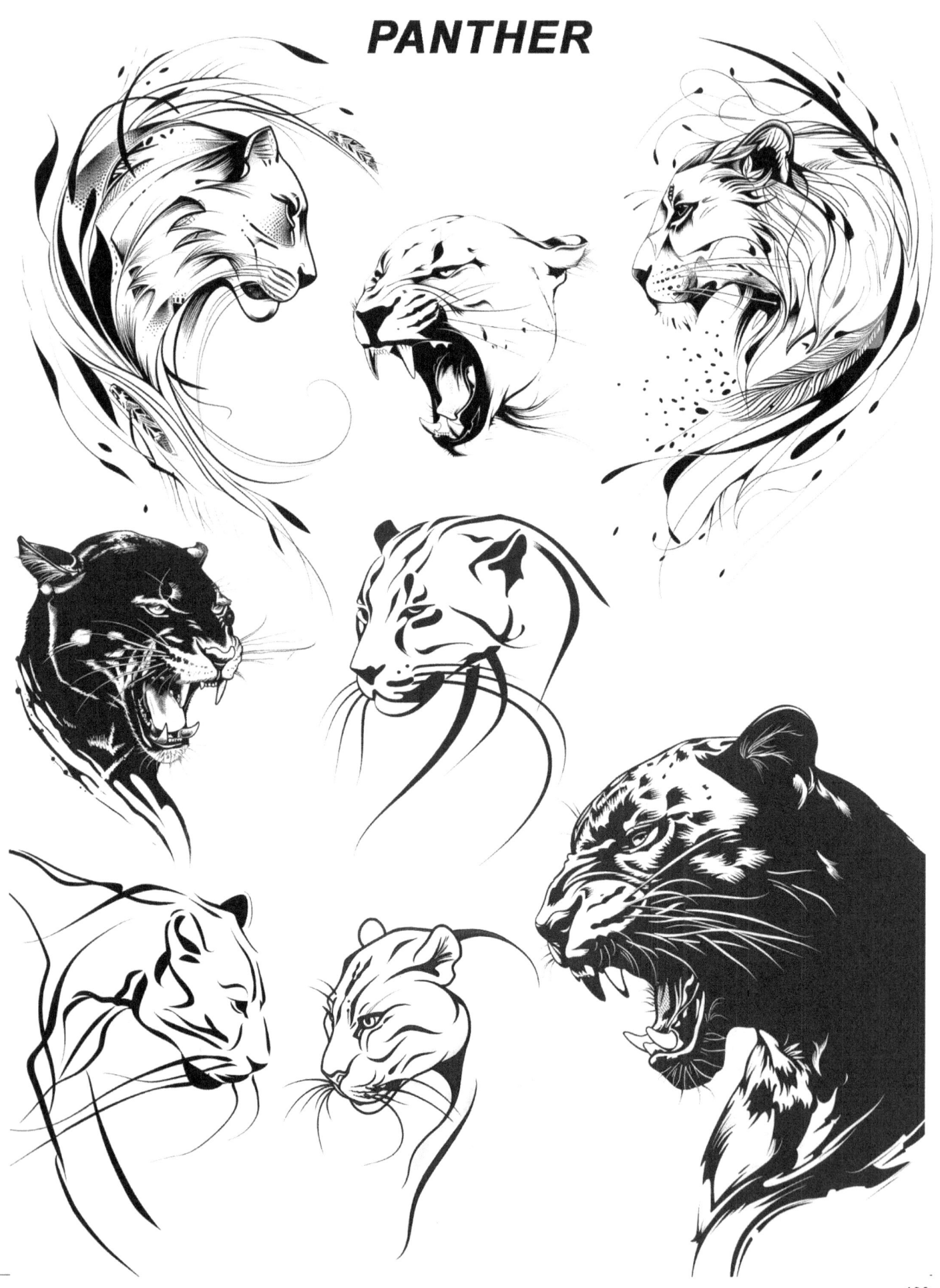

PARROT

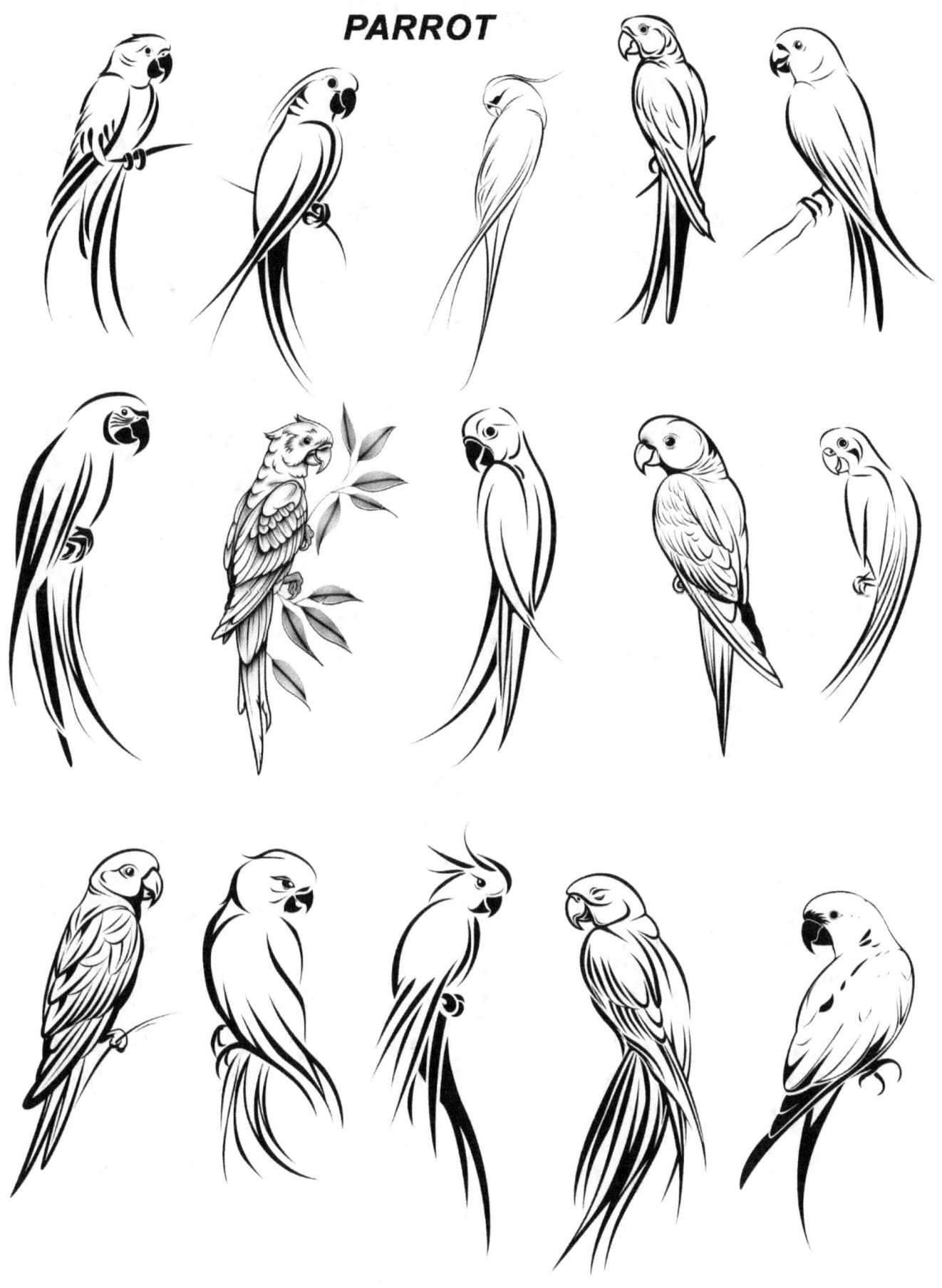

PHOENIX

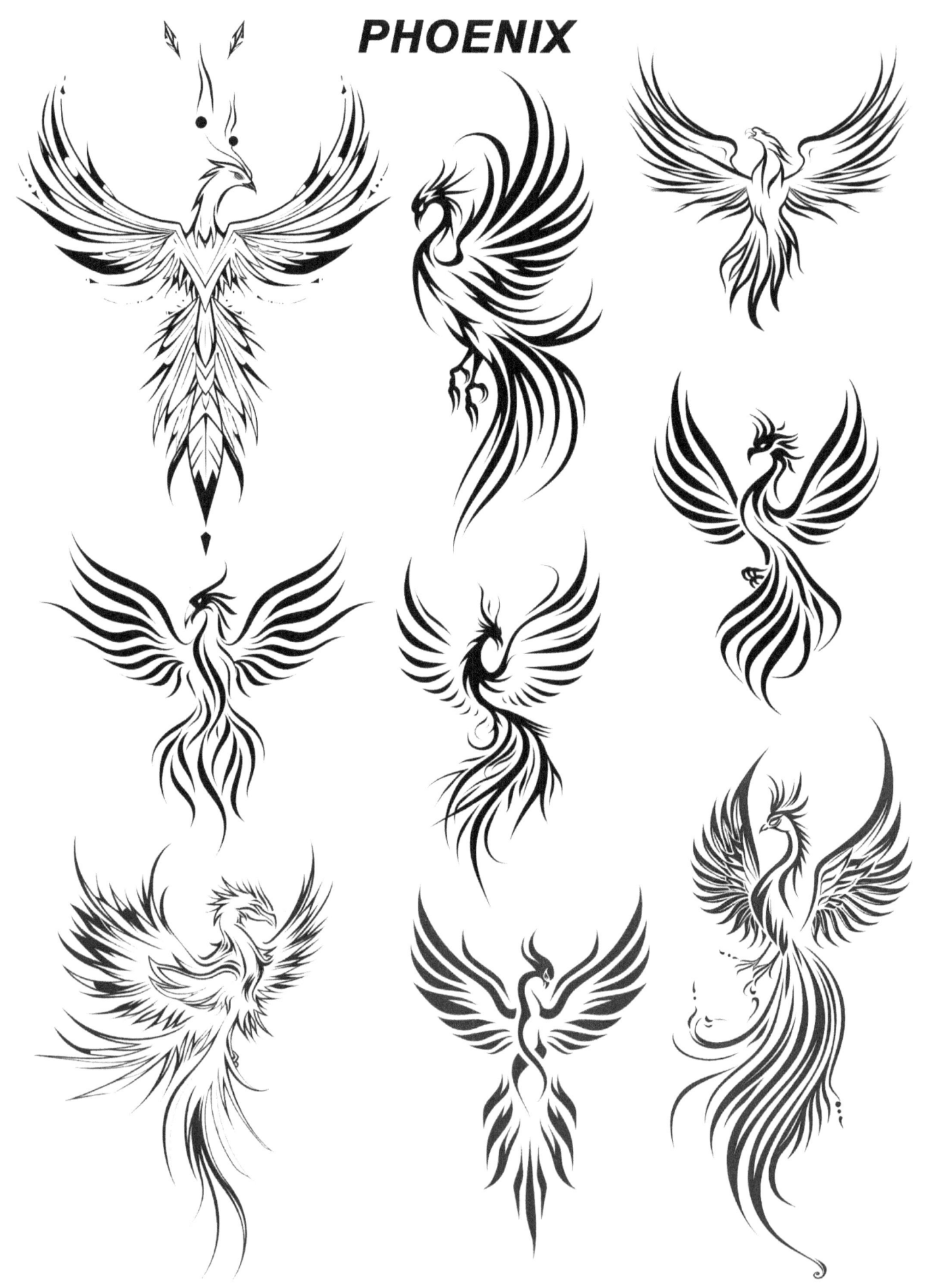

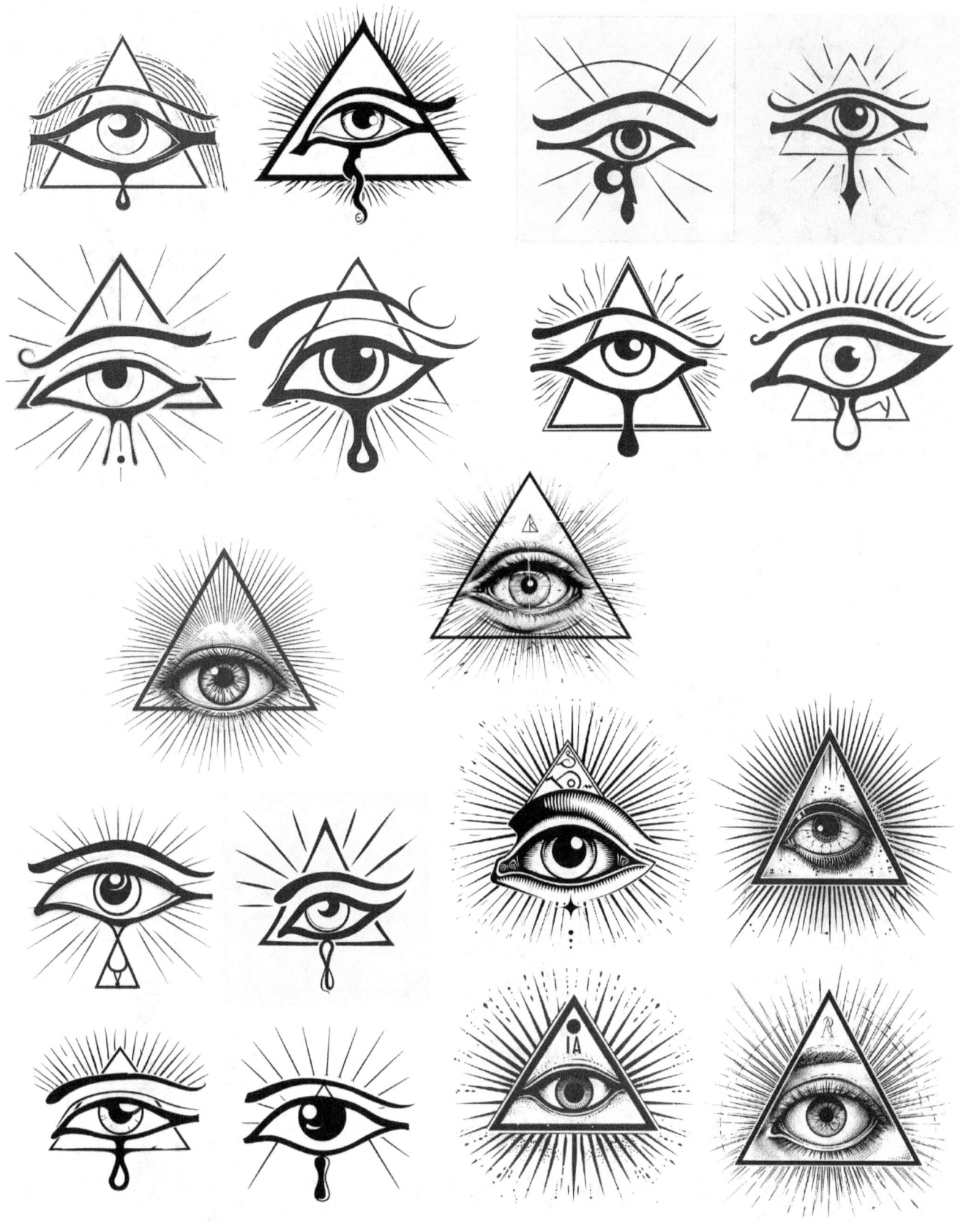

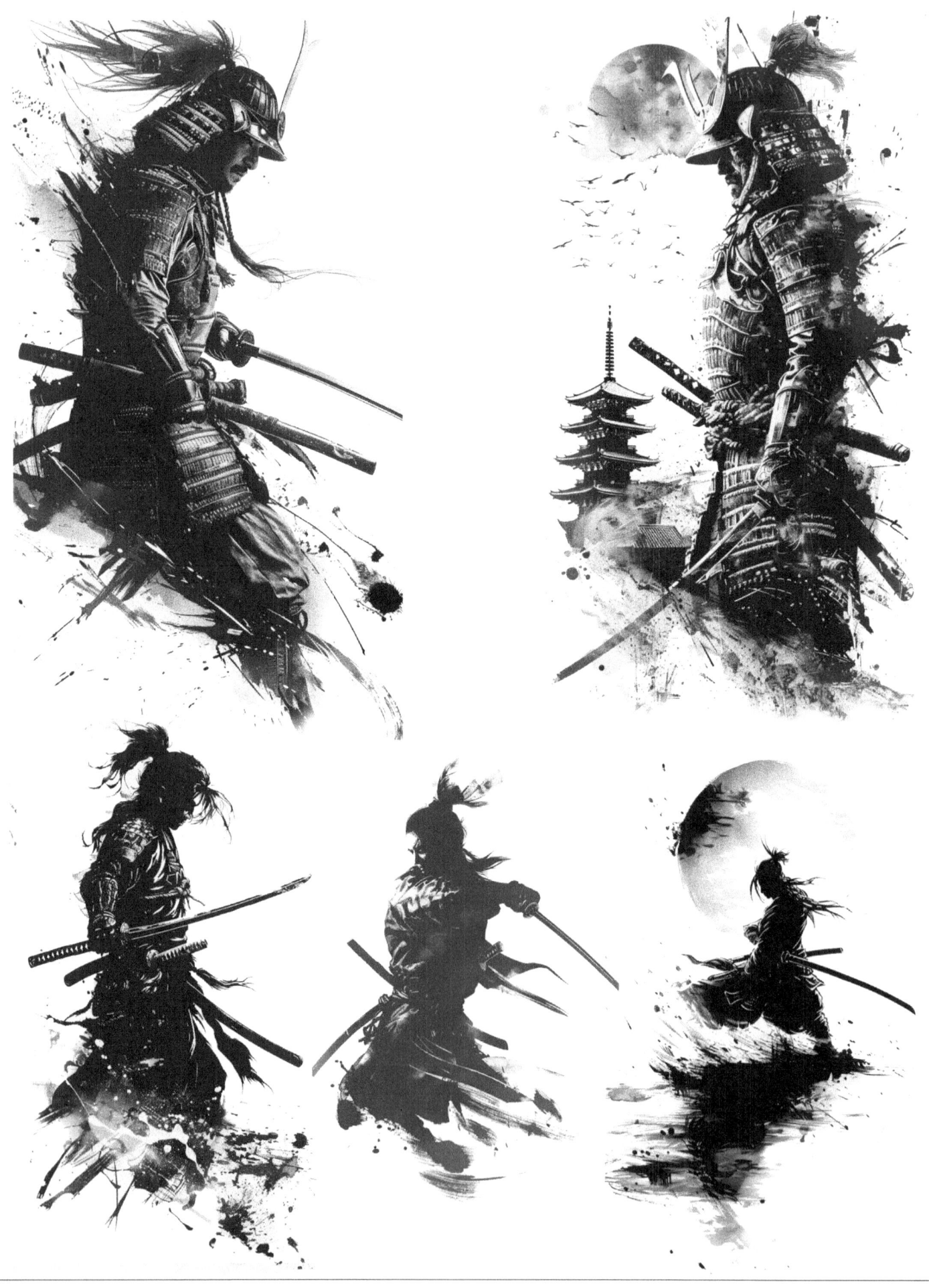

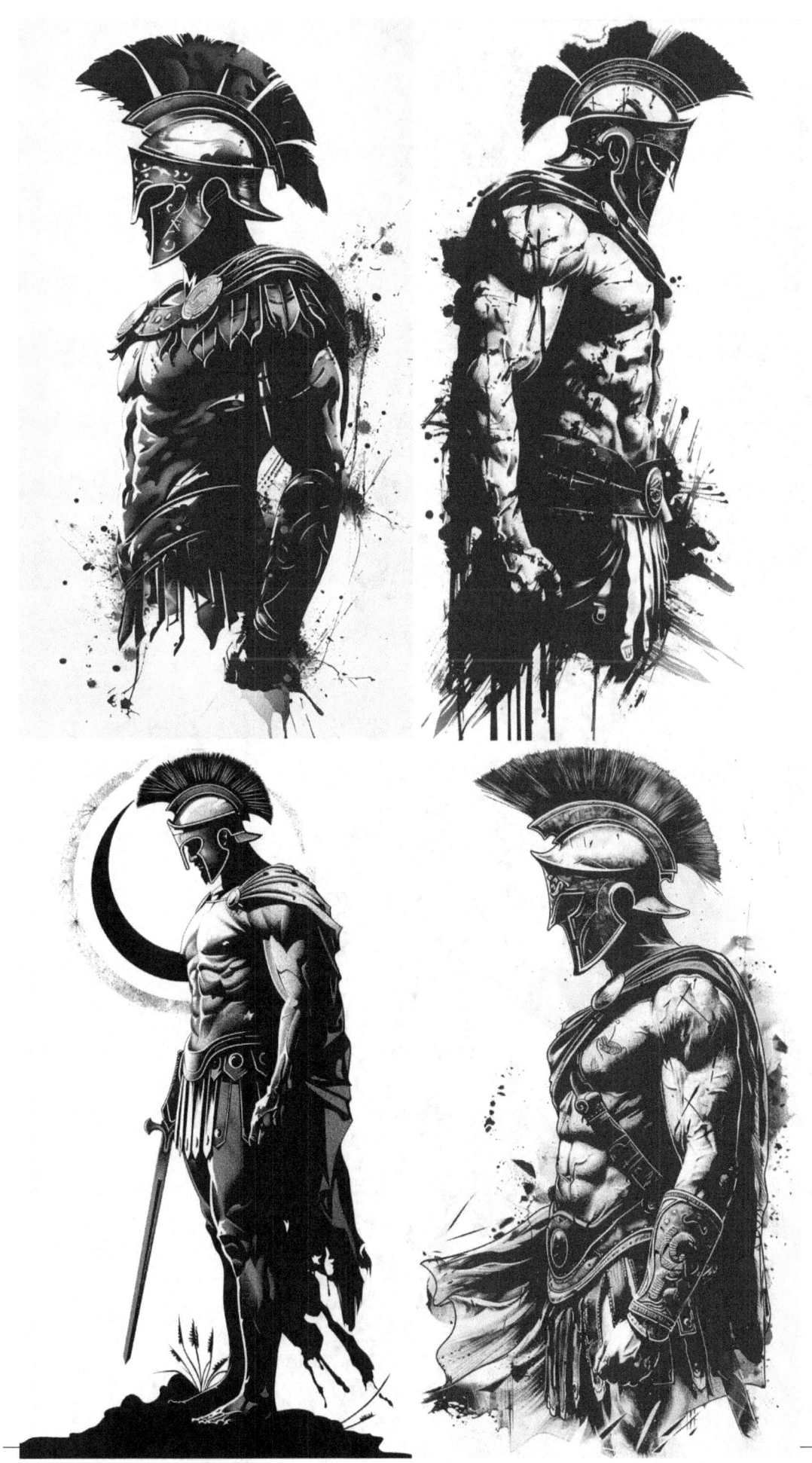

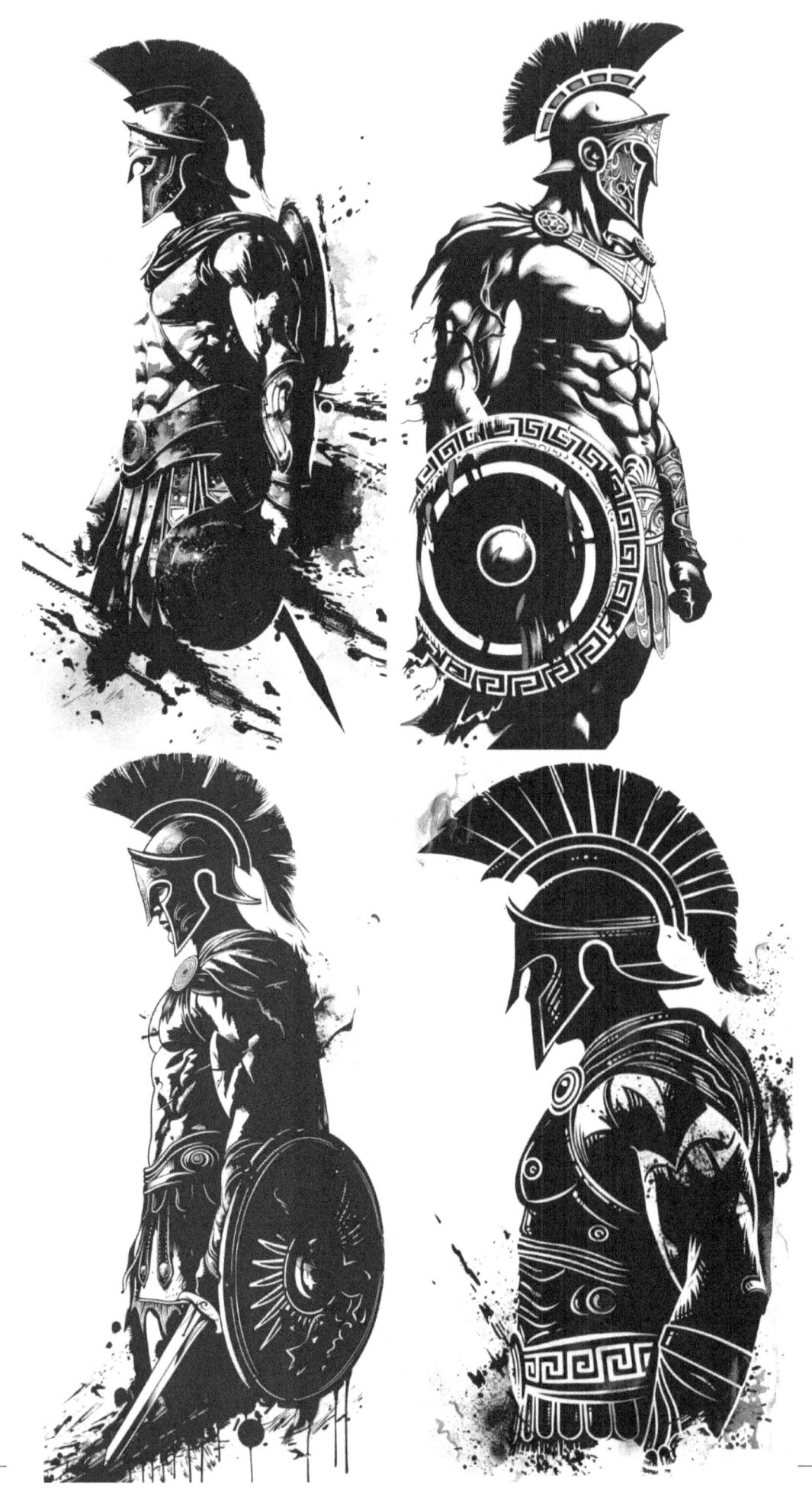

TIGER

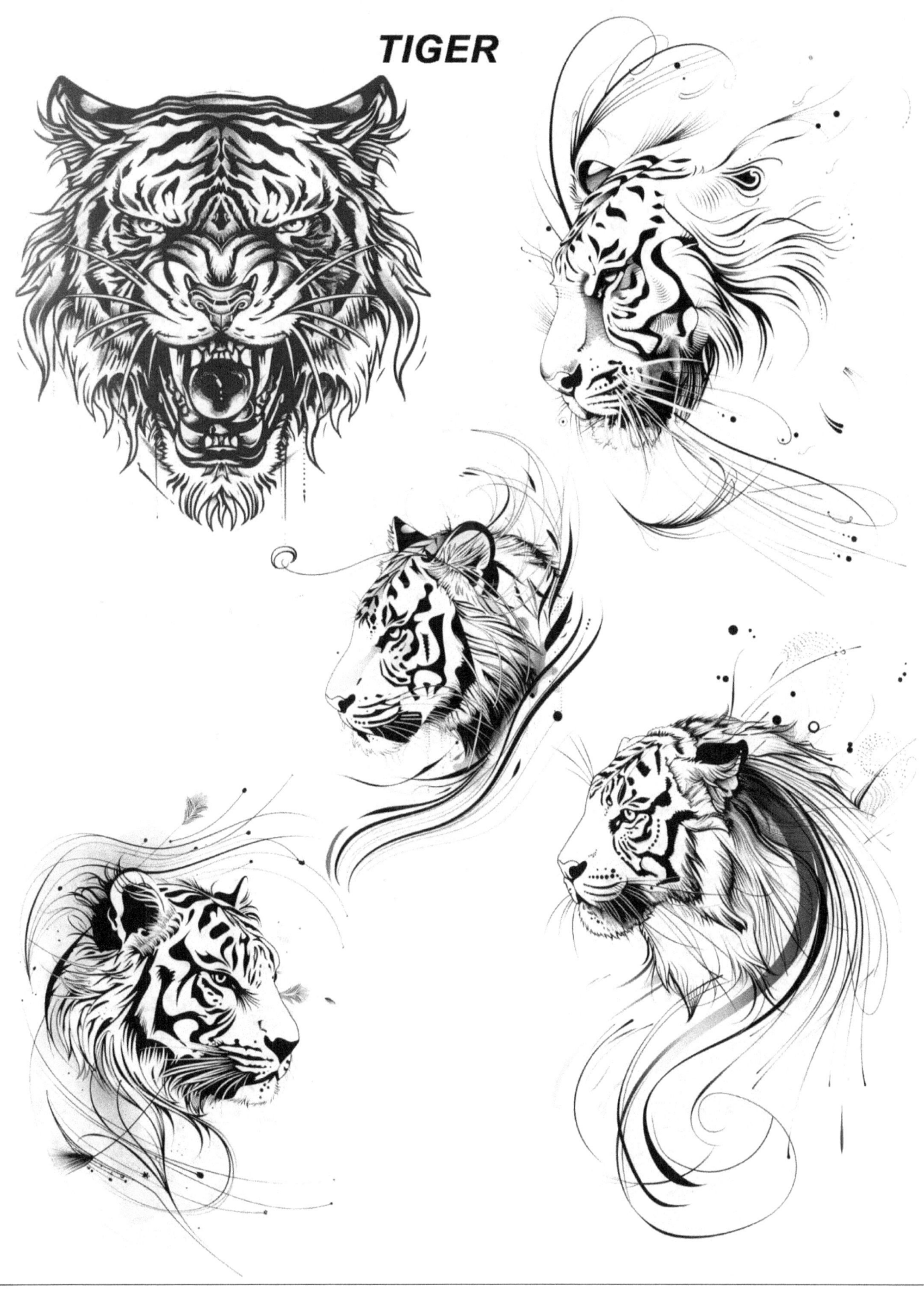

TIGER

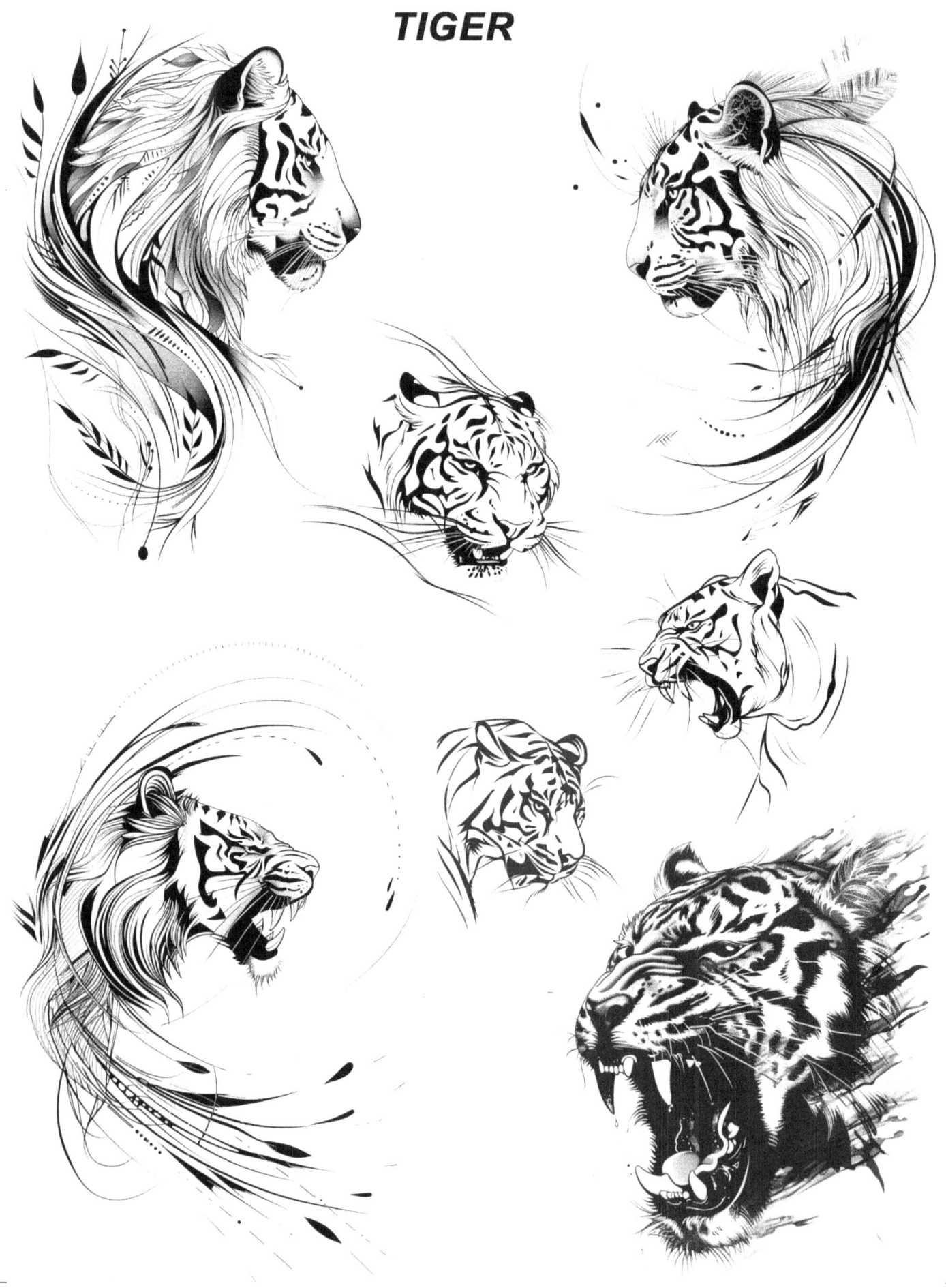

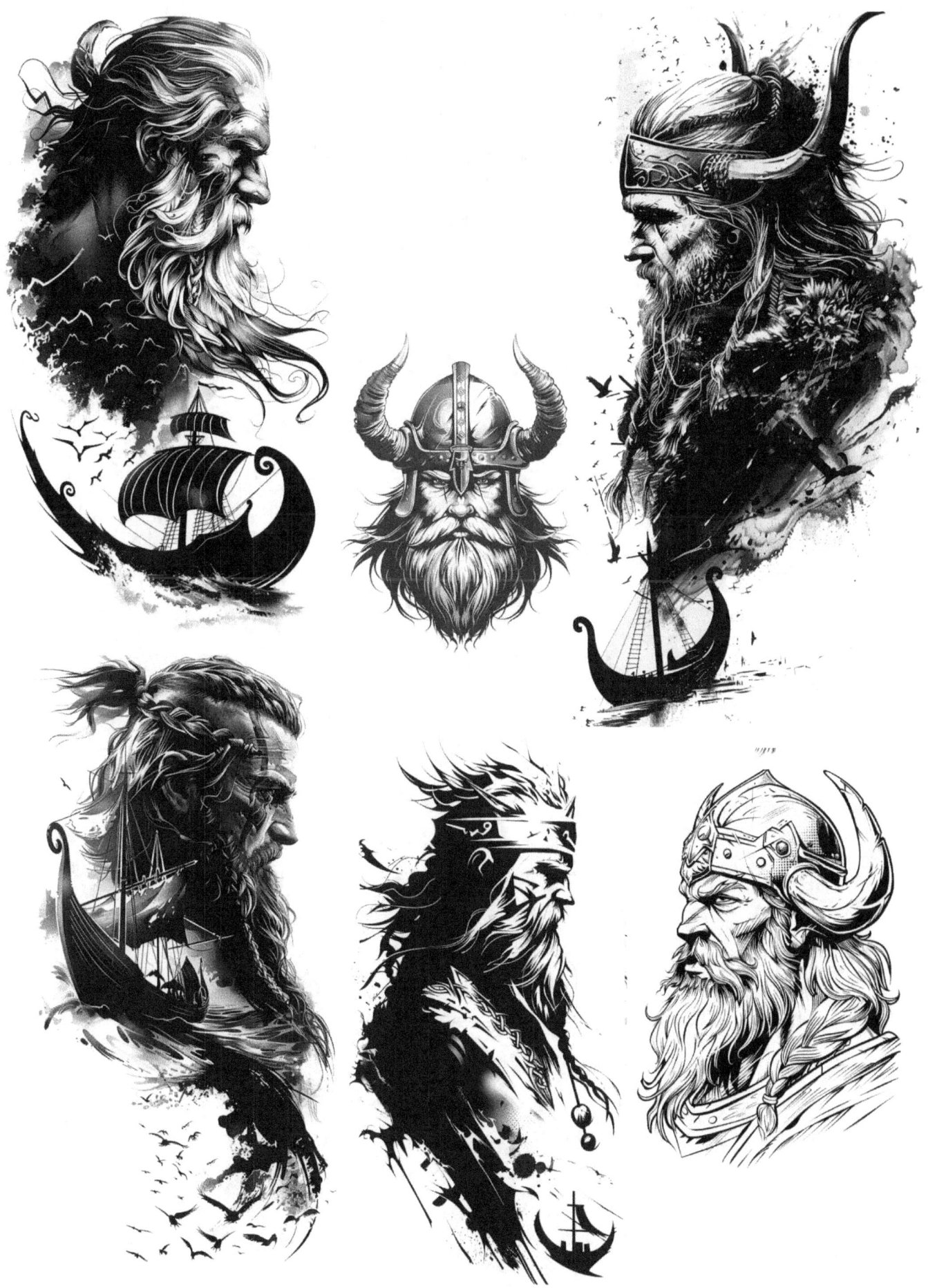

You can find my other books on Amazon here :

https://www.amazon.com/author/alexartbooks

Hope you enjoyed this book and take a moment to leave a positive feedback on Amazon about it,
This will help making out books even better